CW00377113

WHISTLE WHILE YOU WORK

BOB HOWITT

Published in 2004 by Hodder Moa Beckett Publishers Ltd
[a member of the Hodder Headline Group]
4 Whetu Place, Mairangi Bay
Auckland, New Zealand

National Library of New Zealand Cataloguing-in-Publication Data

Howitt, Bob, 1941-
Paddy O'Brien : whistle while you work / Bob Howitt. 1st ed.
ISBN 1-86958-986-6
1.O'Brien, Paddy, 1959- 2. Rugby Union football referees—
New Zealand—Biography. I. Title.
796.3333092—dc 22

Designed and produced by Hodder Moa Beckett Publishers Ltd
Printed in China by Everbest Printing Co., Ltd

Front cover: Photos by Fotopress
Back cover: Photo by Fotopress

Dedication

To my wonderful wife Carolyn for all the sacrifices she has had to make in being both a mother and father to Danielle and Hamish while I have travelled the world living my dream.

Contents

Acknowledgements

The writer would especially like to thank Brian Hewett, Dave Evans and Ian Macfadyen for their vivid recollections of Paddy's days in the police force; Clive Woodward and André Watson for so enthusiastically composing tributes to Paddy (Clive Woodward having to interrupt his World Cup celebrations back in England to do so); Paddy's mother Val for so delightfully recalling the early days (you should have been a journalist); and to Fotopress and the *Southland Times* for the illustrations that have so enhanced the book.

Foreword

Paddy O'Brien is quite simply at the top of his game. He is the number one referee in New Zealand and, in my view, is one of the best in the world.

He reached his position amongst the referees' elite through his excellent communication skills, his ability to work well under pressure, and his integrity and consistency.

Paddy has taken all of those attributes into each of the five England test matches he has taken charge of since I became England Head Coach in September 1997.

While we all respect that the referees are in charge of the test matches for the 80 to 90 minutes that they are played, Paddy's ability and willingness to enter into dialogue with coaches before a game has proved to be an invaluable sounding board for me.

One of the important issues for any coach to address is to get a firm understanding from the match referee as to how they will run the game and what they expect from the teams taking part.

I always make a point of meeting the referee in the week before a test and my exchanges before and after a game with Paddy, while they are always confidential, are positive and open, which is reflected in the way he handles matches.

He has a good dialogue with the players of both sides and my squad have always expressed their respect for him and the often difficult decisions he has to make.

Paddy's credentials are of the highest calibre. He has been the referee of 32 test matches and over 175 first-class appointments, both of which are New Zealand records.

Of the five England test matches Paddy has taken care of since I became coach in 1997 the two that stand out, to me, are the Investec Challenge match against South Africa in 1998 and the Rugby World Cup semi-final against France in 2003.

The South African game had a great build-up. The Springboks were attempting to break the world record for successive wins, held by New Zealand at 17, and we were playing off the back of qualifying for the Rugby World Cup in Huddersfield, a tough and well documented summer tour Down Under and a one-point defeat to the Wallabies the week before.

Some members of the media and former players were saying that I should be removed as coach if we lost. However, none of these issues had any bearing on my preparation, or the squad's.

We beat South Africa 13–7, Jerry Guscott scoring our try, with the side, captained by Lawrence Dallaglio, performing outstandingly. We hadn't beaten South Africa at Twickenham since 1992 and we've now won our last four games against them, which underlines the progress we have made as a side.

The World Cup semi-final against France was always going to be an exceedingly tough game. The media interest was massive and Andy Robinson and I, once again, had a very open, honest and positive dialogue with Paddy before the game, a process I'm sure Bernard Laporte went through as well.

France scored the first try and Paddy handled a challenging game well and made tough calls, with Dominici being sinbinned in the first half and Betsen in the second.

Jonny Wilkinson kicked well, but I was delighted with the overall team performance, which set us up well for the game against Australia in the final.

From my experience of working with Paddy, it would appear he enjoys the test arena and big games as much as I do. I've never seen him affected by the pressure that comes with the territory of refereeing a big game.

You have to be at the top of your game to handle the deciding test in a British Lions series, as Paddy did in 2001, and also to take charge of the Springboks international against the Wallabies directly after the infamous incident when a fan attacked David McHugh at Durban. Once again, Paddy took charge of these games and handled them in his customary professional manner.

Finally, I hope Paddy continues to referee as long as possible. He is professional on and off the field and I wish him, his wife Carolyn and their family all the very best for the future.

Clive Woodward, England Head Coach

Mucking In at Makarewa

It was July 1959 and Valerie O'Brien's pregnancy was beginning to weigh heavily on the mind of Dr Murray Robertson. The doctor was much admired throughout Invercargill, where he conducted his practice, for his caring attitude and gentle nature.

But he was a rugby fanatic and on the afternoon of the 18th he had an appointment at Carisbrook in Dunedin where Ronnie Dawson's British Lions were to engage in combat with the All Blacks in the first of a four-match test series. Dr Robertson had secured a grandstand ticket, a rare treasure indeed. It sat splendidly on his desk, right beside the open diary that reminded him that on the same afternoon Valerie O'Brien was due to give birth to her fifth child.

There was never any question which of these important events should take priority. By the time Dr Robertson set out with his fellow rugby cronies in his trusty Austin on the road north to Dunedin, Valerie O'Brien understood that for the next 24 hours, while almost the entire male population of New Zealand was transfixed on events at Carisbrook, she should remain totally immobile. She wasn't to even think about cooking, hanging out washing or even answering knocks at the door.

What an occasion it was at Carisbrook. The mighty Lions threw everything at the men in black, scoring four wonderful tries. But their nemesis was a Goliath in the

No. 1 jersey called Don Clarke who answered every try with a penalty goal. He landed a couple more goals, for good measure, to give the All Blacks an unbelievable 18–17 win. That such an important rugby international could be won in such a manner sparked outrage among the British media and supporters and, of course, provoked plenty of stimulating discussion among the All Black faithful as well. So much so that Dr Robertson did not return to Invercargill until after midnight, relieved to find there were no messages on his telephone notepad from the O'Brien residence. His instructions had obviously been faithfully followed.

Scarcely had he descended into slumber than the telephone began ringing. Mrs O'Brien was in labour and on her way to the hospital.

'I'll be there as soon as I can,' assured Dr Robertson, struggling to get both eyes open at the same time. When they did finally co-ordinate, he noted it was 3.30 a.m.

Having delivered Mrs O'Brien's four other children, Dr Robertson knew her pattern well enough. A quick check of the situation and he assured everyone within hearing range that the baby would be 'at least an hour', whereupon he took himself off to an adjoining room, curled up and went back to sleep! As a consequence of which, he missed, by two minutes, the birth of Patric Denis O'Brien, who wasn't prepared to wait for the good doctor to overcome his tiredness.

Paddy possessed cherubic qualities — fair, curly hair, blue eyes, dimples and lots of smiles. He slotted naturally into the O'Brien household behind Anne, Margot, Kevin and Casey and would eventually be joined by Danny, Gabrielle, Tim and, after a six-year break, Jeremy ... nine in total.

When Patric, who wouldn't acquire the nickname of Paddy until he was a teenager, arrived the O'Briens were living close to Invercargill city, with his father Ray working at the Alliance freezing works site at Lorneville. With the growing family ready for school, Raymond and Valerie decided to buy their first home, a four-and-a-half acre property at Makarewa, a tiny settlement on the main road about ten kilometres west of Invercargill.

The Makarewa move was a truly great idea, a perfect place in which to rear a large family. They would live there for almost 20 years. They had room to plant a couple of acres of potatoes, which they sold (the early crop at the gate, the main crop in 140 lb bags to the market), in addition to which they ran up to 20 sheep and they also had hens, a cow and even a pig. They also maintained an extensive vegetable garden and grew blackcurrants. Which meant the O'Briens were largely self-sufficient, and it also meant there was always plenty going on to interest the kids. They often made their own bread and ginger beer and every Easter they would drive through to Central Otago and load up with fruit for preserving.

A small, empty paddock adjoined the house where all the children from the immediate neighbourhood came to play, the Dawsons, the McPauls, the Voss's, the Vallis, the Udys and, later, the Henderson boys, David and Paul, the Mortimers and the Grays. It suited everyone just fine, and the parents could tell by the amount of noise and yelling, that the kids were all at O'Briens playing rugby or cricket and, therefore, out of mischief.

Poor wee Gabrielle, a lone female in the midst of six brothers, stoically contributed her bit. But one day she fled inside, seeking the comforting arms of her mother, because, while stationed at first-five, she had dropped a pass that cost her team a match-winning try. Her siblings had rounded on her.

'What are you, a girl?' they yelled scornfully.

When Paddy was about three, one day his 'big' sisters Anne and Margot dressed him in a frock, brushed his curls up nicely and took him over to show their 'new sister' to a rather bemused, elderly neighbour!

The O'Briens' car was an impressively large Vauxhall PAX, perfect because, with its large front seat, nine family members could be ferried to church for Sunday mass or, at Christmas time, transported on the 30-minute drive down to the holiday home, or crib as it was known, at Riverton. Seat belts weren't a concern then. Traffic was light and the speed at which Paddy's father drove was more likely to prompt a 'hurry-up' blast from a following driver than to ever be a traffic hazard.

'Paddy, you sit on Anne's knee,' instructed Valerie. Paddy dutifully obeyed. He'd have sat on anyone's knee to get to Riverton. It was his favourite place.

The crib had three bedrooms. Raymond and Valerie occupied one, the boys piled into another and the girls made themselves at home in the third. An old gramophone player ensured there was always music to listen to.

Young Patric spent all day, every day, rain, hail or shine, on the beach at Mitchell's Bay, directly opposite the crib. He built sandcastles, he climbed trees, he swam, he caught cockabullies, he chatted to whoever was in his company. His mother's chunky sandwiches sustained him through the day and he enjoyed nothing more for dinner than a barbecued sausage. He never had any suntan lotion applied and, notwithstanding his fair skin, cannot ever recall being sunburnt. But, then again, this was the 1960s and the ozone layer was firmly intact; in fact, it's doubtful if anyone in Riverton at the time even knew what the ozone layer was. On Paddy's first day at school, he demonstrated the determination to succeed that would become his hallmark. As his birthday was in July, the school year was well advanced when he started and the 'tiny tots' class efficiently organised. The children were quite used to finishing off small tasks at home.

On his very first day, Paddy brought home a small piece of handicraft which, he assured his mother, 'has to be finished tonight'. Nothing would persuade him otherwise and although his eyes could hardly stay open, he sat at the kitchen table working on it till it was finished ... every last stitch!

Raymond O'Brien supplemented his income growing potatoes, a crop that does particularly well in the deep south. Because of Raymond's commitments at the freezing works during the week, the potatoes were tended to and eventually harvested on Saturdays, with assistance from all the O'Brien children. Well, all except young Patric, that is. His responsibility was to provide regular score updates of the local senior club rugby match, particularly if it featured the O'Briens' favourite team Marist, and to keep his father posted on the outcome of the daily double at the nearest race meeting. Paddy fulfilled this assignment most diligently by standing on a stool in the kitchen and giving the mantel radio his undivided attention.

Raymond O'Brien's formula for investing on the daily double was basic. He always took No. 1 in the first leg and No. 2 in the second. In Paddy's memory, those numbers never came up more than a handful of times over several years. And when they did, the dividend was modest. Mind you, the outlay was only five shillings.

Listening to the rugby commentaries fired Paddy's enthusiasm for the game. The 'voice' of the time was John Howson, later to become Radio New Zealand's premier commentator. Paddy listened enthralled, especially when Marist was featuring. The team's star was invariably Frank Oliver, another who would make his mark on the national scene. Whenever Marist scored, young Patric made a beeline for the garden with the joyous news. He wasn't quite so eager when the opposition was adding to its points tally!

If Saturdays were about potatoes and sport, and for Paddy most definitely not in that order, Sundays were quite a different mix. The O'Briens' were staunch Catholics which meant that there were fairly strict guidelines regarding Sundays. For Paddy, his Sabbath effectively began on Saturday night when he was on compulsory shoe cleaning duty. Given that he had three sisters and four brothers at the time, it represented a demanding commitment. It suited Paddy just fine because among the alternative chores was milking the cow. And that wasn't Paddy's bucket of milk at all; indeed, he hated the outdoor jobs. He'd have happily polished sixty pairs or shoes rather than milk one cow.

Flora St West comprised 10 houses and was a close-knit community. The residents were amazingly talented at sport and every second home, it seemed, owned a racehorse.

The O'Briens subsisted on love, caring and attitude more than wealth. Paddy had to operate with a worn and buckled tennis racket but invariably cleaned up opponents who sported more modern equipment. Many were the occasions during Paddy's sporting days at college when no more than four parents were huddled on the sideline. One would always be his father who could have been working, bolstering his income, but supporting his children was always a higher priority.

Valerie O'Brien was always there for her children. But one afternoon she missed the bus from the city. When seven-year-old Patric arrived home from school, he was devastated to find his mother absent. He burst into tears and was inconsolable until she finally turned up.

Raymond O'Brien was a disciplinarian, one whose reasoned judgments were accepted by his children. One rule he imposed was that there was to be no alcohol consumed in the family car.

Because Casey was an asthmatic, Paddy was always his driver. On one occasion after rugby training, when he drove home from the Marist club rooms, the boys had broken the golden rule by consuming three bottles of beer on the journey to Makarewa. Unfortunately, some of it was spilled, leaving an unmistakable odour in the car, one immediately identified by O'Brien senior. He demanded an explanation. Because Paddy had driven, Casey, the only one who hadn't imbibed, took the rap. Paddy was innocent, he insisted. He and the others had consumed the beer.

Casey was distraught when his father grounded him, not from driving but from playing rugby for the college first fifteen that Saturday. No penalty could have hurt more. It was tantamount to being shown a red card on the rugby field.

Because the O'Briens' financial resources were meagre, Christmas presents were never lavish. One year, Paddy was given a plastic hat with flashing lights on it and some lollies. He thought it was the greatest present ever, the hat becoming almost a permanent fixture on his head for weeks afterwards. Another year, one of his brothers was given a copy of the Peter Snell book *No Bugles, No Drums*. That really was special, and Paddy, who as a youngster only read sports books, was in seventh heaven when he was allowed to borrow it.

As far as Paddy was concerned, the O'Briens didn't want for anything. It wasn't until he was a teenager and accompanied his parents to the service station one day, when his mother paid $10 off their account that he realised they existed precariously close to the breadline. When Paddy discovered that the neighbours had coloured sheets on their beds, while the O'Briens made do with basic white, he decided it was time to upgrade. His mother was mortified when she came outside and found young Patric industriously attacking the sheets on the clothesline with a pot of red paint!

Whenever the neighbours saw any building going on at the O'Briens' property, they concluded it was because Valerie was pregnant again. Which wasn't far from the truth. Finding sleeping quarters for nine children (well, eight really, because Jeremy, the youngest, was pretty much an after-thought) was certainly a challenge. Paddy shared a double bed with Casey, which seemed a perfectly normal arrangement at the time, and it was a case of first up, best dressed.

Because Valerie O'Brien was a regular visitor to the Invercargill maternity home, a variety of babysitters were brought in to mind the children. One of them, a Mrs Bartell, seemed to regard it as her personal challenge in life to tidy up the O'Briens' home and, in particular, to spruce up young Patric. She had an obsession with cleanliness, a quality not high on Paddy's priority list. He found he was forever being dumped in the bath, which he didn't appreciate. Revenge was extracted by throwing stones and objects at the windows. Paddy, for one, was enormously relieved when Mrs Bartell moved on.

Sunday afternoons were for entertaining relatives or going visiting. Paddy's favourites were Bill and Marjory Hewitt, his uncle and aunty, because they possessed a television set, a rare item in Southland in the 1960s. Often in late summer or autumn the O'Briens' visit would coincide with the delayed coverage of a Five Nations rugby match, which represented sheer heaven for Paddy. He would never have believed, as he lay on the floor transfixed by the action from Twickenham or Murrayfield or Cardiff Arms Park that by the turn of the century he would be officiating at such illustrious contests.

Paddy had boundless energy as a youngster and wore out more pairs of shoes and boots than any of the other O'Brien children. Toes were kicked out, heals worn through, all in record time. His parents were convinced the footwear industry in the area slumped when Paddy eventually left home and the police force took over the job of supplying regulation issue to keep him shod.

Alas, he was also injury prone. He became a regular visitor to the Accident and Emergency department at Invercargill Hospital from falling off fences or out of trees. On one occasion he landed on the roof of the hen house and smashed right through it, which didn't do much for either Paddy or the hens. The duty nurse at the hospital at Kew asked on one occasion if young O'Brien had been there before. 'Oh, yes,' replied Mrs O'Brien, 'on quite a few occasions.' The nurse's eyes lit up when she uncovered Paddy's bulky file. 'Ah, yes, I see what you mean!'

To any casual onlooker, Paddy must have looked like a demented butterfly as he darted around the paddock, tackling imaginary opponents, sidestepping them, diving for heroic tries, slotting conversions and dropped goals and celebrating epic victories. What the onlookers didn't see were the world class players in the same paddock. Barry John and Gareth Edwards were often there, Mike Gibson dropped in occasionally and so did JPR Williams. Paddy's team was blessed to have players of the calibre of Sid Going, Ian Kirkpatrick, Ian MacRae, Bill Davis, Kel Tremain and Waka Nathan and, of course, the incomparable Fergie McCormick.

It didn't matter what miracles Johns and Edwards achieved, Fabulous Fergie was always there to ensure a home victory. With no time constraints, often both teams would accumulate in excess of 100 points before Paddy was called in for his evening meal. If Paddy's team was trailing, there was always just enough time for Fergie to slot a late dropped goal to ensure Makarewa remained the Paddock of Pain for visiting teams.

For his 10th birthday, Paddy was presented with a pair of rugby boots and a ball. For many days, it might have been weeks, the boots never came off.

And then came the fantastic news ... Fergie McCormick was coming to Makarewa. FERGIE McCORMICK WAS COMING TO MAKAREWA! It seemed scarcely believable that such a famous All Black, Paddy's hero, would visit such a humble wee settlement in Southland. But it was confirmed. And not only that, he was to be hosted for an evening by the O'Briens. The greatest match-winning All Black on earth was going to be right there in Paddy's home. The power of prayer!

Fabulous Fergie's visit was part of a project by the Makarewa community to raise funds for a new sports complex that would provide squash courts and tennis courts for the local sportspeople. Raymond O'Brien was a driving force behind the fund raising and was the individual responsible for luring Fergie McCormick to the area. One of the fundraising ventures was to have locals try and match Fergie McCormick's best All Black fifteen, comprised of players he'd played alongside. There was a modest entry fee and the prize, which had considerable appeal among a rural community in the early 1970s, was a dozen quart bottles of beer.

Paddy and his brother Casey found the challenge of matching Fergie's fabulous fifteen irresistible, and they had a decided advantage over everyone else because he was going to be dining in their home. Urged on by Paddy, Casey peppered Fergie with questions.

'Sid Going was surely the greatest attacking halfback in the world, don't you think?' asked Casey.

'Yes, I'd always have Sid ahead of Chris,' replied Fergie.

Ahhh, thought Paddy, that's got the halfback position sorted out.

'Grahame Thorne had a fantastic tour of South Africa in 1970,' said Casey. 'But was he a better centre or wing?'

'I'd always have Thorney on the wing with Bill Davis at centre. Billy set up his wingers so well.'

Two more ticked off on Paddy's list.

And so the evening progressed. Paddy's prompting and Casey's questioning got about seven-eighths of the team sorted out before Raymond O'Brien ordered the youngsters to 'give Fergie a break'.

Next day Paddy methodically filled out the entry form, borrowed the dollar entry fee from his mother and slipped it into the special box provided at the local hall. When the entries were marked, only one had correctly matched all 15 of Fergie McCormick's mightiest All Black fifteen. And the winner was ... 12-year-old Patric O'Brien. Who else?

Paddy's father was a non-drinker, so he swapped the beer for a crate of soft drink and proudly delivered it to his sons.

'Guess what I've got here?' he announced on his return home. Paddy and Casey high-fived each other when they realised they'd outsmarted the best in the district.

Paddy's first job was a paper run, delivering the *Southland Times*. It provided a useful source of income and eventually he was able to purchase a new aluminium tennis racket which became his prized possession. One afternoon, he and neighbour Angela Mortimer were at the Doon St bus stop in the city, readying themselves for the trip back to Makarewa. Having grown up together and of the same age, they were best friends; indeed, many in Makarewa predicted they would eventually marry. On this particular occasion, a friendly argument became heated and culminated in Angela throwing Paddy's tennis racket onto the road. Paddy was so outraged, he whacked her.

The bus driver immediately leapt to Angela's defence. He hastened down the steps of the bus, grabbed young O'Brien by the scruff of the neck and frog-marched him backwards into a hedge.

'Boys don't hit girls,' he told Paddy. 'Don't you ever let me see you do anything like that again.'

'But she threw my tennis racket on the road!'

'I don't think you're listening to me,' continued the driver. 'Now you apologise.'

Under duress, Paddy did apologise to Angela, but he wasn't sure the bus driver fully appreciated her unforgivable actions. She'd treated his most priceless possession with disdain. Some things demanded a good whack!

Because Raymond O'Brien worked on Saturday mornings, Paddy's rugby activities were confined to inter-school matches at Sacred Heart Primary School where all the teachers were nuns. Now this could have been a serious impediment but the principal, Sister Xavierus, was a rugby fanatic and organised the first fifteen as efficiently as any male could have.

When Sister Xavierus was assembling her team for the season's most important derby against Waikiwi Primary School, she found she had only 14 volunteers from forms one and two. So she went into the standard four room and singled out Paddy, whose passion for rugby was well known, and told him he was required for the first fifteen. Paddy couldn't believe his good fortune.

Fresh from his achievements in the paddock at Makarewa, he was soon a commanding individual. He became captain of the side, he took the kick-offs and he generally directed operations from his position at halfback. When he scored the winning try in the match against St Peters of Gore, his joy knew no limits. This confirmed that he was going to become an All Black.

In fact, it was in sports other than rugby that Patric O'Brien began to make a name for himself in the 1970s. Although he demonstrated sufficient talent at rugby to win selection (as a No. 8!) in the Southland under-45 kg team that defeated Otago 3–nil, it was in squash and athletics that he commanded headlines in the *Southland Times*.

As a squash player, operating out of the courts his father and a band of dedicated locals had built, Paddy and brother Casey, along with Scott Mortimer, Noel Crosswell and Martin McKelvie won the Southern Districts title in their age group. Their coach and the man who had an important influence on Paddy's sporting development was near neighbour Ted Mortimer. One day, when Paddy was playing Casey, watched by Ted, a disputed point culminated in Paddy throwing his racket against the wall. After the match, Ted Mortimer gave him a clip over the ear.

'If I see that behaviour again,' he warned Paddy, 'you're never playing squash again. You have to learn to respect your opponent.' It was an important lesson which Paddy took on board and has remembered to this day.

Paddy thought he might have a future in squash until he bravely entered the national championships one year and was humbled 9–0, 9–0, 9–0 by Stu Davenport, who was on his way to becoming a New Zealand representative.

The sporting event that Paddy proved a natural at was high jumping. He was making modest but unspectacular progress using the old-fashioned scissors method of clearing the bar, but once Doug Wray, a teacher at Marist Brothers School, introduced him to the Fosbury Flop, where the jumper effectively launches himself backwards at the bar, Paddy began smashing records.

The *Southland Times* reported after one athletics meeting: 'Pat O'Brien thrilled the crowd with his high jumping. He had to overcome some difficulties including a rising run-up and a stiff wind which forced attendants to hold the bar as it rose to 1.94 metres. His performance was a crowd stopper and the whole area watched the young St Pauls jumper give a first-class performance. He earlier won the shot put and discus on handicap.'

Another report records that 'the continuing improvement being shown by Pat

O'Brien should soon see him featuring in higher positions on the national ranking list. He won both the senior and junior high jump titles at the meeting at the Caledonian Ground at the weekend.

'His effort in the poor conditions saw him break the Southland high jump record. His excellent leap of 1.94 metres equates to 6 ft 5 in and should he improve just two inches he will join a select band of New Zealand junior high jumpers who have cleared 2.00 metres.

'The New Zealand record at present is 2.04 metres, held by Terry Lomax of Canterbury.'

Another extract from the *Southland Times* announced that 'Pat O'Brien broke a long-standing record when jumping 1.85 metres in the A grade event at Surrey Park. He beat the record set by Jack Borland in 1952 by two centimetres. O'Brien is only 17.'

He would become the first high jumper in New Zealand to clear 2.00 metres on grass and the 2.04 metres, which equates to 6ft 8in, he cleared overseas (at the Police Olympics in Austin, Texas in 1982) remains the Southland record. The year he contested the high jump at the nationals, he finished third behind Canterbury's Terry Lomax, who went on to represent New Zealand at the Commonwealth Games, and Mark Hudson, who would go on to play rugby for Otago. He then shared first placing with Hudson and Quentin Poulsen at the New Zealand under-19 championships at Hawera, all of them clearing 1.92 metres. Poulsen won on countback from Hudson and Paddy.

Young O'Brien continued to achieve in athletics, and particularly the high jump. By virtue of his natural talent, he earned selection in a national training squad. For some aspiring sportsmen, this could have sparked a flourishing athletics career. But Paddy lacked the necessary motivation. He would explain to a colleague later that 'I could jump, and I did, but it was never a passion.' For Paddy, rugby was supreme. It was the sport about which he was totally passionate.

Yet as a rugby player, notwithstanding the blistering pace that brought him bucketloads of tries, Paddy was never more than a modest achiever. He would concede in later life that his ambition greatly exceeded his ability.

A sevens game he played for Sacred Heart Primary School against Ohai would come back to haunt him for the remainder of his playing career. A fearless tackler until then, he required treatment after lowering Ohai's star player Paul Laidlaw, who would go on to play dozens of matches for Southland. While the shoulder was sore, the full extent of the injury did not become apparent until Paddy executed his next tackle. He had actually broken his collar bone and suddenly he was in excruciating pain, pain like he has never experienced in life before or since.

Although the shoulder duly mended, Paddy was tackle shy for the remainder of his career. He became a jersey grabber rather than a classical tackler. Selectors noticed and it prevented him ever winning the full representative honours he so desperately sought.

But he had his moments. He scored the winning try for Marist in the Galbraith Shield club final against Blues at Rugby Park in 1979, he represented Southland B, sharing in a notable victory over Otago B at Carisbrook, and in the late 1970s he won selection in a talented Southland sevens team, that included such astute performers as All Black Steven Pokere, Kelvin Farrington, Alan Monaghan and the player who caused him such anguish, Paul Laidlaw.

Sevens in New Zealand didn't enjoy the same status then as it does now and the national tournament was staged at Feilding without any great fanfare or television focus, which was probably as well for Paddy. When Southland was playing Counties, Paddy's lack of bulk became evident when he attempted a high tackle on Counties' hardy old campaigner Alan Dawson who lifted him off the ground by the jersey and carried him almost 25 metres to the goal-line for one of the tries of the tournament!

Academically, Paddy was above average but anything that interfered with sport always seemed to him to be a complete waste of time. He used to sit in class in the fourth and fifth forms watching the clock as it crept slowly towards the magic hour of 3.30 p.m. when he could get out onto the field and practise his rugby or his athletics or, in summer, his tennis and his squash.

At primary school, Paddy was always in the top two, proving particularly adept at spelling. When he advanced to Marist College, later to become Verdon College, his infatuation for sport placed him seriously at odds with the headmaster, Brother Roger, who was a brilliant academic. They detested each other from the start.

On the day Paddy left school, at the tender age of 16, Brother Roger refused to present him with the sports award he well and truly deserved for his accomplishments, even though he had set college records in more than one discipline.

What followed represented a fascinating character sketch of two men. The sports master was so angry at the headmaster's refusal to acknowledge young O'Brien that he purchased and had engraved, at his own expense, an appropriately worded medal. After all the other prizes were handed out, he stood up and made a personal presentation to Paddy as 'the outstanding sports achiever'. As the headmaster fumed in the background, the audience gave Paddy rapturous applause.

Paddy's natural intelligence saw him achieve pass marks in English and Geography in the School Certificate examination. Generally though he languished as a student but excelled in communications. He was always interested in people and loved nothing better than to chat to older folks. Coming home from school on the bus, he often chose to sit beside an elderly passenger and engage them in conversation. One elderly Makarewa neighbour told Raymond O'Brien how he looked forward to the children going past in the afternoons because 'that lad of yours always stops for a chat'.

It wasn't just the older generation Paddy related to. He also got on famously well with members of the opposite sex. A highlight of the school year was the annual ball and Paddy had all bases covered as the event approached. Finally, he went to his mother, with a perplexed look on his face.

'There are these three girls I'm supposed to take to the ball,' he said. 'What do you think I should do?'

His mother was brutally honest. 'If you've managed to get yourself into this situation, Pat,' she said, 'you can jolly well get yourself out of it!'

The O'Brien children were always encouraged to give of their best at school, although the choice of their vocation was always left up to them. Paddy's father Ray was born into a farming family and that was always his first love. He started out as a shepherd, but being epileptic had to find more appropriate employment. He eventually became a freezing worker. It was tough, monotonous work, and a job which he would not allow his children to engage in.

Valerie O'Brien had been exceptionally bright at college, achieving 98 in English for her School Certificate. She had ambitions of becoming a writer but eventually settled for being a mother to nine children and a devoted wife to her husband.

The academic achievements of the family were quite notable. Of the nine children, Anne, Margot, Danny, Gabrielle and Jeremy achieved university degrees. Anne attained a BA and LLB and both Grabrielle and Jeremy achieved honours in their degrees. Margot qualified as a nurse and now works for the New Zealand Cancer

Society, while Gabrielle worked for a time in a government department, one of her duties being to write speeches for the then Minister of Labour, Stan Rodger. She is now a full-time mother to two children. Casey is manager of a social welfare department in Melbourne, while Kevin is foreman of a processing plant in Dunedin. Tim is stock manager for the Browning Brothers farming complex in Hawke's Bay and Jeremy is the marketing manager for Lion Breweries in Auckland. Interestingly, Paddy is the only child still living in Invercargill.

About every two years they have an excuse, like a birthday or a wedding anniversary, to come together. Such occasions are always special when the brothers and sisters share stories of their days growing up in Makarewa.

Paddy never aspired to higher education, although he might have hung in at Marist College had he and the headmaster not regarded each other with such utter disdain. So, as a tender teenager, there he was out in the work force.

Neighbour Doug Gray was a principal in the tanning company of Colyer, Watson and Underwood and was influential in getting young Patric a position of office clerk at the princely wage of $26 a week. None of the children ever had problems finding work in and around Invercargill. 'Oh, you're Ray and Val's son,' the employer would inevitably say. 'You'll do us.'

Paddy thought life was pretty cool at 17. Of his weekly pay packet, $10 went to his parents as board, $6 was saved towards a car and the balance went on such essentials as 'fags and booze'.

While Paddy enjoyed this cosy existence, after a year as a clerk he began to think there had to be more demanding challenges in life. And so he applied for a cadetship at the New Zealand Police training school at Trentham, north of Wellington. He met the height criteria, flew through the physical testing and obviously provided sufficient correct answers to the IQ test because he was accepted for the year-long course.

Qualifying for the course was one thing. Committing himself to it was quite another. The prospect of spending a year away from Southland as a teenager suddenly paled and he switched to a three-month course which commenced when he turned 19.

And so, in August 1978, he took off for the capital on what he anticipated would be a great adventure. But there was to be an unpleasant surprise for young O'Brien. The normally super-fit athlete staggered through a two-mile run, coming home an embarrassing last. Something was seriously wrong so he dragged himself along to the doctor.

The diagnosis wasn't good. Paddy was suffering from glandular fever and hepatitis. His 'adventure' was disappointingly cut short. Only a few weeks after his departure, he was back in Invercargill convalescing.

Because the next police training course at Trentham wasn't until January 1979, Paddy, once restored to full health, was given work experience handling light duties with the police in Invercargill. He took to the job like a duck to water.

When he finally completed the course at Trentham, he was presented with a job application form. He was required to complete four spaces indicating the towns or cities where he would prefer to be based. Beside all four, Paddy wrote Invercargill! 'Where else would I want to go?' he replied earnestly when a supervisor inquired if he was being facetious.

One reason Paddy wanted to be based in Invercargill was because of a flourishing relationship that had developed between himself and Ann Wilson, a bank clerk. They had been going out together for more than a year and prior to Paddy's departure for Trentham had become engaged. It was while he was on the course that Ann told him she was pregnant. He was 19 and she was 18. There was only one honourable course of action. In May 1979, they were married at Sacred Heart Church in Invercargill.

Given their tender ages, modern day attitudes would suggest their decision to marry was misdirected. But Paddy prefers to identify all the positives. For a start, it made him grow up quickly. Had it not been for the commitment to Ann, had he remained footloose and fancy free, he's sure he would have squandered his salary on the good life.

Instead, he and Ann rented a police house in Invercargill and eventually saved enough money to purchase their own home, for which they paid $42,000, a not inconsiderable amount of money in the early 1980s. Although the marriage ended in 1984, Paddy doesn't look back with any regrets. The bottom line, he acknowledges, is that they were too young. They soon recognised that they were a pair of individuals with completely different ideals in life.

Out of their relationship came two wonderful children, Kylie and Matthew. Kylie, 24 when she was watching her father refereeing at the 2003 Rugby World Cup, works in human resources in Sydney and has marriage plans for 2004. Matthew, who displays many of the wayward and rather devilish characteristics of his father, completed a pharmaceutical degree at Otago University in 2003. His post-graduate year was being undertaken in 2004 on Australia's Gold Coast.

Paddy would remarry in 1987, this time to Carolyn Wyeth.

Paddy the Policeman

When Brian Beardsley, who was in charge of the Invercargill Police Armed Offenders Squad in 1979, decided his team needed a good work-out he chose one of his newest, rawest recruits, Paddy, to play the part of the offender.

No one would have identified Paddy as a policeman. For the purpose of the exercise, the long-haired 20-year-old, unknown to any of the Armed Offenders Squad, was dressed in flared jeans and a casual top. With his sunglasses on, he could easily have been mistaken for a pop singer.

Only Beardsley, Paddy and the manager of the Esk Street TAB knew the robbery and taking of a hostage (Judy Trimm, a typist from police headquarters) were being staged. When the manager, on cue, telephoned the police to report the 'armed hold-up', giving a wonderfully accurate description of the robber and the car he was driving, Paddy began cruising the streets of Invercargill, eager to give the AOS a run for their money.

The driver of one of the pursuit vehicles identified Paddy's car and ordered him to pull over. Paddy was compliant, until a patrol member approached and ordered him out of the car. Suddenly, Paddy's adrenalin took over. He reacted as if he was starring in the movie *French Connection*, slamming the car into gear and screeching away from his apprehender, driving up and over the footpath to do so. He weaved around a lamp post and was gone.

The police officer, stunned by developments, rushed to his car to call for assistance. He couldn't believe what was happening on a quiet Monday morning in his home town of Invercargill.

By the time the Armed Offenders Squad got themselves organised, Paddy and his hostage were half an hour gone and ensconced in a reserve close to Invercargill known as Thompson's Bush. Eventually, Paddy's car was discovered — and identified as belonging to a member of the well-respected O'Brien family — but by then Paddy and his hostage were camouflaged high up a tree, well out of range of the dog handlers.

The challenge for the AOS had been to apprehend the robber and bring the hostage out alive. By 12.30 p.m. they had made no progress whatsoever. And they were thoroughly embarrassed when Paddy and his hostage, doubling round behind the police ranks, advanced on their assembly point.

'Hi, Brian,' Paddy tossed at Sergeant Beardsley. 'What time's lunch?'

The Armed Offenders Squad received a serious number of demerit points for their handling of that particular exercise while Paddy was identified as a police trainee with a promising future.

But the action hadn't finished. After lunch, Paddy and his hostage were given time to drive to a pre-designated farm shed at Tokanui, 30 kilometres away, where the challenge for the AOS and the police was to get them both out alive. Armed with a revolver that fired blanks, Paddy kept his pursuers at bay for a considerable time.

Unfortunately Paddy's enthusiasm impacted on hostage Judy. Unfamiliar with firearms, he fired off a series of shots so close to Judy, she had to take four days off work with a deaf ear. The stand-off ended with Paddy letting his hostage go after the shed was tear gassed, a nightmare ordeal he knew he never wanted to experience again.

Paddy would spend two years on escort duty, where his main responsibility was helping usher individuals to court either in Invercargill or Dunedin. He and John Hughes, who went on to represent Southland as a lock forward, once decided to see how fast they could drive their police vehicle from Invercargill to Dunedin. It would be regarded as inexcusable behaviour now, and modern speed cameras would curtail such activities, but to officers O'Brien and Hughes it was light-hearted entertainment in the course of duty at that time.

On one journey north to Dunedin, the police vehicle broke down. Paddy, with a limited knowledge of engine workings, was in a perplexed state when the prisoner on board offered to effect the necessary repairs in return for an ice cream. Paddy, aware the individual concerned was not regarded as dangerous, accepted the offer. Both completed the journey satisfied.

One night in 1980 he called on a hotel just outside Invercargill, leaving his car unlocked. When he returned, it was to discover that someone had stolen the radio microphone. Somewhat embarrassed at his own foolishness, he announced that he was returning to the same hotel the following evening. 'And no one's going to pinch anything from my car tonight because I'll be locking the doors.'

When he came back out on this occasion it was to the realisation that someone had got away with the red light off the roof!

When 1981 rolled around, Paddy found himself caught up in the Springbok tour, in more ways than he could ever have anticipated. As a rabid rugby fan, red-necked New Zealander and diligent policeman, he could see no valid reason why the tour should not go ahead. Hell, it was sport, wasn't it, and as a policeman, it was his duty to protect law-abiding New Zealanders.

Personally, Paddy was in his element, defending his countrymen's democratic right to participate in his favourite sport against whomsoever they wished ... until he arrived in Christchurch for the first test. There, he was delegated to march in plain clothes among the second row of protestors, feeding information back to base. Marching in the protestors' front row was his sister Anne. And when the marchers advanced on the main gates of Lancaster Park, there was his brother Kevin, passionately defending his right to attend this sporting occasion by shouting abuse at the protestors. It's no wonder the Springbok tour has never been a topic for discussion around the O'Brien family's Christmas table!

The furthest north Paddy was assigned in '81 was Palmerston North, being saved from having to help defend Eden Park at the time of the third test, when probably the fiercest battles between protestors and police were fought, because his son Matthew had been born.

Paddy, 22 at the time, was an extremely diligent policeman. At a briefing before the

Manawatu-Springboks encounter in Palmerston North, where all the troops were issued with handcuffs and batons, the commanding officer asked if there were any questions. Paddy's hand shot up.

'Yes, what's the problem?'

'I've lost the band off my helmet,' reported Paddy.

'You were obviously a bloody cadet,' said the commanding officer.

'No, sir.'

'I don't think the protestors will notice.'

Paddy would argue that the Springbok tour, however you interpreted the rights and wrongs of it, was a time of growing up for the New Zealand police. The police are better equipped and prepared for emergencies on a major scale as a consequence of the events during that tempestuous winter.

The tour split many New Zealand households down the middle, especially those where policemen were married to schoolteachers. Paddy empathised with fellow members of the force who suddenly found themselves at odds with their partners. After all, his sister was a front line protestor!

Paddy relished his brief moments of leave back in Invercargill because the country's southernmost city remained remarkably peaceful and tranquil, in contrast to the acts of near civil war that were being waged at most of the other Springbok match venues. Invercargill had geography on its side, being such a damnably difficult place to get to from major centres, and it also had a no-nonsense chief of police, Tommy Thomson, who allowed zero tolerance for individuals who sought to disrupt law-abiding citizens from playing rugby.

'This is my town,' he barked at any protestor who crossed his path. 'I don't care what you've got up to in Hamilton, Palmerston North or Wellington, you won't be doing it here.'

One of the protestors' leaders dared to call Tommy Thomson a racist and got clobbered for his trouble.

Tommy Thomson was the last of the old school police bosses, one blindly loyal to his troops. If a policeman was in strife, as long as he was totally honest, Thomson would back him 100 per cent and not allow him to suffer. Paddy saw him as one of a rare breed with a great sense of justice. He still enjoys sharing a beer with his old staff members.

Ask Paddy, more than 20 years on, whether the '81 Springbok tour should ever have gone ahead and he gives an ambivalent answer: 'From a police viewpoint, yes; morally, I'm not so sure.'

The Springbok tour highlighted that many New Zealand policemen were not particularly fit, which led to the introduction of PCT (Physical Competency Test) for all police. It involved a variety of exercises, from pushing a 1500 cwt trailer 10 metres, to lifting a heavy tyre out of that trailer before running 250 metres and then walking along a narrow beam, all in a set time.

As a rugby player, Paddy was one of the fitter members of the force, but he attacked the PCT course with such startling aggression that by the time he'd hurtled through the 250 metres he'd turned an alarming crimson colour and was unable to complete the walk along the bar.

'For God's sake, Paddy,' his boss Ian McFadyen told him, 'this is not the bloody Olympics. Pace yourself. You had twenty seconds to spare.'

A more subdued Paddy completed the course comfortably the next day (and has never failed a fitness test since).

In the wake of the Springbok tour, life back home in Invercargill returned to normal. Well, as normal as a uniformed policeman's life could be. For a while he operated as a court orderly, effectively the judge's gopher, where events were largely predictable. But when he was on duty as a uniformed officer, anything could happen. As they did in 1983 when prisoners began rioting at the Invercargill borstal.

Things had been out of control at the prison for almost two hours before the police were summoned. As Paddy and his boss Ian McFadyen arrived at the scene, three prisoners broke out through the front door. On sighting police, they made a beeline for the drycleaner's shop opposite, with Paddy and Ian in hot pursuit.

The next scene could have been scripted in Hollywood as prisoners and pursuers weaved in and out of blankets and sheets until finally Paddy and Ian cornered two of the escapees.

'The other one's hiding in that corner over there,' said Paddy, demonstrating the instinct that would make him a successful referee.

Slowly, reluctantly, the third prisoner stood up, adopting a threatening pose. In his hand was an unfinished cigarette.

Paddy, who was wielding a long baton, broke the tension by pointing to the cigarette. 'I hope one of us is a smoker and can use that!'

Once the three prisoners were safely back in custody, Paddy and Ian made their way back to the prison where Ian made an attempt to kick down a door behind which confusion obviously still reigned. To Paddy and Ian's great good fortune, the door held strong because it was later revealed that the prisoners on the other side were armed with lethal weapons and one even had a gun.

When, some time later, reinforcements arrived and the situation was brought under control, two prisoners were discovered in an overhead manhole. When they refused to come out, the superintendent of the prison fired a tear gas canister up amongst them. Unfortunately, it fell straight back down, sending Paddy and his colleagues scurrying as the fumes enveloped them.

On another occasion, Paddy and Ian were patrolling in Mary St in the centre of Invercargill when a series of explosions put them on full alert. The source of the activity became apparent when the alarm began sounding at a chemist shop. As they approached, three burglars came running out and piled into a Holden Berlina which shouldn't have been a match for the police department's Holden, but the Berlina was more powerful and maintained an advantage in a high speed chase along the main road to Gore.

At Dacre, the Berlina careered off the road into the scrub where the occupants, mindful the police were close behind, jumped out and hot-footed it in different directions. Paddy, equally swiftly out of the HQ, gave chase, randomly selecting one of the villains who had the misfortune to confront a fence. Paddy arrived as he was clambering over it and delivered a fearful whack over the head with his baton. Notwithstanding the power of the blow, the robber scampered away into the bush.

Paddy let him go, a judgement call he deemed fortunate when he was advised later that one of the individuals concerned was a notorious burglar of chemist shops from Christchurch who was understood to be armed.

That very individual, sporting a significant bruise on the back of the head, was apprehended in north Invercargill the following day. Paddy was summoned and asked to identify him. 'I can't,' he replied. 'It was dark when I hit him. I have no idea what he looked like.' The circumstantial evidence was damning but Paddy, demonstrating the fair-mindedness that would distinguish his refereeing career, refused to compromise himself.

In 1986, Paddy took the decision to join the CIB. He could have chugged along for the remainder of his career as a uniformed policeman, dividing his duties between office routine and rushing to trouble spots when crises occurred.

But Paddy was ready for a fresh challenge, which his entry into the CIB certainly provided. There were three candidates for the position, but Paddy, who had completed a dozen in-service training units, quickly went to the top of the list.

The course that qualifies policemen as detectives is recognised as the hardest in the business, involving no fewer than 24 exams. They are required to know the law inside out. In his new role as a detective, Paddy transferred to Oamaru. It would do wonders for his refereeing career and it would also involve him in a couple of the country's high-profile murder cases.

Paddy and his supervisor, Detective Sergeant Brian Burrows, rushed to the small Central Otago town of Ranfurly one evening when a call came in that a member of the force, Peter Umbers, had been killed. The word was he had been shot and when Detectives O'Brien and Burrows sighted their colleague's body, so badly had he been beaten up, they initially accepted that that was how he had died.

In fact, the 17-year-old responsible, who was in custody when Paddy arrived in Ranfurly in the middle of the night, had bludgeoned Umbers to death with his own baton. The teenager had been trailed by Senior Constable Umbers after robbing a pub. Umbers, unarmed, had pulled him over but somehow as he approached the offender's car, he had had his baton wrenched from him.

Paddy was outraged that a colleague, a decent family man simply doing his job, should be so senselessly killed, especially when it was later revealed that the motive for the robbery was to steal $300 to repay a debt.

Paddy and Brian Burrows were assigned the task of interviewing the offender who prior to their involvement had demonstrated a stubborn reluctance to talk. Detectives O'Brien and Burrows brought their considerable skills to the interviewing room although for almost three hours the suspect, one Richard Lakich, remained mute. Finally, Paddy got him to break his silence by inquiring if there was anything he, Lakich, wanted to ask him.

'Yeah, when did you last have sex?'

'Last Tuesday.'

'Who with?'

'My wife.'

'Was it any good?'

'I'm not complaining.'

It was almost another three hours before Paddy and his colleague finally extracted a confession. Lakich was subsequently convicted of the murder of Senior Constable Umbers and sentenced to life imprisonment. It was no wonder that Detectives O'Brien and Burrows were drained when they finally exited the interview room. They had been at it almost eight hours.

When *North and South* magazine carried a major feature on the Umbers murder, it disappointed Paddy that the only part of the extensive interview with Lakich it carried were those extracts with sexual connotations.

'Hell,' Paddy would explain, 'when you've got a subject as reluctant to talk as this fellow was, you'll say anything to provoke a response. It was sex, which in the context of what had happened was entirely incongruous, that finally got him to open up.'

Another murder that focused the nation's attention on the deep south involved a teenage girl, Kylie Smith, who was taken off her horse at Owaka, raped and killed. It was a case that Paddy, as a father of a young daughter himself, found particularly hard to deal with.

There was a strong resolve among the police to catch the offender and when he was finally locked up, Paddy wasn't surprised to find he had an extensive list of convictions which included being imprisoned for rape.

A local minister had magnanimously encouraged the rapist to come and live with him in Owaka. It was a display of compassion that had tragic consequences.

The only murder that happened in Oamaru during Paddy's three years there involved the stabbing of a young lad at a party by a well-known local, Kelvin McCarthy, who had benefited from a heart transplant as a consequence of a community fundraising venture.

It was while he was working on this case that Paddy first encountered Tim Gresson, the Timaru crown prosecutor. Gresson would come to have an immense impact on Paddy's career as a referee. Although refereeing received a brief mention at the time, their conversation then focused on more sombre issues.

Shortly after his return to Invercargill in 1993, Paddy and his supervising sergeant Tim Haughey drove to the western Southland town of Otautau after learning that an 80-year-old woman had been raped. They arrived at the scene at midnight and soon established that there were three or four likely suspects, with whom they conducted preliminary interviews without extracting a confession. It was their intention to return to Otautau the next day with a full team of detectives.

Down at the local police station drinking coffee a short while later, Paddy was having misgivings about one of the suspects. In what he would come to regard as the best piece of intuition in his 15 years in the police, he suddenly announced that he wanted to interview the suspect called Matheson again. He had a criminal record and there was something about him that was not right.

Paddy drove to his house and brought him back to the police station. Within 30 minutes, he was pouring his heart out about the crime he had committed.

Paddy would say later that the sensation of someone admitting to a major crime equalled the adrenalin rush when running out in front of 80,000 spectators at Twickenham.

That particular incident could have impacted seriously on Paddy's refereeing career, for the next day he was scheduled to control the Super 10 encounter between Otago and Grizz Wyllie's Eastern Province team from South Africa at Carisbrook. After less than three hours sleep, he was on the road to Dunedin. It was, he concedes, a mistake to referee such an important fixture in an exhausted state. His concentration levels were wavering long before the finish, but fortunately it was a one-sided, incident-free game, taken out handsomely by the home side, and no one seemed to notice that the referee sneaked in the occasional yawn!

By the mid 1990s, Paddy was trying to balance his work as a detective with his family commitments and his burgeoning refereeing career. He was only just managing to accommodate them all. His priorities tended to be refereeing, police work and family, in that order, and so in 1995 he made the decision, albeit reluctantly, to take early retirement from the police force.

Paddy treasured his time as a policeman and detective. He labels it the best job he ever had and says he would unhesitatingly support his son, or anyone else, if they announced they wanted to join the police force. But by 1995 after 17 years in the force he was worn out. Stressed out is probably a more accurate description. There were too many 'bread and butter' days when he farewelled his family in the morning and never made it home that evening.

Seventeen years dealing with other people's problems and experiencing the seedier side of life had taken its toll. Within 12 months of his departure from the force his wife Carolyn assured him he was a far easier person to live with. Interestingly, he now avoids reading the court news in the *Southland Times* and hardly ever notices the criminal element in the streets of Invercargill. When he was operating as a detective, he would identify individuals as people he had locked up, interviewed or chased around town!

Paddy prided himself that in 17 years in the force he was only hit once, and that was in somewhat amusing circumstances in Oamaru where he had delivered a speech to the local police. During his talk he disclosed that through staying alert and always communicating he had never been hit.

Following the speech he moved down to the cells where he identified a well known Oamaru troublemaker. Paddy sat down alongside him and was conversing with him until one of the Oamaru police members entered the cell. The local immediately became agitated and went after the cop. Paddy tried to intervene and was smacked in the jaw for his trouble.

Being the sprinter that he was, Paddy always joked that he won all his fights by 100 metres!

In the early 1980s the Southland Police rugby team reigned supreme in the country. Drawing from a staff of just over 100, it won the coveted New Zealand Police Cup off Canterbury and resisted all challenges for five seasons.

The Police Cup is the Ranfurly Shield of police rugby with the rules the same, the holder defending the trophy on its home soil. Canterbury, with three times the staff of Southland, and Otago, with twice as many members, were regularly sent home with their tails between their legs.

Such was Southland's dominance, in an era when Auckland was all-powerful amongst the New Zealand rugby provinces, that the members of the Queen City force decided to fundraise, journey to Invercargill and take the trophy back to its rightful resting place. Able to draw on a staff of 1000, Auckland got the necessary $20,000 together and headed south, determined to put the southern upstarts in their place.

About 1500 spectators turned out for the game which was staged on the hallowed turf of Rugby Park. In charge was one of Southland's big five, Arthur Gormack, who realised after five minutes that he had a serious contest on his hands. When the Aucks, who appeared to tower over their opponents as they ran out of the tunnel, tried some rough-house tactics in the first scrum, it was game on.

Second-five for Southland was Malcolm Dunn, a capable senior player in his day, and it was he who got the Aucklanders wound up when he trampled one of their players in an early ruck. For the next 75 minutes, the Aucklanders were intent on taking revenge. They were so preoccupied with the eye-for-an-eye approach they suddenly realised that, with time running out, they were behind on the scoreboard by a couple of points. They camped near the Southland line, but thanks to some generous refereeing decisions by Mr Gormack, Southland held on for an epic win. David had felled Goliath.

The aftermatch at the police bar looked like turning ugly until an intuitive local copper rang the nurses' home and invited the girls across for a drink. The rest, as they say, is history. Auckland returned home minus the trophy but with pleasant memories of their trip south. The spirit in the Southland Police team epitomised all that was great about rugby. They were probably the closest-knit branch in New Zealand at the time. The boss, Tommy Thomson, was a rugby junkie and just loved those troops who dug deep on the footy paddock, knowing that in the process a rich loyalty towards each other was developing.

The team possessed some pretty useful footballers. Lock Colin Blackie, No. 8 John 'Boof' Hughes and the captain Geoff Clarke all represented Southland. Of the others, Geoff Mason, Colin Millar, Glen Smith, Carl Purcell, Lindsay Dow (who represented New Zealand at softball), Peter May, Barry Taylor, Rob van Keulen, Ian Maccambridge, Athol Soper, Malcolm Dunn, Dave Evans, Ross Jenkins and Paddy O'Brien all played senior club rugby. It was a golden era for police in Southland, all built around the rugby team.

The wins over Otago Police were especially sweet because they gave the Southlanders bragging rights for 12 months, which Tommy Thomson revelled in, leaving his Dunedin-based counterpart fuming.

The footnote to all this is that Arthur Gormack had an honorary superintendent's title bestowed on him after he'd refereed five Police Cup matches in Invercargill, all of which the home team won!

As Paddy departed the force he lamented that the vocation he embraced in 1978 was not the one he was still involved with in 1995. And that, essentially, he considers, is because of the breakdown in New Zealand society. Civil libertarians have got what they deserve. In Paddy's book, you do the crime, you do the time.

Paddy is emphatic that the number of prisoners in New Zealand could be halved if the justice system toughened up on them, if a 12 month sentence meant 12 months of hardship. At present, Paddy sees prisoners having access to drugs, watching colour television, enjoying better meals than they would eat at home, experiencing a better life than they could find on the outside.

'They don't have to be treated like criminals,' says Paddy, 'but all the state owes them is three meals a day. If they had to rise daily at 6 a.m., work hard, exercise, had no TV and drugs were stamped out, people would not want to go there.'

It saddens Paddy that police are more into revenue collecting now than apprehending criminals. He believes the public have been hoodwinked into believing that driving at 120 kph is as serious an offence as committing a burglary. The fine for each is around $300.

When Paddy first donned a policeman's uniform as a bright-eyed teenager in the late 1970s, he says villains knew they would get a smack in the ear if they played up. 'While I don't advocate such behaviour, I never saw anyone worse off for it. The criminals knew if they caused trouble while they were in custody, they would pay for it.'

And if 17- or 18-year-olds had been up to no good, the police would often escort them home to their parents, giving the parents licence to deal with the young troublemakers. 'By the time I exited the force, however, if you indulged in such behaviour, you were more likely to be accused by the parents of picking on their child.'

Paddy's status with the police presented him with a magnificent opportunity in 1992 to undertake his first major overseas tour, accompanying the New Zealand Combined Services rugby team to the UK. He had by then established himself as one of the country's most promising referees and had just broken into the NZRU's top 10. He was thrilled to receive an invitation from the team's coach Gordon Hunter to come on board, and considers that that particular experience was the making of him as a referee.

Hunter introduced him to dressing-room etiquette and appointed him the team's statistician. It was his duty to provide 'Gordy' with relevant statistical information at halftime and again at the conclusion of each match. Whether it was Paddy's accuracy in compiling these figures, or Hunter's interpretation of them, that made the difference is open to speculation, but the New Zealand Services team was stunningly successful, winning all seven matches played by handsome margins.

The Royal Navy was beaten 28–6 at Plymouth, the Police 25–3 at Northampton, the RAF 36–nil at Brize-Norton, the Army 54–10 at Aldershot and the British Combined Services 39–23 at London.

Captain of the touring party was none other than Steve Hansen, who took over the responsibility from an injured Adrian Kennedy. Hansen, a sometimes representative player for Canterbury, would go on to become an outstandingly successful coach of the red and blacks before helping knock the Welsh World Cup team into shape.

The side also included such accomplished representative performers as loose forwards Murray Henderson and John Mawhinney, prop Kerry Pauling, winger Richard Kapa and fullback Jody Smith.

Jody Smith had a reputation as a real speedster, but Paddy was convinced he could outsprint him and boasted this to Steve Hansen one day. Hansen, aware of Paddy's prowess on the track, sensed the opportunity to make a few pounds. He not only set up the match race, along a street near the team hotel in Plymouth, he opened his own 'book', taking bets from virtually the entire squad, all of whom had great faith in their man Smith. But when Paddy reached the finish line first, it was a bonanza for Hansen, who still chuckles about it to this day.

In among the Combined Services matches, Paddy officiated at four local games around England. They were mostly matches like Plymouth against Devon. While his refereeing was appreciated, it's unlikely that anyone observing this fellow attached to the Kiwi Services team would have identified him as someone who, within a decade, would be in charge of internationals at Twickenham and go on to stamp himself as one of the top handful of referees in the world.

Paddy returned from the trip with the greatest admiration for coach Hunter who won the respect of not only his own players but the opposition as well. A couple of years later his Otago team would be cruelly denied an NPC title at Eden Park when Colin Hawke controversially awarded a last-minute penalty try to Auckland. Although Hunter must have been hurting more than anyone, he declined to get involved in the drama and referee bashing that followed.

Paddy's time in the police presented him with magnificent opportunities to travel overseas.

In 1982 he won selection in the first New Zealand team to compete at the Police Olympics at Austin, Texas. He won a gold medal in the high jump, clearing 2.04 metres — the highest he ever jumped — and a bronze medal in the decathlon, where the pole vault was substituted with the 800 metre because hardly any of the police were proficient at the pole vault. Paddy slotted into that category but back in New Zealand in domestic competitions he employed a unique strategy to earn himself points whenever he contested the decathlon. He ordered the bar to be set at a ridiculously low 1.98 metres and high jumped it, throwing away the bar as he approached the obstacle.

In 1984 he again participated in the Police Olympics, this time at Phoenix, Arizona, taking home a silver from the high jump, a bronze from the long jump and a bronze from the 4 x 400 metres relay.

Let's Go Refereeing

Paddy's first experience of refereeing came about in 1982 while he was immersed in his work at police headquarters in Invercargill. At the time, there were five uniformed sections, each involving about 10 individuals and they decided to stage a sevens rugby tournament, inviting the CIB in as the sixth team. Paddy's section bowed out at the semi-final stage, in dubious circumstances, the referee, one Sergeant Dow, being blamed for the loss. Anyway, it left Paddy as a spare part, and being such a rugby nut, he was invited to referee the final. It was completed without incident and he enjoyed the experience.

As he was to travel to the United States later in the year with the New Zealand Police Olympics team, he decided to have a season off from playing the game and, with a minimum of encouragement, joined two other police officers, Rob Hubbard and Athol Soper, at the Southland Rugby Referees Association. He was 23 at the time.

Paddy hadn't taken much notice of those present at his inaugural meeting. He'd been pretty nervous at the time. But as he became more familiar with the Thursday night procedure, he began to assess the individuals who comprised the Southland Rugby Referees Association (RRA). Among them at the time was one of the most accomplished referees in the world, Dave Bishop.

It seemed to Paddy that the membership included a disproportionately small number of young members, as young as himself, that is. Conversely, there appeared to be an excess of 'old fuddies'. That in itself didn't concern him, for he acknowledged that experience in any aspect of sport is an essential commodity, but as Paddy's refereeing career began to evolve, he found those 'old fuddies' started to become an impediment.

The problem with most old fuddies is that they have difficulty adjusting to modern trends. Because they joined the refereeing body at an age when the constitution dictated that no individual could be considered for any appointment above club level until he had served an eight-year apprenticeship, many considered such Draconian rulings should still apply. Even when a newcomer as obviously talented as Paddy O'Brien joined the ranks.

The Southland referees met weekly on Thursday evenings and the rules were that you served your first season on probation with special law tuition being given. At season's end, if you were successful in your examination, as Paddy would be, you were invited to become a fully-fledged member of the association.

Full of unbridled enthusiasm and with a background of senior club rugby, Paddy was tremendously excited when, kitted out in referee's attire, he took charge of the 12th grade match between Collegiate and Blues on a fresh, frosty Southland morning. At the time, the head of the Southland appointment board was Barry Dawson, who at his peak received several New Zealand appointments, including Ranfurly Shield and Lions tour games. He ranked with Dave Bishop as the best referee Paddy had ever played under.

After Paddy's second Saturday of controlling schoolboy rugby, he was walking off the field when Dawson approached him. He had been blissfully unaware of Dawson's presence at the game. He offered Paddy two pieces of advice. One was that the rugby ball always came down following a kick. Paddy, in his enthusiasm, had been chasing every kick as though he personally was required to make the catch. He then advised Paddy not to clutter his mind, at that stage of his refereeing career, with the laws of the game. He advised his young protégé to referee on his instincts. 'You'll pick everything else up as you develop in the role,' he said.

Dawson surprised Paddy by saying he would come and observe him the following Saturday as well. At the conclusion of Paddy's third outing, Dawson said, 'Keep it to yourself, but I am going to appoint you to an under-16 representative match to test you out.'

Paddy was floored. He didn't know what to say.

'There may be some politics involved but leave that to me.'

Paddy was busting to tell someone of his good fortune. After three games refereeing under-12s, he was going to take control of an under-16 rep match. This was bigger than getting a test match appointment!

At the next Southland referees meeting, Dawson announced the upcoming appointments for the Queens Birthday weekend when, traditionally, Town and Country teams squared off against each other from under-16 level through to senior. Sure enough, Paddy O'Brien was named as the referee for the under-16 match.

All hell broke loose. It was Paddy's first experience of the tall poppy syndrome in operation. Several members of the committee, the old fuddies brigade, objected to a probationary referee being put in charge of a representative fixture. Out came the constitution where an obscure sub-section revealed that probationary referees were ineligible to referee representative matches. So before Paddy could announce the wonderful news to his parents, the match was taken away from him, on the grounds that his appointment was unconstitutional.

Paddy was shell-shocked. In his naive way, based on his experiences in several sports, he had believed that if you were good enough you got the job. But that wasn't how things worked within the Southland Rugby Referees Association. Barry Dawson was fuming and there and then resigned his position. He walked out, never to return, which was a tragic waste of talent for Southland rugby.

Paddy went back to refereeing Saturday morning under-12 grade matches, to serve out his apprenticeship. He touch-judged occasionally at senior club fixtures, gaining valuable experience from watching the centre's top referees in action.

It would be four years before Paddy would control his first senior club match, which was rapid promotion by New Zealand refereeing standards. He had impressed on his way through the grades and was certainly regarded by many as a referee with a bright future.

In those days, each provincial union was given the opportunity to submit up to five names to the NZRU to be considered for appointments to NPC matches. Southland almost always nominated its full quota of five, listing in order of merit.

Around the time Paddy joined the senior ranks, the centre was rich in talent. Dave Bishop, boasting international status, was clearly No. 1 — indeed, he would soon become New Zealand's highest-ranking referee — but there were several others who rated highly, notably Kerry Henderson, Bruce Morrison, Murray Jarvis and Arthur Gormack. Waiting in the wings was Peter Tetai with the up-and-comers being Craig Morton and Paddy, both of them in their twenties.

When Barry Dawson stormed out, Peter Culhane, uncle to Simon Culhane who would become a distinguished All Black, took over as chairman of the appointment board where his assistants were Roger Tippen and a couple of country members. While they were all experienced referees, none had distinguished themselves with the whistle. Paddy saw them as an 'old boys' clique, of the variety that haunted English clubs, whose attitude was that until you had served on the social committee and mixed in the right circles, you would be kept in check. Especially if you had turned to refereeing as a successful sportsman and dared to bring a cocky attitude to your new association.

When Kerry Henderson, Arthur Gormack and Bruce Morrison retired, almost simultaneously, it created significant opportunities for the 'young guns' of Southland refereeing, particularly Craig Morton and Paddy. They were seen as challengers for the No. 5 slot. A friendly rivalry existed between them, as you would expect of two ambitious young sportsmen. Unfortunately, members of the association, who were divided on who had the greater potential as a referee, promoted the rumour that there was extreme discord between the two.

Paddy was down to referee the annual Southland Country-Canterbury Country match on a Tuesday, being informed of the appointment five days previously by Peter Culhane who told him that all the selectors would be present to assess him. He implied that an impressive performance could see him promoted to the top five.

Imagine Paddy's horror on the Saturday morning when he opened the *Southland Times* to find the union's top five referees named. Craig Morton was among them. Paddy wasn't.

Paddy could live with the fact he wasn't rated among Southland's best five referees but what infuriated him was that he had been misled. He was obviously never going to be considered for the top five, whether he refereed well in the Country match or not. Always an upfront person, he confronted individuals face to face, whether the news was good or bad. And he expected others to treat him the same, not feed him a line of encouragement then crap on him from a great height.

He was feeling so desperately low, he announced to his parents that he was quitting refereeing. He told them he refused to be associated with a sport where his future could be determined by politics and the attitude of officials of mediocre standing.

In other sports, like tennis, athletics and squash, it was easy to prove who was the best. You either defeated your opponent in tennis or squash and advanced up the ladder, or you lost. And in athletics, if you ran faster or jumped higher than your rivals, you were declared the winner. Your performances were measurable. No one could deny that the gold medal hanging around your neck clearly indicated you were the best in your field. But in rugby refereeing, Paddy was finding that your progress was entirely at the whim of individuals, most of whom had never risen to any great heights themselves.

He didn't want to reach the top because of his social connections. How the hell was sharing a glass of bubbly with the president going to make him a better referee! Paddy was a dyed-in-the-wool sportsman, a particularly ambitious one, and he wanted to be the best on his merits.

Paddy's father Ray offered him sage advice. 'Don't give them the satisfaction of showing them you have been hurt,' he said. 'The best way to beat them is to continue refereeing and take the breaks when they come. Those current selectors won't be there forever.'

Prophetic words, indeed. The following year Don Mowat was transferred from Blenheim to Invercargill as District Commander of Police and with his extensive refereeing background and outstanding lecturing skills, he soon started to make waves in the Southland referees' fraternity.

Paddy was among a group that led the campaign to oust Culhane and co. from the selection committee. With sufficient numbers behind them, they were able to get Mowat and Gordon Dawson installed.

When the next top five list was announced, there, along with Dave Bishop, Paul Johnston and Murray Jarvis were the 'young turks' Craig Morton and Paddy O'Brien. Paddy had made the breakthrough and within two years would be named in the NZRU's first 15-strong development squad.

He wasn't amused when Peter Culhane came up to him at one stage and said, 'Although you didn't appreciate it at the time, we did you a huge favour holding you back when we did.' Yeah, right.

The Southland Country-Canterbury Country match, in which Paddy understood he was to be assessed, is one that stands out in the memory. The Canterbury Country team of the time included such distinguished performers as Robbie and Bruce Deans and Andy Earl, while most of the Southland NPC team came from the country.

In the first minute of the game the Southland fullback was given a searching up and under to contend with. At the instant he called 'Mark', and was about to be engulfed by Andy Earl and seven other rampaging Canterbury Country forwards, Paddy blew the whistle for a fair catch, only to see the fullback look up and drop the ball. For the remaining 79 minutes, he kept being reminded by the Canterbury Country players that he owed them one!

Running touch that day was one of Southland's favourite rugby sons, Leicester Rutledge. He'd given refereeing a try but became frustrated with all the politics involved and moved on to coaching. Southland Country was leading by two points with about five minutes remaining when Trevor Bokser, the southern No. 8, trampled on a player in a ruck. Paddy blew his whistle and was about to deliver a lecture to the offender and issue the Cantabrians with a penalty handy to the goalposts when it was pointed out that the touch judge on the far side of the field had his flag out.

Off Paddy wandered to have a discussion with Rutledge. His report was along the lines that Bokser had been provoked and the fairest and best way to deal with the incident was to warn both captains and restart play with a scrum.

'Who am I to argue with such a legendary character as Leicester?' mused Paddy as he rejoined the players in the middle. He called out both players, delivered a suitably stern warning and set down a scrum. Southland held on for an upset win.

In the changing rooms afterwards, Paddy thanked Leicester for his input and asked what had gone on at the ruck where he said Bokser was provoked.

'Well, actually, Paddy, we haven't beaten those bastards for 10 years and we've been on the end of some shocking referees' calls,' was his reply.

Thank God for neutrality these days, Paddy says, whenever he refers to that incident.

Notwithstanding the tribulations he endured in his early seasons' refereeing, Paddy is proud to call himself a member of the Southland RRA. Two of the association's stalwarts Peter Tetai and Zane Soper contact him before every test appointment, regardless of where that may be, to offer their support.

Craig Morton, who suffered a health setback early in his career, has quit refereeing and is now Rugby Manager of the Southland Rugby Union. Paddy brands him one of life's 'good buggers' who goes out of his way to ensure Paddy receives all the support he needs from his home union. Two members who share the same name, Richard Russell, work tirelessly for the referees and always offer encouragement, as does Murray Jarvis, the former top five member, who keeps the present day boys on their toes with his profound knowledge of the laws and awareness of changing trends.

Whenever Paddy is lining up for the anthems prior to internationals, be it in Auckland or Johannesburg or Paris, he always takes time to reflect on the Southland referees and the manner in which they now support him.

Because of his status, Paddy gets the prestigious appointments now, but he never overlooks the bread-and-butter members who often control two matches on a Saturday before running touch for a colleague. They receive no financial remuneration and seldom get so much as a thank you. But they're there because they love the game and enjoy a pint with their fellow referees on a Saturday evening. They train just as hard as Paddy who knows if it wasn't for their contribution rugby would not flourish in New Zealand the way it does.

Paddy was excited to see a promising young referee emerge out of Southland in 2003, a 30-year-old lawyer by the name of Keith Brown who has made it on to the exclusive NPC panel of the NZRU. He controlled one of the third division semi-finals and, in Paddy's opinion, is a referee with a huge future ahead of him.

Once Paddy began handling representative matches he soon came to the attention of Graeme Harrison, the NZRU's co-ordinator of referees whom in 1990 set up the country's first national development squad. Harrison was concerned that following the retirement of such long-serving individuals as Tom Doocey and Bob Francis there was a dearth of quality referees coming through. So he set out to do something about it, identifying who he regarded as the 15 most promising referees in the country. Among that cluster were Steve Walsh senior, Glenn Wahlstrom and Paddy, who would all go on to referee at test level.

The members of the development squad were assembled in Wellington where they received tuition from the top-ranking referees of the time, Dave Bishop, Lindsay McLachlan, Keith Lawrence and an up-and-coming Colin Hawke. And, naturally, they received favourable treatment in the matter of appointments for NPC matches.

Dear Departed Danny

Of the boys in the O'Brien family, the one least interested in sport was Danny. He would become an accomplished squash player but he was never a passionate follower of sport like Paddy. He was more academically inclined, the clever one.

His nickname when he attended Otago University was Danny Wong, which had racist undertones. It was accepted around the campus that Danny was the only New Zealander as intelligent and dedicated as the Asians studying there, hence the title of Danny Wong.

Paddy used to give him a hard time when he was young because he didn't fit the O'Brien family pattern. He was a softer kid, unadventurous, more interested in a book than a cricket bat or tennis racket. While Paddy was hanging out of trees or making like Fergie McCormick in the back section, Danny would be in his room reading or studying.

Eventually, Paddy and Danny became great mates. Possessed of a rich sense of humour — he could have almost made it as a stand-up comedian — Danny became a great story teller. And although he never embraced sport in the manner of his brothers, he did take up squash and he and Paddy had many epic battles together.

In 1984, Paddy was working as a builder's labourer for three weeks to raise funds so he could make the trip to America with the New Zealand Police athletics team. His mother was due to travel to Dunedin for Danny's graduation when she received news that Danny had had a breakdown. She asked Paddy if he would accompany her.

Paddy was shocked at the state in which they found Danny. He was a mess. It was obvious he was suffering from a mental illness and he was eventually diagnosed with manic depression.

Back in the relaxed environment of the O'Brien family home, Danny made what appeared, on the surface, to be a full recovery and took a job with the accountancy firm of KMG Kendons. He met a charming girl called Charlotte, although their blossoming relationship was put on hold while he took himself off to the UK for a spot of OE. He had been away only a couple of months when the O'Briens received an upsetting phone call. Danny had tried to slit his wrists and been admitted to hospital in London.

Fortunately, a couple of mates from Invercargill, John McGrath and Judith Trapski, were close at hand to comfort and settle him. Along with Brendan Schollum, they made the necessary arrangements to get him back to New Zealand.

Upon his return he again convalesced with his family. As before, he ostensibly made a full recovery, although Paddy and his parents, who were now effectively his nurses, all knew it was only a question of time before Danny became overwhelmingly depressed again.

When the burden of depression was lifted from him, Danny was a truly delightful individual, humorous, a great conversationalist, fun to be in the company of. He was taken on as an accountant by Slink Skins, a company run by former All Black Jack Hazlett. And he became engaged to Charlotte. Maybe, just maybe, Paddy hoped, the storm clouds that tormented him were finally wafting away.

Paddy and Danny had similar features and could have been mistaken for twins. Jack Hazlett was one who was deceived when he attended a cricket match at Carisbrook in Dunedin. There he was surprised to see Danny. Well, he thought it was Danny. It was actually Paddy.

The next day, at work, he confronted Danny.

'How did things go at work yesterday?'

'Fine, I got through everything I had to do.'

'But I saw you at the cricket in Dunedin.'

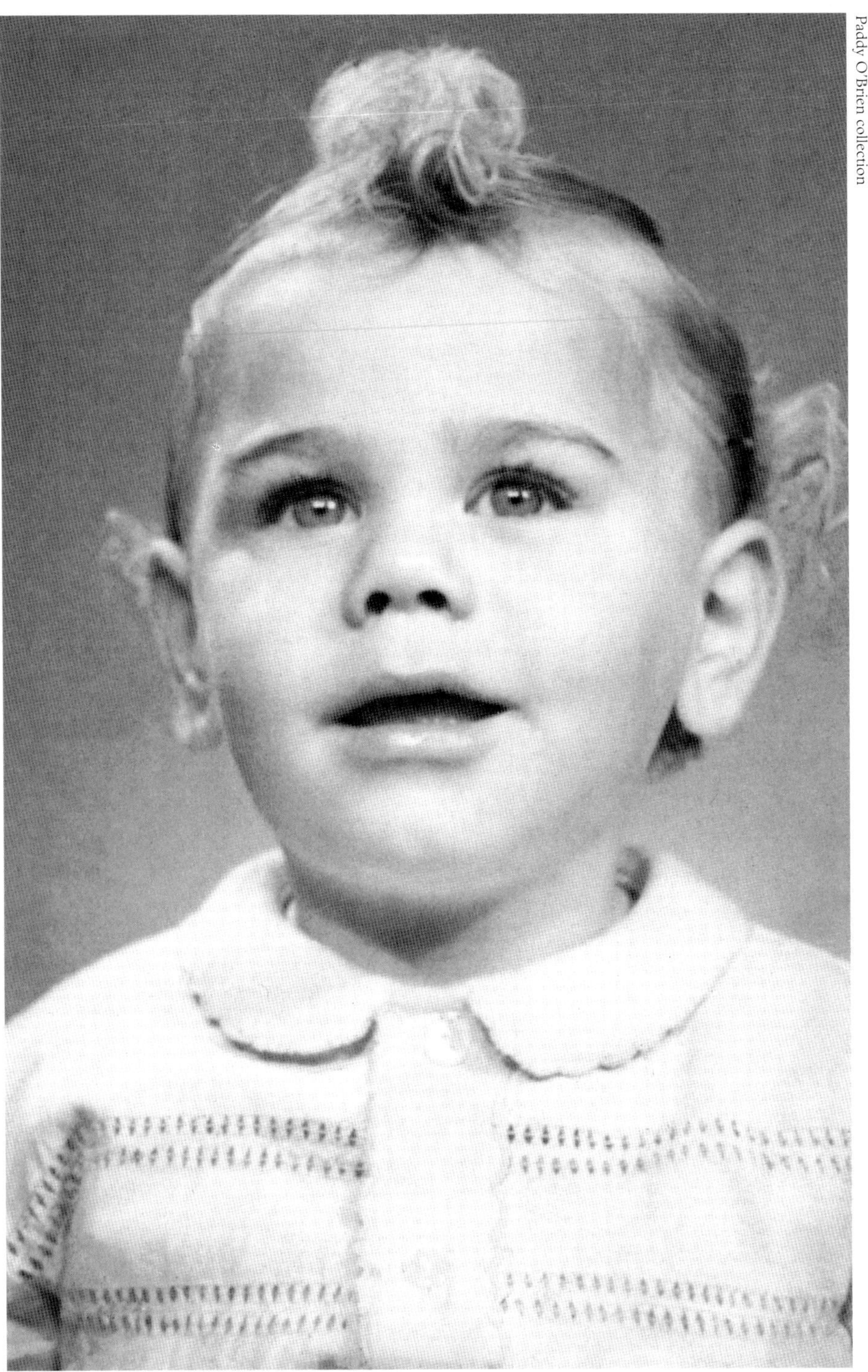

Paddy O'Brien collection

Wow, look at those curls. Patric O'Brien all spruced up for a baby competition. Naturally, he won!

Paddy O'Brien collection

Seven of the nine O'Brien children in 1964. Back row: Kevin and Casey. Front row: Anne (holding baby Gabrielle), Danny, Paddy and Margot.

Paddy O'Brien collection

Obviously long hair was fashionable with the Invercargill Marist debating and public speaking team in 1975. That's Paddy on the extreme left of the back row with brother Danny second from left in the front row.

Paddy O'Brien collection

Super slim Pat O'Brien (he hadn't won the nickname of Paddy then) in full flight for the Marist senior club team in 1979. The previous season he'd been the leading tryscorer in the senior competition.

Paddy O'Brien collection

The art of clearing the high jump bar using the Fosbury Flop technique, as demonstrated by Paddy. He became the first high jumper in New Zealand to clear 2.00 metres off grass.

Paddy O'Brien collection

Paddy and fellow Southlanders Carl Purcell and Lindsay Dow before heading off to Phoenix, Arizona, for the Police Olympics in 1984.

Paddy O'Brien collection

Paddy proudly shows to his children Matthew and Kylie the medals he won at Phoenix. He claimed a silver medal in the high jump (losing the gold on countback after clearing 2.04 metres) and a bronze medal in the long jump.

Paddy O'Brien collection

The first New Zealand referees development squad, set up by Graeme Harrison in 1990. From left: Steve Walsh sen, Glenn Wahlstrom, Hugh Chisholm, Steve Lunn, Paddy O'Brien, Craig Morton, Alister Thorpe, David Bishop (tutor), Colin Hawke, Graeme Harrison (tutor), Barry Smallridge, Hugh Catherwood, Ross Whitmore, Alan Riley, Lindsay McLachlan (tutor).

Paddy O'Brien collection

The Southland Police team that claimed the New Zealand Police Cup off Canterbury and retained it for five seasons. Paddy's the extremely slim fellow third from left in the middle row.

Paddy O'Brien collection

Paddy's younger brother Danny poses with his proud parents following his graduation from Otago University in 1984.

Paddy O'Brien collection

Can you believe that the fellow holding a gun to his hostage would go on to become New Zealand's top referee? It's 19-year-old Paddy O'Brien helping give the Armed Offenders Squad a workout in his first year in the police force.

'You must have been mistaken,' replied a bemused Danny as he returned to his desk.

It was some months before Jack encountered Danny and Paddy together and realised that it had been a classic case of mistaken identity.

In April of 1987, as New Zealand was completing preparations for the inaugural Rugby World Cup, Danny took himself off to the North Island for a brief holiday during which he visited all his brothers and sisters. Although no one suspected it at the time, it was Danny's way of saying goodbye.

On his return, Paddy noted that he had never seen him look better. Paddy, delighted that his brother was in such robust health, was in high spirits himself, having just been allocated his first senior refereeing appointment which was coming up the last Saturday in May.

The Thursday immediately prior dawned fine. Danny, now back home, had taken himself off to work at Slink Skins while Paddy had headed for police headquarters, where, because he'd tripped over a railway sleeper in Gore the previous weekend following his refereeing assignment and split the webbing on one hand, he was confined to light duties manning the phones. Their father Ray was busily labouring away at the freezing works where the major topic of conversation was the All Blacks' spectacular 70-point thrashing of Fiji in World Cup action the previous afternoon.

Life that particular day appeared so normal and uncomplicated that, for the first time in many, many months, Valerie O'Brien decided to risk a shopping trip to the city. So when Paddy phoned to leave a message for Danny saying he couldn't play squash that afternoon because of his damaged hand, no one answered the phone.

The previous day, Danny had telephoned all the members of his family except Paddy and engaged them in pleasant conversation. He assured them all his health was great, that he had, in fact, never felt better.

It was because he was in such robust health that Danny formulated the plan he did. He was terrified of being plunged back into depression. He never wanted to experience that dark abyss again. He would exit this world feeling wonderful.

He completed a normal morning's work at Slink Skins, before announcing that he was heading home for lunch. There, he completed his parents' tax returns, as normally and as meticulously as he always had. Then he obviously let himself into the garage.

Jeremy, a third former at Verdon College was first home, a little surprised to find his mother not there. He parked his bike in the garage without noticing anything untoward.

When he entered the kitchen, however, he found the note Danny had written. He rushed back to the garage and saw Danny in the car, not knowing whether he was dead or alive. In an agitated state, he shot across to the neighbours, bursting through their door to announce the emergency.

It was immediately apparent to Mrs Devery, the neighbour, when she entered the garage that Danny had not survived. She telephoned the police.

It was Paddy who fielded the call. 'Paddy, it's Mrs Devery here. Something terrible has happened. Your dad's dead.'

Well, that's what Paddy thought she said. In her shocked and emotional state she had stumbled over Danny's name and, to Paddy, it sounded like she was telling him his father was dead. Paddy was instantly galvanised into action. A police union meeting was in session upstairs. He burst in, declaring, 'It's an emergency, give me the car keys' and before anyone could determine what the emergency was, Paddy was gone.

As he sped towards Holloway Street, ignoring the speed limit, a million thoughts were tumbling around in his head. Had he dropped dead at work? Had there been an accident? Had Mum been with him when he died? Saturday was to be his senior club refereeing debut which his father was so looking forward to. He couldn't be dead, not before Paddy's big day.

Bystanders reckon the police car was on two wheels when it rounded into Holloway Street, screeching to a halt outside O'Briens. Paddy was directed to the garage and it took him just one glance to realise that it was not his father that was dead, but Danny.

Paddy went into overdrive. As a policeman, he was trained to act decisively and positively in moments of crisis. He blotted everything out of his mind except those matters which now demanded his urgent attention and action. In rapid succession, he telephoned the priest, comforted Jeremy and their neighbour and arranged for the police to locate his mother. They established she had caught a bus from the city centre. When she stepped from the bus she was met and comforted by the priest.

Paddy then had the doleful task of contacting his many brothers and sisters and breaking the news to them.

Because the weekend immediately approaching was the Queen's Birthday holiday weekend there were difficulties in arranging the funeral, but eventually it was set for the Tuesday.

When Paddy finally had the opportunity to sit down and contemplate the days ahead, it was to the realisation that the funeral would come 72 hours after he was scheduled to make his senior refereeing debut and 24 hours before Invercargill staged its first rugby test, the World Cup contest between Wales and Canada. Paddy briefly considered forfeiting his refereeing appointment but then reasoned there was little point in sitting around at home moping. The game would focus his attention.

Given Danny's tender age, the funeral at the Sacred Heart church could have been a melancholy event but Valerie and Ray O'Brien requested that it be a joyous occasion. Demonstrating enormous courage, they treated the service the way they knew Danny wanted it to be. 'He made a choice,' Val declared, 'and we must respect that. He will find peace where he is going.'

A massive number of mourners attended the funeral. They filled the church and spilled over into the grounds outside. Danny's fiancée Charlotte was there. Just one week earlier, they had bought a house which they had planned to live in.

Paddy held his grief in check until the funeral. Putting his police training into effect, he had operated like an automaton since finding his brother dead. Now he let the tears flow as the full realisation that he had lost a brother and a soulmate swept over him.

He remembered how Danny always used to say, 'Paddy, you've done so well in sport, but I'm hopeless.'

Paddy never bought that. He told Danny that he himself was envious of guitar players. 'People say how lucky I am to referee important matches in front of big crowds. But, you know, I'd swap that to be able to play the guitar.'

It still tears at Paddy that he never had the opportunity to say goodbye to his brother. Because they were so close, he suspects Danny knew that if he tried to proffer any sort of unusual gesture, Paddy would have immediately suspected he was up to something. Like his mother, Paddy understood Danny's desperate decision. He will argue with those who claim suicide is a coward's way out. Danny was the victim of an illness he believed he could never overcome. If he had died of cancer or in a car crash, everyone would have understood. Suicide is seen quite differently. But in Paddy's mind, his brother died bravely.

Spiritually, Danny has never departed Paddy's life. Although depression doesn't get a look in with Paddy, who believes that no matter how gloomy today's events may be, there's nothing a good sleep can't right, he recalls Danny on the occasions when things aren't going too well in his world.

When he contemplated his future, in the empty days that followed the funeral, Paddy determined that life, for him, had to go on. He gathered a fierce resolve from the experience, a determination to succeed for himself and his brother. When Paddy and Carolyn's first child was born in 1991 they named her Danielle in memory of Danny.

Danny had always lacked confidence. On the surface, it oozed out of Paddy, the ultra ambitious one. Whenever he watched, on television, a Five Nations match with Derek Bevan in charge, or an NPC fixture with Tom Doocey or Dave Bishop on the whistle, Paddy, exhibiting not a little arrogance, convinced himself that he could do a better job than them.

When Graeme Harrison brought his Development Squad together, he invited Colin Hawke and Lindsay McLachlan to address the gathering. Both talked of the trauma associated with turning in a bad performance.

Paddy didn't empathise with those comments at all. 'The obvious solution is not to have a bad game,' he mumbled to himself. 'I haven't had a bad game yet, and I don't intend to start.'

Paddy's bad day, and it would be a really, really, really, really, really bad day, was eight years away. In the meantime, Southland's up-and-coming refereeing star would survive on natural talent, fitness, sound advice and a decent dollop of cockiness.

'If You Need Any Help, Just Ask!'

1988–97

It's fair to say Paddy's entry into the ranks of representative rugby refereeing wasn't without incident. He debuted in familiar surroundings, Invercargill's Rugby Park, on 27 June 1988 when Southland took on Otago in a heap of matches from age grade events through to the premiers.

Paddy, hyped for the occasion, having been appointed to the main game, couldn't wait to signal the start. To all those who inquired if he was nervous, he nonchalantly assured them he was eager to go. So eager, that instead of making a quiet, dignified entrance on to Rugby Park behind the captains, Mike Brewer and Dave Henderson, he ran, sprinted in fact, and promptly fell over the sand bucket.

He could hear the spectators laughing as he cannoned onto the muddy turf. He was uninjured but his pride was dented and his pristine shorts were now two tone, brown and white! There would be more dignified entrances over the next fifteen seasons as he went on to rack up almost 200 first-class performances.

What Paddy failed to notice, in striving to regain his composure, was that the mud had clogged the whistle he'd been carrying in his hand. So when he went to signal the start of his first-class refereeing career, no sound emanated.

'Sorry, guys,' he announced to the players, 'Won't be a moment.' Fortunately, he had a spare whistle on him.

Notwithstanding the inauspicious preliminary, Paddy gave a competent performance as Otago, coached by Laurie Mains, eked out a 15–10 victory against a gritty Southland team which languished in second division at the time. His career was on the way.

At the aftermatch function, Don Mowat, head of selectors for Southland referees, assured him the spectacular entrance on to Rugby Park was probably the best thing that could have happened. It relaxed him.

Three months later he had control of the Counties-Southland match in Invercargill, a game Counties slotted in between its NPC first division fixtures against Canterbury and Otago. Counties won a highly entertaining contest, that produced eight tries, 37–19. Word began to filter around afterwards that the referee in charge had something going for him. Paddy O'Brien of Southland was starting to make an impression.

The NZRU was sufficiently impressed with the newcomer from the deep south to appoint him to a brace of NPC third division matches when the 1989 season rolled around.

The first of these was at Greymouth, West Coast against Wanganui, on a bleak afternoon when the rain fell in torrents from a leaden sky. Paddy quickly came to appreciate that, when vital championship points were at stake, not every outing for him would be a bed of roses.

The Wanganui players took one look at the deadball zone that was littered with stones and declared they weren't going to play. Paddy, accustomed to conciliatory negotiations as a detective, managed to convince them otherwise after first arranging for local officials to clear as many of the stones from the field as they could prior to kick-off.

Wanganui possessed a powerful front row and was obviously determined to make it count. But as they drove, fractionally early, into the opening scrum, the local front three suddenly stood up. As they did so, one of the West Coast props brought his knee up into the face of his opponent.

Paddy O'Brien, 2003 vintage, would go straight for a yellow card, possibly even a red one. But back in 1989, on the occasion of his NPC debut, he was gobsmacked to encounter such brutality at the first scrum.

He penalised the offender and gave him a stern talking-to. If he was guilty of anything, he thought, it was leniency. And so he was surprised when the West Coast referees' assessor approached him after the game and commented that he would progress far in the game refereeing like that.

'What was the first penalty for, anyway?' asked the assessor.

'For the West Coast prop putting his knee in his opponent's face,' replied Paddy.

'Well, what was he expected to do when they drove in high and early?'

Paddy didn't have an answer to that, but events became a little more obvious soon after when it was pointed out to him that the prop in question was the referee assessor's son!

In the report that was submitted to the NZRU, referee O'Brien was categorised as being of C quality (A being outstanding and D poor). In the comments section, the assessor asked why his union was being sent referees 'from outposts like Southland'.

Back on his home turf, Paddy handled a non-competition fixture between Southland and North Harbour, choosing to ignore the occasional infringement to allow play to flow. It was how he'd played his rugby and it was how he wanted the matches over which he had control to unfold. At this stage of his career, he was determined to be a players' referee.

Frano Botica certainly appreciated Paddy's positive approach. In electrifying form, he set up countless tries, North Harbour running in 10 altogether in the process of hitting the half-century mark. But if Paddy and Frano were delighted with the relaxed manner in which the game unfolded, not everyone was. Some of the veterans of the Southland RRA were most unimpressed with what they interpreted as their referee's cavalier approach. Rugby was a game bound by laws, several of which they considered their representative was ignoring. There was much tut-tutting.

If the O'Brien style didn't go down big in the Southland RRA clubrooms, it impressed an individual who carried far more clout, a gentleman who would soon aspire to the NZRU and go on to become chairman of the International Rugby Board's referees committee, Tim Gresson.

Gresson was chairman of the South Canterbury union when Paddy breezed into Timaru to handle his second NPC appointment, the home side against Nelson Bays. Paddy had encountered Gresson, who was Timaru's crown prosecutor, in a professional capacity while working on a murder case, but he never suspected Gresson would have such a massive influence on his refereeing career. All the same, he was pleased when Gresson congratulated him on his performance that day. It was only when Gresson began to progress up the administrative ladder that Paddy realised how calamitous it could have been for him had he flunked his assignment that afternoon in Timaru.

Gresson says that having known Paddy as a promising young detective, he was looking forward to his performance as a referee. 'The ground in Timaru is very close to the grandstand and you can hear everything that is going on, and it was obvious that Paddy possessed great man management skills. The art of refereeing is the art of communicating and Paddy managed that marvellously. He was very obviously a referee on the way up.'

By 1990, Paddy the policeman was living in Oamaru where he offered his services to the North Otago Referees Association. Initially, he wondered how he could possibly aspire to major appointments from such a modest base. As the duffer of the third division, North Otago claimed just six senior clubs and 15 referees.

Paddy quickly appreciated that size isn't everything. Attitude counts for far more. Where the 'old boys' in the Southland organisation had persisted with a let's-keep-him-back attitude, the North Otago clan couldn't have encouraged him more. In Paddy's words, they 'pushed hell' out of him. He was amazed and delighted at the difference in attitude. Former first-class referees in John McDonald and Keith Gawn, the then No. 1 Henry Aubrey and the secretary Dick Cleland all recognised that in Paddy they had a member of exceptional talent destined for higher places and gave him every encouragement.

While his work as a detective sometimes impacted on his sporting commitments, Paddy completed two more NPC third division appointments in 1990, Nelson Bays against West Coast at Nelson, and South Canterbury against Horowhenua at Timaru.

His first big break came in 1991. After handling the NPC second division match between his old province Southland and Thames Valley at Invercargill, he was allocated the Canterbury-Hawke's Bay first division game at Lancaster Park. Paddy expected he was being 'broken in' with a game that Hawke's Bay, promoted from second division the previous season, was expected to lose by a wide margin.

In the event, the game produced a thrilling 31–all draw. Graeme Harrison told Paddy later that upon hearing the result Bob Francis, who was in his car heading to Masterton at the time, almost drove off the road. He was enormously relieved to learn that it was Hawke's Bay's resolute play and not Paddy O'Brien's refereeing that had made this possible! In fact, Paddy was warmly congratulated on his performance and returned home with that warm fuzzy glow that successful sportsmen strive for.

He reflected on the fact that to that point he'd controlled 14 first-class fixtures without a failure. He felt pretty damn smug about that. Perhaps there was even a tinge of arrogance involved.

That would pretty soon change. Midway through 1992 he flew to Wellington to take charge of the New Zealand Universities match against an England B team that included such emerging stars as Tony Underwood, Phil de Glanville, Neil Back, Ben Clarke and Martin Bayfield.

An international fixture it might have been but the atmosphere at the old Athletic Park registered only marginally above zero. The weather was grotty, the surface sticky and the attendance no more than 4000. It was the last tour undertaken in which lineout forwards stood shoulder to shoulder, producing the inevitable skirmishes. In the first minute Martin Bayfield and Steve Surridge were involved in a dust-up.

Paddy blew his whistle. 'Come here,' he said, pointing to Bayfield.

'No, you come here,' was Bayfield's defiant response.

And to his everlasting embarrassment, Paddy did. It's something he says he would never do now, as it represented a sign of weakness. The moment he yielded to Bayfield's command, he knew he'd lost control.

In his 15th game, he'd made his first mistake. And it was a whopper. He came off Athletic Park feeling like a sucked-out jube, certain he'd blown his career. He doubted he would get another opportunity.

'Hard luck,' said Bob Francis, 'I'll phone you tomorrow.' To Paddy, those words carried ominous undertones.

As he journeyed home the next day, he remembered Lindsay McLachlan warning Colin Hawke to be prepared for the black day when things would go horribly wrong. Paddy had somehow believed he would be exempt from such an experience, that refereeing was a breeze. Players loved him. Adversity for the man from Invercargill was never a consideration.

Well, at Athletic Park it had ensnared him. Why would the NZRRA want to persevere with such a weak-kneed referee? Senior club fixtures at Centennial Park in Oamaru would probably be his lot from now on.

Bob Francis phoned. 'What happens to me now?' asked Paddy.

'Well, one dud game won't kill you, but two more like that will.' Bob gave him an assurance that he would remain high up the pecking order but would be eased back in with second and third division matches.

Very obviously, he had slipped a couple, perhaps several, notches down the pecking order. He faced a challenging time re-establishing himself.

He knew how fortunate he was to have people like Bob Francis and Tom Doocey backing him. They understood that every referee had the occasional bad day at the office and they wouldn't cast anyone adrift on that score.

Out of misfortune often comes strength. The Athletic Park experience was valuable for Paddy. It made him appreciate that by surrounding himself with his peers, he could survive any traumatic happening. He realised that if he maintained a superior, arrogant attitude, his colleagues would snigger at him when he stumbled, but if he was loyal, humble and sensible, they would always be there when he needed them.

Paddy was relieved to be awarded second and third division appointments at Timaru and Ashburton, games that were completed without incident or controversy. Then he knew he was back in favour when he was posted to Hamilton for the Waikato-King Country first division game.

On the morning of the game, he thought he would check out Rugby Park, a ground completely unfamiliar to him. He had only ventured a few metres on to the lush turf when the groundsman appeared. Paddy reached into his pocket for a silver fern, with the intention of making a small presentation.

'What the f—- are you doing out there?' bawled the groundsman.

'I'm Paddy O'Brien, the referee.'

'I don't care if you're the Prime Minister. Get off my f——— ground!'

It wasn't until the aftermatch function that the opportunity presented itself for Paddy to finally hand over the silver fern to the groundsman. In the process, he complimented him on the state of the Rugby Park surface. They became friends for life!

Waikato fielded an awesome set of forwards that year, captained by the man who would become All Black coach, John Mitchell. Around him were such experienced campaigners as Warren Gatland, Steve Gordon, Graham Purvis, Duane Monkley and the notorious Richard Loe.

'If You Need Any Help, Just Ask!'

Paddy's first encounter with Loe was an unsettling one. Very much a hands-on referee, Paddy was accustomed to organising players at the front of the lineout, often gently pushing them back beyond the five-metre mark. But when he placed his hand on the chest of Loe, the front-rower snapped, 'You're assaulting me!'

Paddy wasn't sure whether to take him seriously or not. Then, towards the end of the match, Paddy made a minor blunder. 'Sorry, guys, I got it wrong,' he said. Loe glowered at him. 'Yeah, well don't bloody do it again!'

After the final whistle, Loe came to him and said, 'You should have seen the look on your face!' He realised then Loe was just having him on.

At the opposite end of the friendliness scale was Matt Cooper, another of Waikato's All Blacks. Paddy was standing alongside him at one stage during a break in play when Cooper inquired if it was Paddy's first first-division game. 'No, it's my second,' replied Paddy. 'Jeez,' said Cooper, 'you've got a big future.' Paddy beamed and has included Matt Cooper in his dream team ever since.

Early in the 1993 season came an experience that Paddy has incorporated in his after dinner speeches ever since. The venue was Levin, the occasion, an historic one for local residents, the first time a Ranfurly Shield match had ever been staged in the Horowhenua. Mighty Auckland, possessor of the prized log 'o wood for an unbelievable eight years, was taking the shield on tour.

Paddy had never attended a shield game and admits he was 'sucked in' by the happenings of the day. The kid from Makarewa watched the shield parade through the main street of Levin wide-eyed, identifying many of the famous figures of Auckland and All Black rugby. The realisation he would be refereeing superstars like Sean Fitzpatrick, Robin Brooke, Grant Fox, Inga Tuigamala, Olo Brown and Craig Dowd produced a huge adrenalin rush. They were his heroes, individuals he felt obliged to address as 'mister'.

Out in the middle of the Domain as the teams inspected the ground before kick-off, on a gloriously sunny April afternoon, Paddy, in magnanimous mood, introduced himself to the respective coaches and captains.

'Is this your first Ranfurly Shield game?' inquired Auckland's esteemed leader Fitzpatrick.

'Yes,' beamed Paddy.

'If you need any help, just ask.'

What a nice fellow, thought Paddy. He would quickly come to appreciate how Fitzy won an international reputation for his gamesmanship and ability to manipulate referees.

Horowhenua fielded a schoolboy at first-five, Carlos Spencer, who would make such a spectacular impact that coach Henry would initiate an offer for him to transfer to Auckland that he would find impossible to resist.

But of more immediate concern to referee O'Brien were the happenings in the front row where All Blacks Brown, Dowd and Fitzpatrick were confronting formidable opponents in Graham Hurunui, captain Kere Akuhata and Willie Fletcher. By third division standards, the Horowhenua front row was an awesome one; indeed, by season's end, that trio plus wonderboy Carlos would guide Horowhenua through to second division status.

Anyway, because Fitzy and co. were encountering unexpectedly tough opposition, which resulted in several scrums collapsing, the Auckland captain rapidly decided it was time for his new mate, referee O'Brien, to tidy things up.

'Paddy, sort it out, or I will!' snapped Fitzpatrick.

Paddy nodded. He felt like Schultz in the TV programme Hogan's Heroes. 'Yes, my kapitan. Whatever you say, my kapitan!'

When the next scrum collapsed, he instantly penalised Horowhenua. And when the scrum after that collapsed, he penalised Horowhenua again.

He acknowledges now that, thoroughly intimidated by Fitzpatrick, he was functioning with no thought for Horowhenua. Inexperienced as he was in the machinations of front row play, he was simply blaming everything on the home side, because Fitzy had told him to sort it out. He admits to extreme embarrassment now whenever he recalls the occasion.

It had no bearing on the final outcome, Auckland an overwhelming 80–17 victor, but he feels he owes Messrs Hurunui, Akuhata and Fletcher a sincere apology.

If Paddy was feeling fragile after his first encounter with Fitzpatrick, it only intensified when the Auckland skipper approached him at the aftermatch where Paddy was deriving a buzz from mingling with, and talking to, many of New Zealand's, and indeed the world's, most celebrated rugby players.

'Just one word of advice, Paddy,' he said. 'Don't always listen to what the players say to you.' They were words that would come back to haunt Fitzpatrick.

Notwithstanding the Fitzpatrick experience, Paddy retains vivid memories of the

Horowhenua shield match, not least because of the try that the 'shy wee Maori boy' Carlos Spencer scored.

Responsible for administering referees throughout the land in the early 1990s was Graeme Harrison, a genial individual operating out of the NZRU in Wellington, well qualified for the position, having refereed to international level himself. He knew the qualities to look for in an emerging referee and was responsible for 'discovering' several individuals who would go on to referee at the highest level. Among them were Colin Hawke, Steve Walsh senior, Glenn Wahlstrom and Paddy. He referred to them affectionately as 'his boys'.

Once NZRU appointments were determined, the selectors at the time being Harrison, Gresson and Tom Doocey, it was usually a week before they were made public, having first to be approved by council. Gresson, who represented the NZRU, was a man of high integrity, as you would expect of a crown prosecutor, who remained tight-lipped. But Graeme Harrison, without actually divulging confidential information, always managed to convey to 'his boys' what they desperately wanted to know.

The phone calls to Paddy would come religiously at 8.45 on a Monday morning. And in the course of discussing genuine refereeing business, Harrison would drop in a question like, 'Have you been to Napier lately?' Paddy always responded with a 'No'. 'Well, they tell me it's very pleasant there at this time of the year.'

Phone call completed, Paddy would immediately refer to the season's fixture list and identify the upcoming NZRU fixture in Napier.

When Graeme dropped that hint in 1993, Paddy realised he would be handling the British Lions game with Hawke's Bay. He much appreciated the advance warning because it gave him time to mentally prepare for his first international appointment.

In being awarded such a prestigious game, Paddy was, in boxing parlance, fighting above his weight. It was accepted that the appointees for the Lions games would come exclusively from the NZRU's Top Ten list. And Paddy wasn't a member of that elite group. The significance of the appointment was rammed home when Colin Hawke phoned him. 'Keep your head down,' he said. 'There are a couple of referees out there, members of the Top Ten, who are hurting.' He did.

Others who were allocated non-test matches on that Lions tour were Lindsay McLachlan, Alan Riley, Grant Lempriere, Jim Taylor, Colin Hawke, Mike Fitzgibbon, Steve Walsh senior, David Bishop and Terry Marshall.

Paddy struck a beautifully sunny day at McLean Park to enter the ranks of international referees. At halftime, Paddy, like the British Lions and probably most of the 15,000 spectators, anticipated a clear-cut victory for the tourists. Although they were fielding their mid-week selection, captained by Stuart Barnes, who was to make his mark as a television commentator, the Lions were patently in control at 17–5.

But a most remarkable transformation came over the game in the second half. Led dynamically by hooker Norm Hewitt, who had scored the first try, Hawke's Bay rattled on 24 points without reply to claim a 29–17 win.

The fans went wild. So did the players, that evening. A victory over the Lions is a rare event and the Hawkeye Guys celebrated in style. And Paddy, relieved that the contest had unfolded without controversy, joined in. He admits to getting 'beautifully sloshed', something that was permissible in those wonderfully amateur days. He recognises that, as a full professional now, being seen tipsy after a game would seriously impact on his career. But in those balmy days, the socialising was as much a part of rugby as the game itself.

A fortnight after his Napier performance, Paddy was handling another international contest, Manu Samoa against Marlborough in Blenheim. By fulltime, the muscles in his shoulder were feeling the strain after he'd signalled an incredible 20 tries to the Samoans who shattered all sorts of records in winning 128–nil.

For Paddy, it was the commencement of a warm relationship with the Samoans. They'd infiltrated New Zealanders' hearts, probably the entire international rugby fraternity's hearts, in fact, at the 1991 World Cup and after his initial association with them in Blenheim, Paddy understood why. He found them wonderful, humble people and he came to treasure any assignment that took him near Apia.

Paddy would come to incur the wrath of many Auckland supporters when results started to swing against them in clashes with Canterbury. But in 1993, Auckland, oozing All Blacks, was supreme while the red and blacks were pretty much at the bottom of the heap and their NPC clash in Christchurch produced a predictably one-sided result in favour of Graham Henry's mighty team.

About 10 minutes after the start, as the ball was advancing along the Auckland backline, Paddy chanced to look back as the forwards were exiting a lineout, just in time to see Sean Fitzpatrick delivering a backhander to his rival Matt Sexton.

Paddy blew his whistle and penalised Fitzpatrick. 'I'm not having that,' he warned the Auckland skipper.

Fitzpatrick began protesting and was marched 10 metres for his trouble.

'You're a bloody quick learner!' he observed as he retreated. Remembering events at Levin back in March, Paddy felt he'd definitely arrived as a first division referee.

Paddy was off to Wanganui for the NPC third division final in October, a history-making day for Horowhenua. With Carlos Spencer the cool hand at first-five, the Levin-based team upset Wanganui to win promotion to the second division for the first time in the union's history.

It was a magical day, 6000 crammed into Spriggens Park to cheer on two sides comprised exclusively of homegrown talent. The atmosphere was vibrant. To Paddy, it was heartland rugby at its finest, a classic example of why the grassroots is so important. He knows it would be tragic for New Zealand rugby if, because of professionalism, that was ever lost.

In 1994 Paddy was living back in Invercargill, working with the Invercargill CIB. His rapid progress as a referee was confirmed when he was given the French touring team's match against a New Zealand XV at Wanganui. It was a game from which he would emerge wiser.

Approximately five minutes from the finish, with the game hanging in the balance, he awarded the New Zealand XV a penalty from a 50-50 situation at a ruck. It presented Shane Howarth with the opportunity to win the game, but his kick was astray and the French hung on for a victory.

Paddy's assessor was Bob Francis who called him aside afterwards and, after complimenting him on his general handling of the game, quizzed him as to why he had awarded the late penalty. Paddy gave him a none too convincing answer.

'Paddy, when a game is that close,' said Francis, 'let it be the players who resolve the outcome, not the referee.'

It was a lesson he absorbed and one he has abided by ever since. He'll still award a penalty at the death, regardless of the scoreline, if the infringement is blatant, say, a punch, obvious offside or a hand in a ruck. But in what referees regard as 50-50 situations, which generally occur at rucks following breakdowns, Paddy will now leave players to scrap to the death in their eagerness to achieve victory.

It was something that came to mind in the 79th minute of the World Cup final in Sydney in 2003 when André Watson, officiating, issued a controversial penalty against the England front row, allowing the Wallabies to take the game into extra time.

André had refereed superbly until choosing to penalise England for a technical offence in the final minute. Paddy, who had been close to refereeing the final, felt there must have been a better way of handling that situation at that stage of the game.

From his youngest days, Paddy had regarded the Springboks as the ultimate opponent. Now he was off to Athletic Park in Wellington to referee their game against Wellington. What's more, in the grandstand as a spectator, would be Welshman Derek Bevan, who'd controlled the 1991 World Cup final and who was regarded by many as the top-ranking referee in the world. He was in New Zealand to handle the All Blacks' two tests against France.

The Springboks were everything Paddy expected them to be, and more. They were confrontational, extremely physical, to the extent of being brutal, and their captain Francois Pienaar, until he was stretchered from the field unconscious, placed extreme demands upon him.

It was not an occasion for a fainthearted referee. Far from being intimidated, Paddy found the experience inspirational; indeed, he would look back on this contest as the one that ignited his taste buds for operating on the international stage.

After appearing in danger of losing at one stage, the Springboks finished with a full head of steam to win 36–26. Among the vanquished were a 21-year-old fresh on the representative scene, Tana Umaga, and a 33-year-old in the twilight of his career, Steve McDowell.

Paddy received a 'Well done' from Derek Bevan after the game but because he regarded the Welshman with such awe, he declined to engage him in conversation.

The NZRU, invited in 1994 to name a referee to control two World Cup qualifying matches in Kuala Lumpur, selected Paddy, who found himself winging towards Asia for his most exotic refereeing appointment yet. Notwithstanding the language difficulties he encountered, where he was grateful for the universal signals the IRB had promoted, the event remains firmly etched in his memory for positively bizarre reasons.

It was the tournament in which Hong Kong humiliated Singapore 164–15, with Hong Kong fullback Ashley Billington scoring an incredible (world record) 10 tries. Then in the final, in which Japan defeated South Korea, the Korean captain, having completely lost the plot, kicked a Japanese player in full view of Referee O'Brien. Paddy was about to cause a sensation by showing him a red card when it became apparent the said captain was seriously injured. So savagely had he lashed out at the opponent that he'd broken his leg in two places.

Watching him exit Petaling Jaya Stadium on a stretcher, Paddy, in a fine display of humanitarian understanding, elected to leave the red card in his pocket!

Getting Even With John Eales

Paddy was immersed in his work at CIB headquarters in Invercargill on the morning of 3 April 1995, a Monday, when Graeme Harrison phoned.

'Got anything planned for this coming Saturday?' Harrison asked in a matter-of-fact manner.

'No, nothing out of the ordinary,' replied Paddy, thinking he was about to learn of a refereeing commitment at Dunedin or Oamaru.

'Do you reckon you could get yourself to Johannesburg in time for Saturday's Super 10 final between Transvaal and Queensland?'

'You're joking.'

'Not at all. You've been appointed. Congratulations. You'll need to be in Sydney by 9.30 tonight to pick up the South African Airways flight to Johannesburg. Good luck.'

Good luck? Hell, he was going to need heaps of that just to make the connections to get himself to South Africa in time. He had to pack and get from Invercargill to Christchurch to Sydney in less than 12 hours. It was going to be a full day.

Paddy made it, of course, and enjoyed the experience of refereeing in front of almost 70,000 fans at a sun-drenched Ellis Park. It was a challenging afternoon for him. The Transvaalers were beaten 30–16, twice narrowly missing tries as they surged over the goal-line from five-metre scrums. Paddy was ideally positioned to adjudicate, ruling that Reuben Kruger had lost possession of the ball on the first occasion and that the Queenslanders had prevented the ball being grounded on the other. Not unnaturally, he was roasted by the crowd for these decisions.

The turning point for the Queenslanders, whose pack included a young John Eales, was a 90-metre dash to the goal-line by halfback Peter Slattery.

As Paddy exited the field, content with his performance on a demanding afternoon, a person he later identified as Louis Luyt, the boss of both Transvaal and South African rugby, berated him, virtually labelling him a cheat. And when he retreated to the referees' room, his two touch judges spurned him, conversing among themselves in Afrikaans.

Following his verbal assault on Paddy, Louis Luyt entered the Transvaalers' changing room.

'How could the referee not award that try?' he asked his captain Reuben Kruger.

'No, Louis, the referee was right. I lost the ball.'

Luyt was magnanimous enough to offer Paddy an apology at the aftermatch function. Not many individuals on earth have ever enjoyed that privilege.

Because he was staying at the same hotel as the Australians, Paddy, short on colleagues in a town he'd never visited previously, joined them in celebrating their great win. It was a night of high revelry, culminating in Paddy being thrown, by one John Eales, into a fountain.

Paddy thought it was a great joke, notwithstanding the drenching he received, but next morning Queensland's coach John Connolly apologised to him most profusely for Eales' 'outrageous' behaviour.

'Don't worry,' said Paddy, 'I'll get him back.'

The opportunity for revenge against an unsuspecting Eales would come later that same year when Paddy was running touch at the Wallabies-Argentina game in Brisbane, the referee being fellow Southlander, Dave Bishop. It was Paddy's job to inspect the Australians' boots. He gave them all the okay except for Eales' pair. With a straight face, he told him they didn't meet legal requirements and that he'd have to change them. It was causing consternation because the giant lock didn't have a spare pair, when Paddy re-entered the dressing room and told him the score was now one–all. Eales broke into laughter. 'Touché!' he said.

Part three of their good-natured rivalry would surface in an unlikely context, midway through the crucial and deciding third test of the 2001 Wallabies-British Lions series in front of almost 100,000 spectators at Stadium Australia in Sydney in 2001. The atmosphere was electric, the game on a knife edge. With the scores locked together and players on both sides striving to achieve that vital little extra, Paddy penalised Australia at a ruck. Eales, a look of disbelief on his face, disentangled himself from the action and said to Paddy, 'I thought you'd paid me back!'

While Paddy was starting to make his presence felt on the international scene, he hadn't yet achieved elite refereeing status. Above him still were Dave Bishop and Colin Hawke, who represented New Zealand at the third Rugby World Cup in South Africa. Bishop had the distinction of controlling the important quarter-final clash between Australia and England at Cape Town and also the play-off for third between France and England at Pretoria. It was four years to the next World Cup. It was a quiet resolve of Paddy's to be involved.

In July 1995, Paddy made his first visit to the Samoan capital Apia to referee the annual Samoa-Fiji match. Culturally, he considered, it was at the opposite end of the spectrum to Twickenham. No Rolls Royce boot parties here, no committeemen in striped blazers, no massive grandstands, no baths in the dressing rooms, no officious gentlemen checking accreditation.

This was rugby Samoan style ... scorching temperatures, happy spectators in brightly coloured attire who found as much to laugh at in the game as to applaud, fans in trees striving for a view of the action. Paddy loved every minute of it. He concluded it might just be his favourite place to referee rugby.

Back in wintry New Zealand, he handled the King Country-Canterbury NPC game at the Domain in Te Kuiti, another cultural experience. King Country, coached at the time by Pinetree Meads' young brother Stan, was punching above its weight in first division and pulled off a massive upset, downing the red and blacks 48–28.

To this day, Paddy believes King Country won the game by intimidation. Led by their Fijian World Cup representative Philippe Rayasi, the King Country players began hitting their more illustrious opponents with a succession of spot tackles that eventually caused the southerners to start shying off the physical confrontations.

The Canterbury line-up abounded in talented performers, players like Andrew Mehrtens, Daryl Gibson, Mark Mayerhofler, Tabai Matson, Richard Loe, Mark Hammett and Con Barrell, plus skipper Mike Brewer who was thoroughly disconsolate at the final whistle. The loss was extremely costly for the Cantabs, ultimately costing them, by a solitary point, their place in the play-offs.

As rugby contemplated a new age of professionalism, Paddy was winning a reputation as a referee of high-scoring contests. His let-it-flow philosophy meant there was usually a proliferation of pointscoring when he was involved. NPC examples in 1995 were 58–30 (Canterbury against Waikato), 60–24 (Otago against North Harbour) and 60–26 (Auckland against North Harbour).

At the conclusion of the domestic season, Paddy was off to the United Kingdom to handle the touring Fijian team's fixtures against Wales in Cardiff and Ireland in Dublin. For the Cardiff game, his touch judges were from Ireland, Alan Lewis and Ronnie McDowell, two hearty, humorous individuals who helped Paddy relax because they were still cracking jokes less than an hour before kick-off. It was the first time he had dealt with Northern Hemisphere referees and he was relieved to find them so supportive, as well as such great company. He had arrived in Cardiff a little apprehensive, having heard stories about overseas touch judges willing New Zealand referees to perform badly.

While Paddy was thrilled to experience the hallowed turf of Cardiff Arms Park, as any New Zealander with a sense of rugby tradition would, he was rather overwhelmed by the number of committeemen, bedecked in club blazers and ties, who attended the aftermatch function. He began to appreciate why Welsh rugby was labouring in the modern era.

One of the touch judges for the Dublin game was Derek Bevan who Paddy soon discovered possessed an impish sense of humour. In seeking to develop a good-natured rapport with him prior to the match, Paddy said, 'Now, Derek, I want you to write down the names of all those spectators who boo me today.' 'It might be easier,' came back Derek, 'to list those who don't.'

Paddy found Bevan the perfect assistant, totally supportive. He was, Paddy came to appreciate, there for the cause, an individual who never wanted to appear more important than anyone else in the room. It was that humility that had obviously helped to take him to the apex of the refereeing tree. Paddy filed it away as a lesson never to be forgotten.

Professionalism was in the air when 1996 arrived — for players if not referees —

bringing with it the Super 12, an exotic new competition designed to annually pit the best provincial teams of New Zealand, Australia and South Africa against each other. It created great excitement and Paddy was flattered to be awarded the first Super 12 contest, between the Wellington Hurricanes and the Auckland Blues at Palmerston North, an historic event because it represented the inaugural game of professional rugby.

Paddy considered it a huge honour. Whether his performance on the night was good, bad or indifferent, he realised he would always be remembered as the individual who refereed the first professional rugby match. Appropriately, his boss Graeme Harrison was at the ground. He would have been so proud, Paddy knew, because one of 'his boys' had won the appointment.

What an occasion it was ... fireworks, cheerleaders, a great cacophony of sound. Paddy did his bit and so did Graham Henry's mighty Blues, who would go through to take out the first title. The Blues came with a barnstorming finish at Palmerston North to win that opener 36–28. In what was a night of firsts, Blues' skipper Zinzan Brooke made an unusual contribution by landing his team's only conversion.

Two weeks later, Paddy tried to telephone Graeme Harrison at his office but got only his answer phone, which struck him as being a little odd. So he called the Harrison residence. Graeme's son Grae answered.

'Is Graeme there, please?'

'No,' answered Grae. 'Who's calling?'

'It's Paddy O'Brien. We usually have a chat on a Monday, but I haven't heard from him today.'

'I'm not sure how to tell you this, Paddy, but Dad's dead.'

Paddy was devastated. Graeme, an immaculately-attired person who kept himself fit, had appeared, to Paddy, to be in the best of health the last time he had seen him. But a sudden heart malfunction, that could not be remedied in time, brought about his death.

Four of Graeme's star pupils, Colin Hawke, Steve Walsh senior, Glenn Wahlstrom and Paddy, joined Grae and Grae's wife Dellys as pallbearers at the funeral in Wellington. Graeme was only 62 and his untimely death stunned the refereeing world.

Paddy, who still corresponds with Graeme's widow Kath, felt as though part of his life had been ripped away. His Monday morning chats with Graeme had become an essential part of his week. To him, Graeme had brought style to rugby refereeing and had possessed man management skills second to none. His infectious enthusiasm had rubbed off on to many of his 'boys'. He preferred one-on-one telephone conversations to faxes and letters. Paddy wonders how he might have coped in the modern electronic age. But back in the 1980s, his methods worked wonders for aspiring referees like Paddy.

Paddy's first encounter with one of the true characters of rugby, Ian McIntosh, came in Brisbane where his Natal Sharks team upset the Queensland Reds to qualify for the final of the Super 12. It was the establishment of a mutual understanding the pair had for each other. While some found him intimidating, Paddy admired McIntosh's passion for rugby, although he came to appreciate that it was important to remain clear of him for at least an hour after the final whistle until his emotions subsided.

The 1996 All Black trial at McLean Park in Napier provided Paddy with his sole encounter with the then All Black coach John Hart, in somewhat bizarre circumstances. The shadow test fifteen that Hart was coaching, operating as the President's XV and captained by Sean Fitzpatrick, was expected to win handsomely against the Barbarians line-up captained by Todd Blackadder.

But at halftime, the Barbarians, operating with typical underdog bravado, were in front, which prompted an unexpected outburst from Hart as the players and officials were readying for the re-start.

'Take a good look at yourself,' he barked at Paddy. 'The game is becoming a shambles!'

What he really meant, Paddy thought later, was that the wrong team was winning, and somehow the blame was being lumped onto the referee. At the time, Paddy, still comparatively naive at this lofty level of the game, nodded compliance. He concedes that a comparable comment in 2003 from any coach would bring a response along the lines of , 'And f— you too!'

When Paddy lobbed into Rotorua in June 1996 to referee Scotland's game against Bay of Plenty, Mt Ruapehu was erupting spectacularly, which made for an almost surreal afternoon of sport. A perpetual haze hung over the city while the surface at the International Stadium was covered in a black ash which continued to fall from the sky throughout the game. Paddy began the game wearing a handsome new jersey — white, with a green collar and black silver fern — which by fulltime look as though it had been dragged across a bonfire. No amount of washing back home ever restored it to its pristine whiteness.

When Fiji and Samoa engaged each other at the National Stadium in Suva a month later, the smart money was on the Samoan team. Coached by BG Williams since about 1990, Samoa had been the dominating force among the Pacific Island nations. But the Fijians that afternoon were unstoppable. Paddy doubts they have ever played better; indeed, he cannot recall any team he has refereed making fewer errors while attacking so consistently for 80 minutes. The final scoreline was an incredible 60–nil!

Beegee afterwards was virtually speechless. 'I'd love to blame the referee or something,' he said, 'but I can't. The Fijians simply blew us away.'

In October of 1996, Paddy was appointed to the Auckland-North Harbour NPC game at Eden Park. With the two unions between them claiming 16 representatives in the All Black team which had just created history by defeating the Springboks on South African soil, he expected this would be a great occasion, mates against mates. Wrong!

As the first lineout was forming, Ian Jones, North Harbour's lanky lineout ace, told Paddy he wanted a wider gap down the middle. A reasonable enough request, thought Paddy, who requested that the two lines of forwards create greater space between them.

Sean Fitzpatrick, who had been preparing to throw the ball in, reacted startlingly. Placing the ball on the ground, he adopted a teapot stance, hands on hips. 'Paddy,' he said, mockingly, 'Ian wants a bigger gap!'

The realisation came to Paddy that while these guys had been brothers in arms on the tour of South Africa, back in an NPC context, they were now deadly enemies. Which they proved by sniping away, caustically in many instances, throughout the game.

Paddy managed to keep a lid on things until a scrum was about to pack down on the halfway line, barely 20 seconds from the final whistle, by which stage Auckland was overwhelmingly ahead 69–27. Fitzpatrick, rugby's master of provocation, commented to Zinzan Brooke, loudly enough for the North Harbour players to hear, that this was an appropriate moment for Auckland to try its new move.

'Which one's that, Sean?' responded Zinzan.

'The 50-metre pushover try!'

It was too much for the North Harbour players. The scrum erupted in a flurry of punches, the forwards of both sides involved in an ugly all-in.

Paddy had had enough. He blew his whistle for fulltime, turned and headed for the changing room, leaving them to it.

Frank Bunce ranged alongside, offering a handshake. 'Jeez, Paddy,' he said, 'I don't know how you guys do it!'

A fortnight later, Paddy was back at Eden Park refereeing his first NPC final, Auckland against a Counties Manukau team that included the tryscoring phenomenon Joeli Vidiri and should have featured Jonah Lomu as well, except that Jonah had been suspended, unluckily many (including Jonah) considered for a spear tackle in the semi-final against Canterbury.

Counties Manukau, coached at the time by Mac McCallion, was extremely competitive in the first half through the efforts of iron man Jim Coe, making his 196th appearance for the union, and inspirational leader Errol Brain. But, as Paddy at close range observed, 'Class took over from arse' and Auckland romped away to a 46–15 victory and its fourth consecutive first division title.

The NZRU was satisfied with the manner in which it had converted from amateurism to professionalism during 1996. It was a year of bedding-in and the general consensus was it had won the battle.

Now it was time to consider paying the referees. When Graeme Harrison had raised the issue at the beginning of the season, Colin Meads, a former board member, had commented that if referees were given 'thirty bucks and a pie' they'd be happy. It was a typical throwaway line from Pinetree. But as 1997 loomed, the question of professionalising the referees was an item demanding the NZRU's attention.

Paddy's first assignment in 1997 was a prestigious one, England against Scotland at Twickenham for the Calcutta Cup, one of the longest-surviving international fixtures. It was his first Five Nations appointment. It would not, he presumed, be enormously different from the NPC final at Eden Park. Twenty thousand more spectators, perhaps, the air temperature a bit cooler, the grass a bit longer, a few more academics involved. But rugby was rugby, a biggie in Auckland surely not significantly different from a biggie in London.

Or so Paddy thought. He would return home far more enlightened.

When two nations like England and Scotland, that once fought bitter wars along their borders, engage each other at national level, particularly in rugby, there is an intensity of fervour that always takes New Zealanders by surprise. Graham Henry, for one, admitted in his autobiography that he had no concept of the passions involved until he began coaching Wales. At Twickenham in February 1997, Paddy was amazed to learn that hundreds of Scottish supporters had travelled south with no prospect whatsoever of purchasing tickets to get into the ground.

An attitude Paddy often detects in his homeland is that rugby standards and passions overseas come nowhere near New Zealand's. He concedes it's a mindset he might have been guilty of himself until, through his refereeing appointments, he gained first-hand experience of the game in the UK and France. The major fixtures there, like the Calcutta Cup, possess a rich history which New Zealand cannot match.

While the pace of the Twickenham contest gave Paddy no problems, mentally he found it one of his more challenging assignments. Predictably, England began to assert its superiority and towards the finish began to pressure the Scots mercilessly. In their desperation to hold them out, the Scots persistently infringed, to the point where Paddy finally awarded a penalty try.

As he exited the hallowed turf, given 'Well dones' from Kiwi colleagues Colin Hawke and Steve Walsh, who'd run touch, Paddy sensed that he had completed his role satisfactorily.

Up in the president's room an hour later a blazered official approached him.

'Penalty try, O'Brien, what was that about?'

'Persistent infringing. It's covered in the laws.'

'How dare you. Do you appreciate that the Calcutta Cup has been in existence for 126 years and that is the first occasion a penalty try has ever been awarded?'

'Oh, really?'

Paddy made sure he didn't raise the topic of penalty tries for the remainder of the evening! You broke with tradition in England at your peril.

From there, it was off to Dublin for the Ireland-England international, this time with Paddy and Steve Walsh running touch for Colin Hawke. Operating as a threesome certainly took the agony out of international travel. It guaranteed companionship while in 'Hawkeye', a seasoned traveller, Paddy and Steve benefited enormously from someone who'd done it all before. Colin Hawke was able to pass on invaluable advice to his less experienced countrymen. It included warning them off reading newspaper reviews of their refereeing performances. 'Your ego naturally directs you to match reports,' he told Paddy and Steve, 'but journalists in the UK have no scruples. If you read them, you run the risk of becoming depressed. Do yourself a favour and stick to the glossy magazines.'

When Colin Hawke and Paddy returned to New Zealand, it was to the exciting news that the NZRU were presenting them with contracts to become the country's first professional referees.

Some 18 months earlier the All Blacks had been offered mouthwatering sums if they rejected equally tempting offers from WRC, the Australia-based organisation that wanted to establish itself as the controlling body for professional rugby, and signed with the NZRU.

What the NZRU put in front of Messrs O'Brien and Hawke wasn't half as tantalising, but referees' boss Keith Lawrence explained that if they had confidence in the national body and were prepared to survive on modest wages in the interim, in 12 months' time, when funds were available, their salaries would be inflated to a realistic level.

Messrs O'Brien and Hawke took the NZRU at its word and they weren't to be disappointed. When 1998 rolled around, their salary packages were adjusted appropriately. The days of amateurism were now well behind them.

Somehow, during the 1997 Super 12 championship, Paddy finished up refereeing matches involving the Natal Sharks three matches in a row, at Albany, Christchurch and Auckland, a sequence of appointments that left Paddy and the South Africa players bemused. Before the first of those encounters, against the Chiefs, Sharks' coach Ian McIntosh made a point of confronting the referee.

'Paddy,' he said, 'you're our favourite referee. But there's just one thing.'

'What's that, Ian?'

'Can we have an even penalty count?'

The penalty count, as it transpired, favoured the Sharks by 11 to 9, McIntosh's men registering a clear-cut victory by 33 points to 15, an excellent result for a South African team on New Zealand soil.

Before the midweek game against the Crusaders in Christchurch (in those early days of the Super 12 championship, players didn't have the luxury of a full week's break between fixtures when touring) McIntosh again made a point of searching out Paddy.

'I'm pleased we've got you again, Paddy.'

'There's only one problem, Ian,' came back referee O'Brien.

'What's that?'

'Well, because the penalty count favoured the Sharks 11-9 the other day, you realise the first two penalties today will have to be against your team. You insisted on an even count, remember!'

McIntosh produced a strained smile and headed back to his dressing room.

Christchurch presented a completely different ball game. Paddy had cause to issue a red card to prop Stu Loe and when the Crusaders contrived to remove another front-rower, the final stages were played out using the farcical Golden Oldie (no push) scrums. The game finished in a 16–all draw.

McIntosh didn't display the same exuberance he'd shown towards Paddy at Albany. But he wasn't doleful either. After all, after two outings in New Zealand, his team hadn't lost.

But things would be a lot different at Eden Park where, again, before kick-off, McIntosh confronted Paddy.

'You weren't quite so good in Christchurch,' he told him. 'I want you to referee like you did at Albany last weekend.'

Paddy didn't offer a reply.

By halftime, the Sharks were down by 20 points against the front-running Blues ... and Mac was fuming. Paddy saw him coming down the tunnel and hastened into the referees' room, shutting the door behind him. McIntosh banged on it. 'You're a bloody cheat!' he hollered.

Tensions rose during the second half, to the point where Paddy had to call the captains together and warn them that further violations would incur red cards.

When Joeli Vidiri subsequently high-tackled the Sharks' hirsute winger Cabous van der Westhuizen, Paddy sinbinned him. It was a decision he later regretted. 'I should have sent him off,' he would tell his colleagues.

Mac came looking for him. Paddy, always desperately eager to avoid coaches in the emotional moments immediately following a game, said curtly to him, 'We'll talk later, Mac.'

Paddy was relaxing at the aftermatch function when McIntosh, much calmer, caught up with him, bearing two pints of beer. 'You know, Paddy,' he said, 'You're still our favourite referee, but we've got to talk!'

McIntosh explained that the perception in South Africa was that the Springboks did not get a fair deal when playing in New Zealand and Australia. Paddy assured him that the fact he did not dismiss Vidiri from the field was a poor decision, not bias.

Notwithstanding his emotional outbursts, McIntosh remained one of Paddy's favourite personalities because of his sharp rugby brain, his great commitment to the game in South Africa and his geniality. His record with the Natal Sharks was outstanding.

His quick wit was often reserved for referees. When Australian Wayne Erickson, not one of McIntosh's favourites, was walking through the gates of King's Park, Durban, on one occasion, he encountered McIntosh driving out.

They exchanged courtesies. 'How are you, Wayne?'

'I'm fine. Nice car you've got there.'

'It would be a lot flasher if it wasn't for pricks like you!'

One of Paddy's more challenging appointments came at the Sydney Football Stadium in July 1997 when the Wallabies took on England. It degenerated into a front row nightmare, the sort of contest referees dread. Paddy, becoming more desperate by the minute, worked through his full repertoire of fix-it remedies. He tried defusing the trouble with free kicks and penalties and by lecturing all the props and threatening them with dire consequences. Nothing worked.

During the second half, Australia was awarded a penalty at a scrum five metres from the England goal-line. John Eales, the Aussie captain, decided he didn't want the three points on offer and advised referee O'Brien he would take a scrum instead.

'You're joking!' said Paddy, but he couldn't convince Eales otherwise.

As a consequence of that incredibly messy encounter, Paddy was left with a reputation as a referee who had trouble with scrums. It was something he urgently needed to address and the individual who enlightened him and gave him the formula by which he has confidently refereed scrums ever since is, ironically, someone who played representative rugby as a back, Steve Hansen.

A hugely successful coach with Canterbury before he took on the almost impossibly daunting task of preparing the Welsh national team, Hansen addressed administrators and referees at a Sanzar seminar in Perth. Paddy was there with Colin Hawke and, as Hansen described the mechanics of scrummaging, it all became wonderfully obvious to him.

Until then, Paddy admits that, probably like many other referees, he was hugely ignorant of what was happening in the darker recesses of the front row, with the consequence that many free kicks and penalties, though delivered with authority, were based on pure guess work.

Paddy's refereeing doctrine does not allow him to guess at happenings on the rugby field and yet, until Hansen educated him, because assessors and officials were pressuring top referees to 'sort out the scrum shambles', he admits he many times 'pinged' a front-rower without having the vaguest idea of what had happened.

A key word for referees as they progress through the ranks is credibility. Until his visit to Perth, Paddy knew that however players might regard his control of all other aspects of play, he was struggling to earn credibility at scrum time. What Hansen provided for Paddy, and all the other Sanzar referees fortunate enough to be in Perth, was a check list.

At the pre-engagement, as the front rowers prepare to come together, Hansen explained, the loosehead prop can be compared to a plane taking off. That is, he should effectively be heading up. The tighthead prop, in contrast, should be dead square, providing a solid shoulder for the loosehead to butt on to.

If the opposing packs are too far apart when they prepare for engagement, that can cause problems, so often Paddy will urge them closer. And then he checks the binding, ensuring that each prop has his hand where it's supposed to be.

This is how Paddy illustrates his requirements to the players with the small numbers on their backs in the dressing room in the shakedown to kick-off. He reaches an agreement with the front rowers which is non-negotiable once they are on the field.

Notwithstanding these preparations, scrums sometimes still fold in and collapse or crab awkwardly acrossfield. But now, unless he identifies an individual deliberately contravening his specified method of engagement, he won't deliver any penalties. He's prepared to re-set the scrum three or four times, if necessary, to get it right, if, based on his Hansen-defined checklist, the front rowers are performing their roles properly.

Sometimes, after Paddy has penalised a particular prop for incorrect binding, a member of the hard-done-by team will protest, claiming the scrum has collapsed for a different reason. While that may be so, asserts Paddy, he's comfortable with his decision because he knows his ruling is factually correct. He likens it to two kids stealing from a lolly jar. The one who is apprehended protests that he's being victimised while the other has got off scot-free. 'Maybe,' says the apprehender, 'but I'm dealing with you.'

Thanks to Steve Hansen, Paddy now has a picture of what the scrum should be like before the ball is put in. If it's distorted in any way, he knows it's wrong and looks for the causes.

In 1997, the IRB introduced a merit-based international panel of referees, applying it for the first time in the Tri-Nations competition. New Zealand's representatives were Paddy and Colin Hawke. Paddy was allocated the South Africa-Australia match at Pretoria, gulping when he discovered that his assessor would be Steve Strydom who had slated him in the South African press after he failed to issue Joeli Vidiri with a red card for his dangerous high tackle on Cabous van der Westhuizen in the Super 12 match at Eden Park five months earlier. This would not be the only occasion Strydom would taunt New Zealand referees.

Prior to Paddy's departure for South Africa, he was engaged in a video hook-up with the UK-based referees co-ordinator for the IRB, Steve Griffiths who expressed the desire that with the introduction of the merit-based panel the difference in interpretations between northern and southern hemisphere referees, that had previously existed, would disappear.

During question time, Paddy expressed his concern that the individual who would be assessing him at Pretoria had openly criticised him earlier in the year. Unbeknown to Paddy, Steve Strydom was in the studio listening to the discussion!

As it turned out, the Springboks achieved a massive, record-breaking victory over Greg Smith's hapless Wallabies at Pretoria (the final score being 61–22) and Strydom gave Paddy an excellent review.

The Paddy and Zinny Show

1997–99

The semi-finals of the NPC first division in 1997 were dramatic affairs, but they involved contrasting brands of drama. At Hamilton, where the two Big Js, Joeli Vidiri and Jonah Lomu, caused mayhem, Counties Manukau staged a barnstorming finish to overwhelm Waikato, coming from 15–37 down in the last quarter to claim a breathtaking victory. At Lancaster Park, where Canterbury hosted Auckland, the drama was more of a personal nature, Zinzan Brooke versus Paddy O'Brien.

Auckland, under the masterful guidance of Graham Henry, had been the dominating force in New Zealand rugby for many seasons and was chasing a fifth consecutive NPC title, while in the guise of the Auckland Blues, effectively Henry's NPC team plus Vidiri, they had emphatically taken out the first two Super 12 championships.

There were a couple of significant developments en route to the Christchurch semi-final. At least, Paddy now deems them significant, although he fancies that at the time because of Auckland's omnipotence, probably no one else noticed. Or if they did notice, they didn't care.

The wheel nuts on the mighty Auckland machine had been loosening ever so slightly. In the absence of the team's cluster of All Blacks, the side had stumbled against Taranaki. If that result was understandable, less easily explained away were the losses against Canterbury and Waikato, after the team was restored to full strength.

They were costly defeats, for Waikato not only took vital championship points, it snared the Ranfurly Shield while the loss to Canterbury secured for the red and blacks the all-important home advantage for the semi-final.

Zinzan Brooke, Auckland's heroic captain, then felt compelled to make the rather untimely announcement, prior to the Christchurch game, that if Auckland qualified for the final, it would be his farewell appearance in the blue and white jersey as he was off to join the Harlequins club in London.

Graham Henry certainly didn't appreciate Brooke going public when he did. He wrote in his autobiography that 'Zinny was having trouble getting focused' having been 'in deep negotiations with the Harlequins club'.

Any prospects of a fairytale ending to Brooke's celebrated career with Auckland were spoiled by an extremely well-drilled Canterbury team and a referee named O'Brien.

Auckland-Canterbury contests are always tight, tense affairs. And this game was no different. What was different, though, was that this time Canterbury was the equal of Auckland in almost every aspect. The scrum was as solid, the lineout was as efficient, the defence was as water-tight — neither goal-line being breached in the 80 minutes — and Andrew Mehrtens was every bit as accurate a goalkicker as Adrian Cashmore.

For the Aucklanders, there was no way through. And that caused Brooke, as captain, immense frustration, a frustration he began to take out on referee O'Brien.

Paddy has reviewed the tape of the game and is at peace with himself over his decision-making. He considers he refereed the game accurately and fairly. It irks him that Zinzan's aggressive attitude provoked screaming on his part, behaviour he knows he would never resort to now.

Although both Brooke and Graham Henry have been critical of Paddy's performance — Henry implying in his autobiography that O'Brien was probably influenced by the NZRU's desire to break Auckland's stranglehold on the NPC — Paddy has no doubts about where the fault lay: Zinzan lost the plot. He is emphatic that Brooke spat the dummy big time. 'Things weren't going his way and he got completely out of control. His behaviour cost Auckland the game.'

At 15–all, which was obviously a crucial stage of the game, Paddy blew up a ruck in which Mark Hammett, the Canterbury hooker, finished up on top of his illustrious opponent Sean Fitzpatrick. As they untangled themselves, Hammett did 'a Fitzy'. He levered himself up by placing his elbow on Fitzpatrick's chest. No penalisable offence that; it was, indeed, something Fitzpatrick had fashioned into an art form. But on this occasion, Fitzpatrick was the individual feeling the elbow. And he resented it, to the extent he began lashing out at Hammett. Whereupon, Paddy penalised him.

It represented a changing of the guard. And the Aucklanders, who for so long had been the masters of gamesmanship or one-upmanship, or whatever you want to label it, were now finding themselves being unsettled by the guys in red and black.

At one stage of the second half, Zinzan hollered at Paddy, 'Come on, come on, you're a f——- joke!'

Paddy barked back at him, 'We'll see who's right!'

Paddy was saddened at the way things unfolded that night, because he had been, and remains, a great admirer of Brooke as a player, rating him an outstandingly skilled individual. In Paddy's opinion, the only ones who come close to him are John Eales and Jonny Wilkinson.

He knew Zinzan as a player, not as a friend. What he discovered that night was that Zinzan was a winner who not only hated losing — Zinzan's competitiveness being legendary — he didn't know how to lose.

Until that embattled contest at Lancaster Park, Auckland had never lost when Paddy was refereeing. Mind you, such had been Auckland's (and the Blues') dominance of New Zealand rugby since the mid-1980s, there were precious few referees under whom they had lost.

But the Brooke-O'Brien fracas at Christchurch, vividly captured live on television and replayed endlessly, resulted in Paddy being branded. Many in the media, including outspoken talkback host Murray Deaker, found it easier to apportion the blame for Auckland's downfall to the referee than to acknowledge the cracks that were beginning to appear in the Auckland machine.

If Aucklanders were developing a complex about the whistler from Invercargill, it wasn't a problem again until the final of the Super 12 rolled around in 1998. The Blues and the Crusaders had stamped themselves as the two best teams in the competition and had prevailed in two thrilling, high-scoring semi-finals, against the Highlanders and the Sharks, respectively.

Eden Park was the venue for the final. And Paddy O'Brien was appointed referee.

Before he flew from Invercargill to Auckland, Paddy told his wife Carolyn he was confident this game would remove the monkey from his back. The Blues, with the home advantage, were firm favourites and Paddy fully expected them to win.

Well, they didn't win and two refereeing controversies only added fuel to the beliefs of Messrs Henry and Deaker that Paddy O'Brien was, consciously or sub-consciously, part of an NZRU conspiracy to redress the balance of power in New Zealand rugby.

In the post-match assessments, following the Crusaders' exciting 20–13 victory, Paddy was, in the eyes of most Aucklanders, guilty of (a) denying the Blues a penalty try when the Crusaders began deliberately collapsing a series of defensive scrums and (b) awarding James Kerr the matchwinning try when Blues halfback Junior Tonu'u appeared to be held back by a Crusaders defender.

Paddy's name had featured prominently in the build-up to the game, particularly on the radio programmes hosted by Murray Deaker who referred his listeners back to the NPC semi-final of the previous season, sowing the seed that the Blues could be up against more than just 15 opponents at Eden Park.

As with the match in Christchurch seven months earlier, Paddy was happy with his performance. In reviewing the tape of the game, he didn't detect any errors on his part that influenced the outcome. But in the emotional wash-up that inevitably followed, given that the Crusaders' victory represented a major watershed in New Zealand rugby, some critics, Deaker most prominent among them, preferred to focus on conspiracy theories involving referee O'Brien rather than acknowledge that there was a power shift evolving. Or that, for once, guru Henry might have been outsmarted as a coach, by Wayne Smith who used his reserve bench far more intelligently.

Paddy is disappointed that anyone would think he made a ruling in such an important contest, or any contest for that matter, because he wanted one team to win. It outraged him when coach Henry implied in his book that O'Brien's reluctance to award the Blues a penalty try at Eden Park that afternoon somehow had its origins in the board offices of the NZRU where they were sick of Auckland and the Blues' dominance.

He has a straightforward formula for the awarding of penalty tries and it has nothing to do with what administrators, national or regional, or coaches or spectators might want:

'If I have to think about whether a penalty try should be given, I don't award it. Likewise, if I have to think whether a player should be ordered off, he stays. I don't hesitate to make the decisive, I suppose you could say ultimate, decisions when they need to be made. I know instantly if a player's actions warrant a send-off and I take the appropriate action. That day at Eden Park, Auckland spent an extended period on attack in the second half and a number of scrums collapsed, but I never saw anything happen that justified a penalty try.'

Naturally, Paddy listens to talkback and reads the papers. It startled him, in the wake of the Super 12 final, to hear people implying the referee probably wanted his South Island team to win.

Well, he has a message for those people: He doesn't give a toss who wins any match he referees. His only concern is for the accuracy of his own performance.

'It's very obvious those critics have no appreciation of the psyche of a referee. Colin Hawke was perceived as being anti-Otago and, after those performances at Christchurch and Auckland, I was somehow seen to be involved in a conspiracy to benefit South Island rugby. That isn't how we operate. I can assure you no official of the NZRU ever spoke to me along those lines and, if he had, I would have been outraged and would certainly have reported him to my boss, Keith Lawrence.

'Those critics who tried to imply that I somehow manipulated the result detracted from the Crusaders' mighty achievement in winning. They went into the game as underdogs and demonstrated enormous resolve and character to win. I didn't feel they got the credit they deserved for winning both their semi-final and final away from home. Results over the next several seasons, when the red and blacks reigned supreme, confirmed that this was a meaningful moment in New Zealand rugby, although a lot of people were so busy searching for excuses, they missed the significance of it.'

Murray Deaker had polarised his listeners, convincing them Auckland could not win as long as Paddy O'Brien was refereeing. Paddy, while irked at this line of rationale, put up with Deaker's diatribe, until he implied one afternoon that Paddy was a cheat. Then the Irish came out in the man from Invercargill.

He tried phoning Deaker, although initially he couldn't get through. He eventually came up with a home number and when Deaker answered, he didn't hold back.

'You can accuse me of anything you like,' said Paddy, 'but never ever call me a cheat, for that I'm not.'

Once Deaker recovered from the initial assault, he asked Paddy if he was prepared to come on his radio show.

'Yes,' said Paddy, 'any time. You tell me when you want me.'

'Right, what about seven o'clock tonight?'

'I'll be waiting for you.'

Under Paddy's contractual arrangements, he required NZRU permission before he could speak to, or through, the media. But when he telephoned Keith Lawrence, it wasn't so much to seek Lawrence's approval as to advise him what he was doing.

Lawrence was concerned at what an obviously fired up Paddy might say on Deaker's programme, which beamed out nationally, so he referred him to Jackie Maitland, who was in charge of the NZRU's media relations. She was obviously concerned Paddy would say the wrong things and tried to swing him round to the politically correct way to handling the interview.

Maitland was dealing with the wrong person. Paddy was a Southlander brought up to tell it the way it is. He was horrified at the spin Maitland was wanting him to put on his story.

As far as Paddy was concerned, the Maitlands of this world operate by what they've read in a textbook. He and Maitland fell out big time.

'Her gobbledygook was the sort of stuff that was spewing out of the All Black camp in the run-up to the World Cup in 2003,' he would say later. 'That's not how I've been brought up. Down south, we say it the way it is.'

And that's exactly what happened on the Deaker show.

Deaker began by saying that rugby followers, certainly those north of the Bombay Hills, had the perception Paddy was a cheat.

So Paddy challenged Deaker to supply facts, not perceptions.

'You prove I'm a cheat,' he demanded. 'You give me statistics that show I've favoured teams opposing Auckland.

'People can accuse me of being incompetent, but as a referee I have never been dishonest since I took up the role.'

When Deaker opened the lines to his listeners, not one criticised Paddy or gave him a hard time. Quite the opposite, in fact. Many called to offer support.

Paddy's approach had worked. Not only did he win the public over but from that moment he and Murray Deaker became firm friends. They developed an excellent relationship and Paddy is now regularly interviewed on the programme, not to explain away his problems but as New Zealand's foremost referee.

On the delicate issue of referees manipulating events, Paddy does have one wee confession to make about a game at Loftus Versfeld, Pretoria, in 1998 between South Africa and Wales. The game was won by the Springboks by 96 points to 13, a humiliating scoreline for a proud rugby nation and one which would help propel Graham Henry into the Welsh coaching role.

Paddy says he never thought he'd referee a match where the home team topped 90 points yet the referee was booed off the field.

When the Springboks hit 96, the crowd began chanting, 'We want a hundred!'

Paddy looked at his watch and saw there was approximately a minute of injury time remaining. In normal circumstances, where the result is still in doubt, or bonus points are at stake, he would play out every last second before blowing his whistle for no-side.

On this occasion, he elected to give the Springboks 'one last chance to get one hundred points' and when a South African player was ankle tapped and knocked on, he signalled the end of the match, knowing there were still a good few seconds left on the clock. Far from being content with a record demolition of Wales, the South African fans took exception to the fact that the referee had curtailed proceedings with time, albeit just a handful of seconds, still showing on the ground clock and began heartily booing him!

That evening Paddy visited a bar in Pretoria with his touch judges, Colin Hawke and Englishman Brian Campsall, where they encountered a group of hugely demoralised Welsh supporters. One of them came up to Paddy to tell him that he had made one glaring error.

'What was that?' asked Paddy.

'You gave the Springboks a try from a chargedown. That was a knock-on. You should have set a scrum.'

'I'm afraid you don't know your law book very well,' said Paddy. 'A chargedown doesn't constitute a knock-on.'

The Welshman persisted. 'No,' he said, 'it was definitely a knock-on. The try should never have been given.'

'Well, look, I'll tell you what,' said Paddy. 'I know I'm right, but just this once I'll make an exception. I'll disallow that try, so the final score will now be only 91!'

'Awwh,' growled the Welshman, 'you bloody referees, you always have the last say!'

Although the Pretoria fans might have been a little disgruntled that Paddy didn't allow their team to notch up the century against Wales, he found himself, somewhat uncomfortably, being described as Springbok coach Nick Mallett's favourite referee.

It seemed that every time he had the whistle, the Springboks scored a handsome victory. He was refereeing when the Boks gave Greg Smith's Wallabies a record 61–22 battering at Pretoria in 1997, he was in charge when they crushed France in Paris later the same year, an historic appointment for Paddy for it marked the last occasion the Parc des Princes Stadium was used for a rugby international, and then came the 96-pointer against Wales.

Paddy was astute enough and experienced enough not to be influenced by such comments. His philosophy is that most results and trends in sport are cyclical and circumstantial and have little bearing on which referees are involved. The Blues' demise at the hands of the Crusaders wasn't his doing — someone had to referee the game — and nor was the Springboks' rise to glory. It was purely coincidental that an Invercargill referee was involved each time. And Paddy had long since learnt not to take his own press too seriously.

Ironically, Paddy would be the referee when the Springboks' stunning sequence of international victories under Mallett came to a halt, against England at Twickenham. Had the Springboks won, they would have surpassed the All Blacks' record of 17 consecutive test victories, which prompted one critic to ask why a New Zealander was appointed to control a game when a New Zealand record was at stake. To that, Paddy simply answers that the doubter has obviously never refereed. 'He doesn't understand a referee's psyche. We don't give a damn about records when we take the field to referee. Our solitary concern is to be accurate, consistent and on our game.'

If England's 13–9 victory sounds like a dull contest, it was anything but. Paddy rates it one of the most enthralling encounters he has ever refereed, comparing it to a chess match and says it had the potential for 10 tries but, in the event, only one was scored.

Like the Blues-Crusaders final at Eden Park, it was a contest of immense significance. It marked the start of South Africa's and Mallett's downfall on the one hand, and the commencement of an astonishing run of success for England and its coach Clive Woodward on the other.

Paddy considers Woodward to be one of the most misunderstood people in rugby. New Zealanders see him as an emotional individual when his team is performing and the media has painted him as pompous and arrogant.

But from Paddy's dealings with him, nothing could be further from the truth. He is one of the few coaches who insists on an early meeting with the referee before a major encounter, so he can put into practice what the referee has explained to him. Paddy has found him a humble and dignified man and was appalled at the way the Australian media treated the England team, and its coach, during the 2003 World Cup. In Paddy's view, they proved on and off the field under Woodward's leadership that they were the ultimate professional team.

If ever there was a display that illustrated O'Brien's neutrality, it came late in the 1999 Super 12 campaign, when the Hurricanes engaged the Highlanders at Athletic Park. Being from Southland, O'Brien is regularly ribbed about the Highlanders being his team. Well, if ever the southern men needed a modicum of parochial support from a referee, this was it.

Going into the final round of qualifying matches, the Highlanders were second in the competition, a point behind the Cape Town-based Stormers. Although they had already qualified for the play-offs, a victory was essential for Tony Gilbert's team to secure the all-important home semi-final.

The game was decided on a disputed try which Paddy awarded to Hurricanes' halfback Jason Spice. The Highlanders players insisted Spice had gone into touch before grounding the ball and, not unnaturally, it provoked outrage among the Highlanders fans.

Without the benefit of a video referee at the time, O'Brien was guided by his touch judge, Paul Honiss, whom he rates the best in New Zealand in that role. Between them, they were satisfied that Spice's grounding of the ball constituted a fair try.

But the wailing went on in the deep south. How could you be sure he was in? Paddy was asked more times then he'd care to remember.

'Well,' he replied, 'as far as a referee is concerned, the player's in until it's proven he's out. And, with no electronic assistance that afternoon, no one could prove to the touch judge or me that he was out.' It was a try then, and as far as Paddy is concerned, it's still a try now.

The Hurricanes' 21–19 victory condemned Gilbert's men to an arduous trek through to Cape Town for their semi-final where they performed heroically, overcoming jetlag, weariness and a formidable opponent studded with Springboks to register a stunning 33–18 victory.

But there would be one journey too many for the gallant Highlanders. The exhausting return flight from Cape Town to Dunedin, via Perth, Sydney and Christchurch, sapped the players' energies, and although they fought bravely in the final at Carisbrook, the fresher Crusaders (who quickly recovered from their three-hour flight home from Brisbane) emerged triumphant.

The outcome might have been quite different if Jason Spice's try had been disallowed. But it wasn't. And that's all there is to that!

Train Smash at Toulouse

The rugby world's focus in 1999 was solidly directed towards the fourth World Cup, hosted by Wales. But the World Cup isn't exclusively a players' domain. Referees are an integral part of it, too, and while New Zealand's leading players were striving desperately to win selection in John Hart's squad of 26, the nation's best referees were doing their utmost to win appointment to the elite 16-man panel that would control the World Cup fixtures.

Paddy O'Brien, Colin Hawke and Paul Honiss all made it, Paddy quietly confident he would be selected after a satisfactory handling of the Wallabies-Springboks Tri-Nations international at Brisbane's Suncorp Stadium in July.

If he was thrilled to win recognition as one of the world's top 16 referees, he was over the moon when he landed the plum assignment of refereeing the tournament opener between host nation Wales and Argentina at the newly-completed Millennium Stadium. The world was smiling on the man from Invercargill. He had arrived big time on rugby's world stage. He was feeling like a perfectly-tuned athlete arriving at the Olympic Games. A gold medal beckoned. Only injury surely could prevent him from achieving the ultimate.

Oh yeah? Looking back on it now, O'Brien cringes when he recalls how naively ambitious he was when he arrived in Cardiff ... 'Instead of focusing totally on the assignment at hand, I made the error of looking ahead, contemplating a quarter-final appointment. I had never played any sport without wanting to win and I went to the 1999 World Cup with the sole objective of advancing as far as I could. I certainly wasn't there to enjoy myself. I probably wasn't mature enough to know the tournament situation and appreciate that I was simply a member of a team, along with 15 others. My attitude was all wrong.'

Paddy came satisfactorily through the World Cup opener which was won by Graham Henry's Welsh team. It was an unremarkable game producing a predictable result. Paddy made no glaring mistakes and received a pass mark from the IRB assessors.

In those early days of October, life was a bunch of roses for Paddy. In relaxed mode, he watched Colin Hawke control the South Africa-Scotland match at Murrayfield, a game in which New Zealander John Leslie came to grief, and Paul Honiss referee the one-sided Australia-Romania game in Belfast, as he began his mental preparation for his next assignment, France against Fiji at Toulouse.

In an average year, New Zealand professional referees control about 25 matches of consequence. Twenty of them pass pretty quickly into oblivion from a referee's viewpoint, meaning there is nothing exceptionally good or bad in the arbiter's control of the game. They would gain a pass mark from any assessor.

After three of the other matches, the referee would come off the field feeling eminently satisfied, knowing he had contributed to a cracking game of rugby, that there had been no controversial moments, no disputed tries. Nothing, indeed, that would see the referee branded anything other than a good bloke. An assessor might be inclined to add 'outstanding display' in the comments section.

And then there are the other two matches. They are the ones where the referee wishes he had never got out of bed. A lot of referees refer to them as 'train smashes'. Paddy's train smash came at the Stade Municipal in Toulouse. And as rugby train smashes go, it was right up there.

Paddy cannot identify any factor or sequence of events that affected his handling of what was a vital pool match between France and Fiji. The French had arrived at this encounter after muddling performances against Canada and Namibia while the Fijians, coached by yet another New Zealander, Brad Johnstone, were in overdrive, having racked up 67 points against Namibia and 38 against Canada. There was a lot at stake. The winner would advance straight to a quarter-final in Dublin while the loser would have to take on England in a repêchage encounter at Twickenham.

Sometimes referees can be unsettled in a foreign environment, but on this occasion Paddy had two English-speaking touch judges, fellow Kiwi Colin Hawke and Tappe Henning from South Africa, to assist him. They were colleagues. He couldn't have asked for a better support team.

The first blunder of the afternoon was a crude headbutt by a French player which Paddy missed. He couldn't be blamed but, unfortunately for him, Messrs Hawke and Henning missed it too.

Then came an injury break following a penalty award to the French. Paddy placed the ball on the mark while the injured player was treated.

When, some minutes later, he blew for play to re-start, French halfback Stephane Castaignede caught the Fijians by surprise. Tapping the ball to himself, he bolted unchecked through to the goal-line, to the delight of his team-mates and the French spectators. It was a daringly intuitive act by the French halfback. Paddy wasn't having a bar of it.

'You can't do that,' he told Castaignede, 'you indicated you were taking a shot at goal. No try. You must take the kick at goal.'

As a distraught Castaignede was pleading for the decision to be reversed, Paddy realised his error. Touch judges Hawke and Henning were stationary on the sidelines. They weren't behind the goalposts because Paddy hadn't directed them there. And that was because French captain Raphael Ibanez had not nominated a shot at goal at all. A concentration lapse had led to a calamitous mistake.

Nowadays, Paddy says he would bounce back by admitting his mistake and putting it instantly behind him. But at that moment at Toulouse, he was devastated. He was embarrassed and rattled. And worse was to come.

One of the principle precepts of Paddy's refereeing philosophy is that he never guesses what might have happened. Early in his career he recognised the danger for referees of assuming anything. Unless you see it with your own eyes, you don't rule on it. At Toulouse that afternoon, he transgressed his own golden rule.

A punishing spot tackle from a Fijian player dislodged the ball from a French defender. First player on the spot was another Fijian who grabbed the ball and plunged across for what television replays established was a legitimate try. In a game where the final scoreline was 28–19, it was a crucial moment. Paddy presumed the ball had gone forward and disallowed the try. He ordered a scrum, French ball. He was wrong, horribly wrong. The French supporters didn't mind at all. The Fijian players and support staff were aghast.

Then came a series of five-metre scrums with the French applying pressure on the Fijian goal-line. After a couple of collapses, Paddy ran to the goalposts and awarded France a penalty try.

He acknowledges now that had he applied the Steve Hansen theory, he would never have made that decision. A penalty try was not justified. But Paddy, thoroughly befuddled by this stage, gave one anyway.

Never has Paddy been so relieved to blow a whistle for fulltime. Although his touch judges were sympathetic, he knew in his heart he'd failed this assignment, even without the video replay which would identify more blunders than he was immediately aware of.

'Often you'll make one bad mistake in a game, sometimes two,' Paddy confesses. 'Collectively, what happened that afternoon was a disaster. I couldn't even begin to account for what went wrong. You can't defend the indefensible.'

Paddy can't read French, but he didn't have to. The name O'Brien kept jumping out of the headlines at him while he waited sombrely at Toulouse Airport the next morning for his flight back to Cardiff.

Ann-Marie Cole, wife of Australian referee Andrew Cole, who was the fourth official at Toulouse, is fluent in French and when they joined Paddy at the airport, she volunteered to interpret some of the newspaper comments. Paddy knows she tempered the translation ... 'She knew I was hurting.' Paddy rates Ann-Marie 'the jewel in the crown' among referees' wives. Again in 2003, along with her husband, she was a great friend to all the referees.

Back at his Cardiff base, the phone was running hot. Every call was from a journalist. And they were not, Paddy recalls with gallows humour, ringing to say well done!

Brendan Telfer of New Zealand Radio Sport was one of the callers. He seemed taken aback when Paddy instantly confessed he'd lost the plot and had had a shocker. 'I think Brendan expected me to defend myself, but I couldn't.'

Stephen Jones of the UK's *Sunday Times* would write that O'Brien 'at least had the balls to say he got it wrong'.

Paddy's World Cup had come to a shuddering halt. The selectors advised him they would not be allocating him any more pool match appointments for 'his own mental state' plus that of the teams he would have been refereeing.

The man from Invercargill, who'd stood so proudly at Millennium Stadium thinking of his family and fans back home prior to the tournament opener, initially felt the appointments panel were treating him harshly. He didn't believe that overnight he'd gone from being a quality referee to a dud one. Like the rider thrown unceremoniously from a horse, he wanted to climb back aboard straightaway. But he concedes now, with the benefit of hindsight, that the appointments panel acted correctly.

He needed time to heal. And the individual who made him appreciate this was NZRU board member Tim Gresson, who was intimately involved in the World Cup in his position as chairman of the IRB referees' committee.

Mid-morning on the day the appointments for the quarter-finals were to be announced, with Paddy clinging to a slender hope he would still be in contention, Gresson called on him at Jury's Hotel in Cardiff.

'Can I come in?' he asked. 'I shouldn't be here,' he told Paddy. 'But I wanted to let you know you won't be doing a quarter-final. Dick Byers and Dave Burnett were prepared to have you involved, but I felt it wasn't in your interests. I wanted to convey this news personally. If you feel like punching anyone, punch me, not them.'

Paddy says it took 'big balls' for Gresson to front him as he did. And although it 'hurt like hell' at the time to know he'd failed in his objective to progress at least to the quarter-final stage of the tournament, he knows that Gresson was acting in Paddy's own best interests.

Paddy considers that Gresson's actions in Dublin demonstrated that he was a person of complete integrity. He demonstrated that integrity on many other occasions, which had people like Syd Miller and John O'Neill waxing lyrical about his contribution to rugby and the values he brought to the game.

New Zealand referees were at least represented in the quarter-finals in '99 with Colin Hawke winning the appointment to control one of the 'big ones', the game between Graham Henry's Welsh team and Rod Macqueen's Wallabies at the Millennium Stadium.

The All Blacks were drawn to play Scotland at Murrayfield. Obviously, New

Zealanders couldn't be involved there, and Ed Morrison of England was given that game. The other two matches, either one of which in different circumstances Paddy might have been in charge of, involved South Africa against England in Paris, and France against Argentina in Dublin. Derek Bevan, the great old trooper from Wales, was assigned to Dublin, leaving Jim Fleming of Scotland to control operations at the magnificent Stade de France.

While hugely disappointed at the unexpected turn of events, which now had him hanging around Cardiff for three weeks as a spare part, Paddy realised he still had an important role to fulfil, as a support person for Colin Hawke. Paddy and Hawkeye were brothers in arms. They had come through the ranks together, taken the knocks together, become professionals together and, what was most important, they understood each other's situations. Paddy was enormously grateful to have Colin around in the week following the Toulouse episode. He was, in Paddy's words, 'absolutely superb'.

Paddy himself was grateful for the encouragement and support he received during those lonely weeks in Cardiff from Bob Francis and his wife Eva. Bob, as a former international referee and long-serving administrator, at the World Cup in an official capacity as an assessor, provided a much needed shoulder for Paddy to lean on. Although it was Eva who contributed most.

She was like a surrogate mother, not just to Paddy but to many of the other referees staying at Jury's Hotel. Almost every morning at 6.30 a.m., Bob, Eva and Paddy would stride out from their hotel. The crisp morning air was good for the lungs but, more importantly, Eva's calming conversation was good for Paddy's soul. 'Those walks alongside Eva were better for me than sessions on a psychologist's couch,' he confesses. 'Bob and Eva could have said this is a guy who can't hack it. But they didn't. They gave me hope. They convinced me that once I came through this, I would be a better referee.'

Over the next four years, Bob and Tom, as referee selectors in New Zealand, would be totally supportive of Paddy and ensure he reached his potential at the 2003 World Cup. Paddy says lesser individuals could have wiped their hands of him. Jim Fleming offered words of comfort. He recalled how he'd sent a wrong player off at his first World Cup tournament. It was something he took a long time to live down.

Memories of Paddy's unfortunate performance had only just begun to recede

Paddy O'Brien collection

Paddy's wedding to Carolyn Wyeth in Invercargill in 1987. Making up the wedding party, from left, are best man Dave Evans, Matthew, Kylie, bridesmaid Nicky Barron and Carolyn's niece Carmen Haynes.

Paddy O'Brien collection

The New Zealand Combined Services team which completed an undefeated run through England in 1992. Paddy (extreme left, back row) accompanied the team which was coached by Gordon Hunter (second from right, middle row) and captained by Steve Hansen (fourth from left, front row).

Paddy O'Brien collection

Paddy with the inaugural Steinlager New Zealand Referee of the Year award in Wellington in 1995. With him is the NZRU director of refereeing Graeme Harrison.

Fotopress

Paddy's first major overseas assignment, the Five Nations match between England and Scotland at Twickenham in 1997.

Southland Times

Paddy tosses a coin to decide who would speak first at an Invercargill Licensing Trust luncheon in 1996, himself or the famous Wallaby David Campese. Overseeing the toss is ILT assistant manager Gary Muir.

Paddy O'Brien collection

André Watson from South Africa, Paddy O'Brien from New Zealand and Alan Lewis from Ireland at the Hong Kong sevens tournament in 1996. It was the first time Paddy and André had encountered each other.

Fotopress

Paddy enthusiastically signals a penalty goal to Southland during the 1997 NPC clash with Otago at Invercargill, a game in which Southland scored an upset 22–20 win.

Fotopress

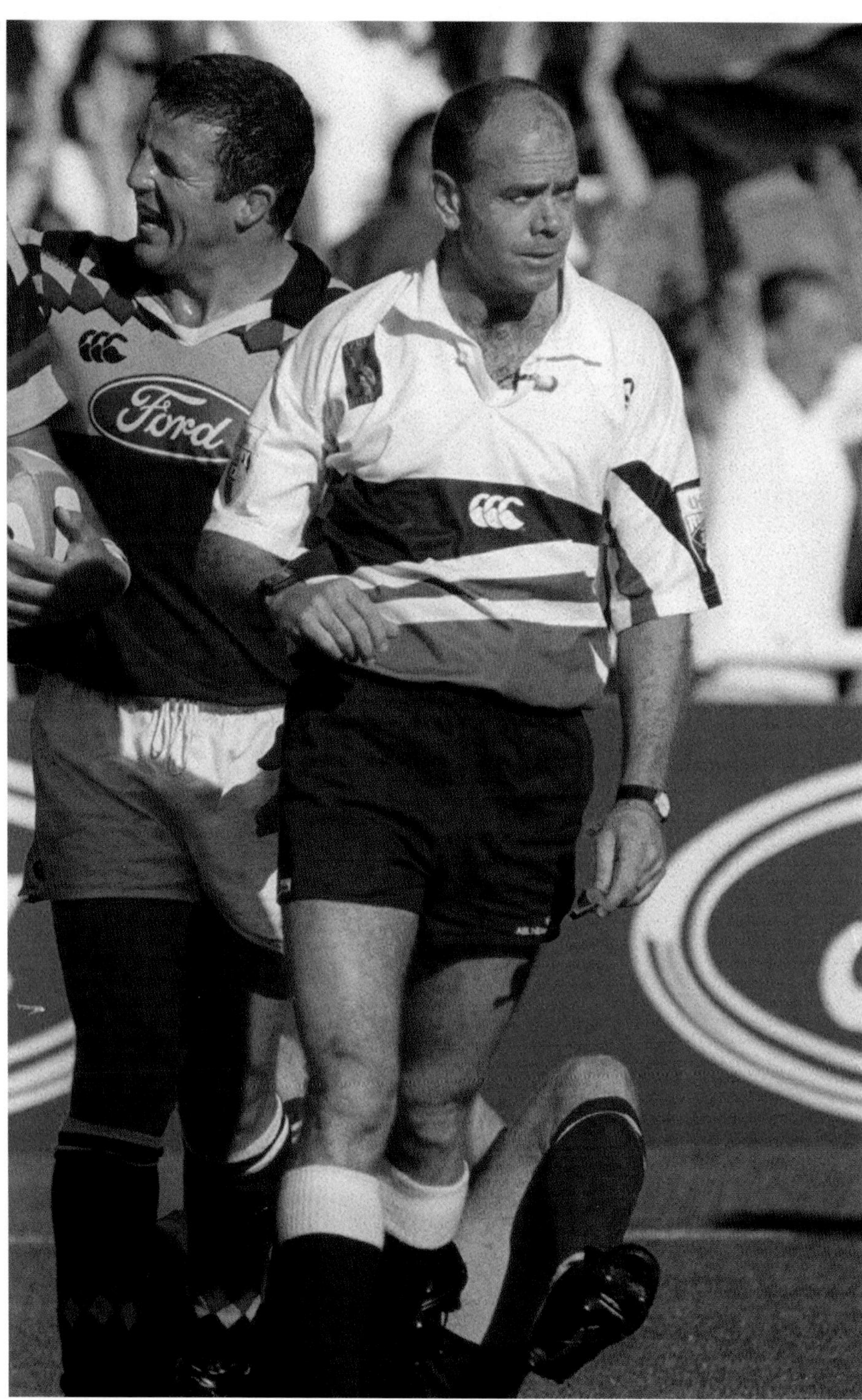

Sean Fitzpatrick shows his delight after Paddy awards Auckland a try during the 1997 NPC. It wouldn't be long before Auckland fans started believing they couldn't win with Paddy refereeing.

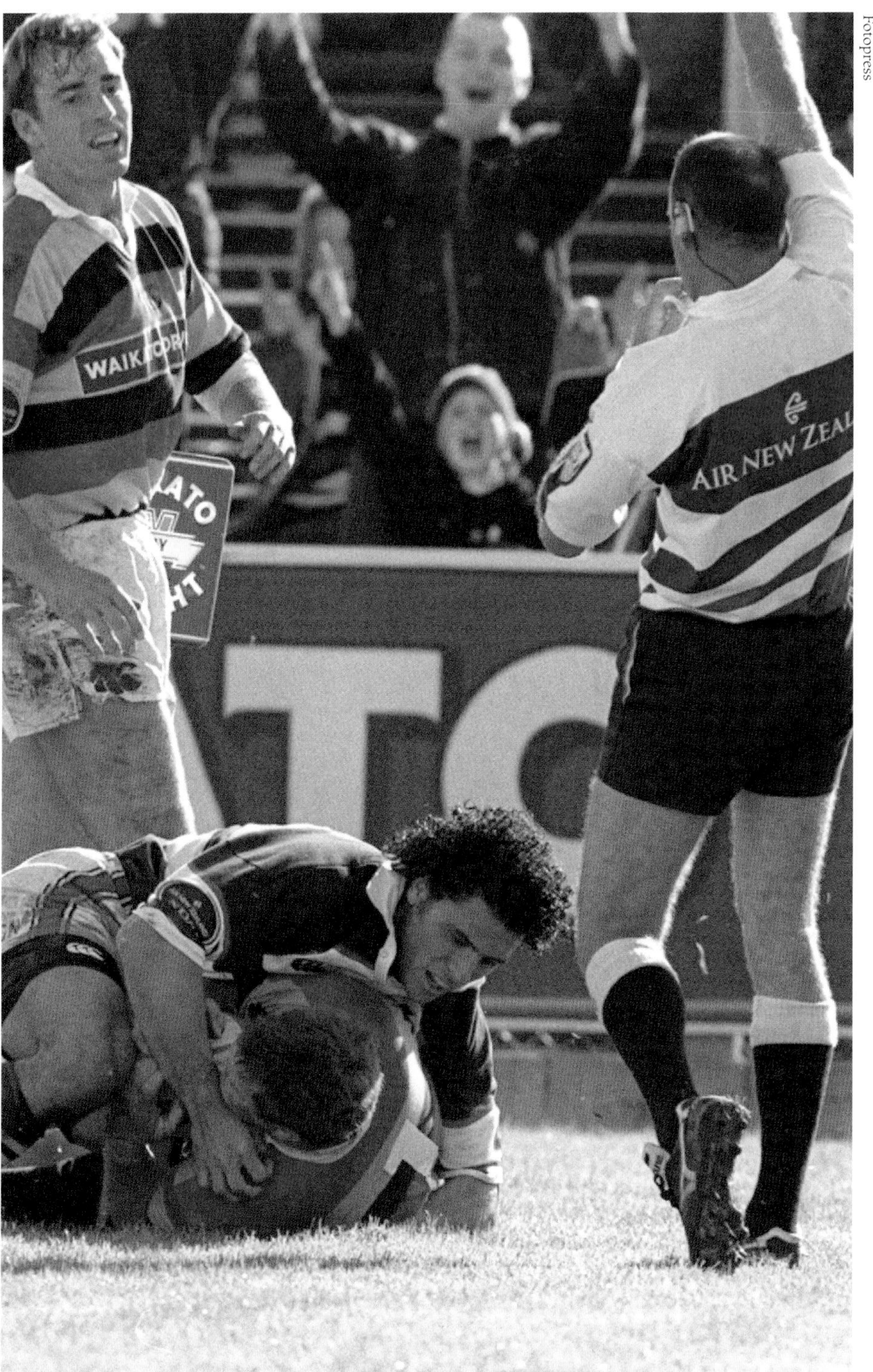

Fotopress

Waikato prop Michael Collins is awarded a try by Paddy at Hamilton in 1998. It helped the Mooloo men to a 24–23 win over Auckland, allowing them to retain the Ranfurly Shield.

Fotopress

Nothing like a wig to give a referee a little anonymity! Paddy at the 1998 Steinlager awards dinner in Christchurch.

when the blowtorch swung squarely onto Colin Hawke at the Millennium Stadium. He awarded George Gregan two highly controversial tries, the second after failing to recognise an obvious knock-on by Tim Horan.

Although Hawke's errors would not have prevented Australia advancing to the semi-finals, the Welsh fans were so incensed they were still booing long after the final whistle. The scoreline was only 17–9 when Horan knocked on and somehow the Welsh must have regarded that as a sort of moral victory against the tournament favourites. When the score jumped to 24–9, they somehow felt outraged. And referee Hawke copped the full blast of their wrath.

Paddy lost respect for the Welsh over their treatment of Colin after the game. 'They were never going to win that game. Colin's mistake towards the finish meant they lost by seven points more than they should have, but the whole Welsh nation seemed to blame him for the loss. No one would speak to him at the aftermatch function and one committeeman had even spat at him as he was leaving the field. When you see people that fervent, you worry about the future of the game. It was a sad reflection on a once great rugby nation, a shame for me personally because I have the utmost respect for the Welsh referees I've worked with, Derek Bevan in particular.'

Someone called Gareth Roberts wrote of Colin Hawke in one Welsh paper that, 'He should get the next plane home, and take his mate O'Brien with him — the rugby world does not need them.'

If New Zealand rugby followers were feeling a little sad about Paddy and Colin's misfortunes, it was nothing to the trauma that would afflict the nation when the All Blacks were unceremoniously bundled out of the tournament at the semi-final stage. Up 24–8 and seemingly in control against the French, a team they'd hammered 54–7 five months earlier, John Hart's men came crashing down 31–43.

There had already been discussions back in New Zealand about which city would organise the ticker tape parade for the conquering heroes.

The tournament had turned rotten for New Zealand. Nothing had worked out the way it was planned, although there was a tiny consolation prize for the Kiwis with Paddy being chosen, along with England's Ed Morrison, to run touch in the final between Australia and France at the Millennium Stadium.

Once the All Blacks were eliminated, the opportunity was there for a New Zealander to referee a World Cup final for the first time (that honour previously going to Kerry Fitzgerald of Australia, Derek Bevan of Wales and Ed Morrison of England), but unfortunately Messrs O'Brien and Hawke had accumulated too many demerit points. South Africa's André Watson got the job instead.

Paddy says Watson was unquestionably one of the best referees at the tournament and thoroughly merited his grand final appointment. Derek Bevan had said that to go all the way, a referee needed 'scars on the back' and he considered André had those scars.

Prior to the final, the referees and touch judges visited both dressing rooms, the touch judges being responsible for checking the players' boots. They all shook Rod Macqueen's hand and wished him well and advanced to the French dressing room. André Watson addressed the front row, in his fractured English way, and shook the hands of Jean-Claude Skrela and Jo Maso, the French coach and captain. Everything to that moment was routine but then Ed Morrison suddenly engaged in a full body embrace with Skrela, and said to him, 'You've got to do it for the northern hemisphere'.

Paddy was shocked. He thought maybe he was being a bit precious but he found Morrison's behaviour incongruous. After all, weren't touch judges, like the referee, supposed to be neutral?

Watson, still youthful, gave an excellent performance in the final (won 35–12 by Australia) in difficult and trying circumstances. As with most World Cup finals, the teams didn't care whether they won by one point or twenty. And they certainly weren't there to entertain.

The French had obviously played their final against New Zealand and never looked like winning. At various stages, Paddy noted from the sideline, they resorted to dubious tactics. On two occasions, John Eales complained to Watson of eye gouging and testicle grabbing. Paddy considers that Watson's mature attitude saved the game from degenerating into a farce.

Seated in business class on the long flight back to New Zealand, Paddy encountered Kevin Roberts, advertising guru and NZRU board member, indeed, the one whose idea it was to decorate the plane carrying the team to Britain with pictures of the All Blacks. Roberts was sitting even further forward in the plane.

'They tell me you've been getting some flak back home,' he said to Paddy.

'Yeah, but not as much as you.'

The conversation terminated at that point.

When he arrived at Invercargill Airport, Paddy was feeling vulnerable and wanted to get into his car as quickly as possible and head home. As he was waiting for his luggage, accompanied by Carolyn and his children, an oldtimer approached him, shook his hand and said, 'We're proud of you. Don't listen to all that crap on the radio.'

Paddy appreciated that he was home again, amongst Southlanders, real people. He knows if he'd refereed the final and become big-headed, that same fellow would have told him he'd missed a knock-on!

As he readjusted to life with Carolyn and his children, Paddy realised that he needed to make a reassessment of his refereeing future. If he was going to continue to put this amount of pressure on himself, then maybe he needed to look at another sport.

In hindsight, Paddy knows that the Toulouse experience was the making of him as a referee. 'I know it's no consolation to Brad Johnstone and the Fijian boys but I learnt so much from that game. Some teams I can think of would be bitter at what went on that day, but Brad simply said he'd seen Paddy referee better. The facts stand on their own, and I gave a poor performance.

'I realise now that I went to the World Cup for the wrong reasons. Instead of just enjoying what I was doing, I was anxiously working towards a quarter-final appointment. That was a huge mistake.'

Getting Back on Track

Paddy was still coming to terms with his poor performance at the World Cup when by chance, early in 2000, he met Lewis McGill, head of Sport and Recreation at the Southern Institute of Technology in Invercargill.

At the time he encountered McGill he was contemplating some tertiary study at the Institute. A casual conversation developed into a close relationship that would have a major influence in turning around Paddy's fortunes on the paddock.

He and McGill initially spent hours looking at videotapes and listening to commentaries to understand where Paddy could improve his onfield performance. McGill identified that it was important for Paddy to be more relaxed in pressure situations. He concentrated on Paddy's mindset and the manner in which he prepared for matches. Priorities were identified with McGill emphasising the need to control the controllables while setting aside those things that were uncontrollable.

A referee can control his physical and mental preparation but he can't control a hail storm five minutes before kick-off or two teams that are determined to play silly buggers. He can control how he deals with such behaviour.

Paddy and Lewis McGill took a while to settle into a relationship where they completely understood each other's roles, but once that was achieved Lewis McGill became of immense value to Southland's No. 1 referee. As their association developed and prior to McGill transferring to New Plymouth, he became Paddy's training partner. Being 10 years older, he couldn't push Paddy physically, but, rain, hail or shine (and Southland during the winter months tends to experience more rain and hail than shine) he was always there to ensure Paddy adhered to the schedule set for him by his new fitness trainer Dan van der Westhuisen.

Many a time as the hail pelted down and a biting southerly whipped around Surrey Park, Paddy would hear Lewis saying, 'Will Peter Marshall or Dave McHugh be doing this?' Paddy knew bloody well they wouldn't be and it drove him on to the conclusion of that session.

Since McGill's departure for New Plymouth they have kept in touch by e-mail and telephone and Paddy says he will be part of his 'team' until the day he hangs up his whistle.

Van der Westhuisen got involved simply through being a member of Lewis's staff at the Institute in Invercargill. Prior to 2000, Paddy achieved fitness by grinding out the kilometres along Southland roads and relied on his speed to carry him through refereeing appointments. But as Paddy was getting older, the game was getting faster and becoming a greater challenge.

Van der Westhuisen was his lifesaver. They sat together and planned the season ahead. Through his new adviser, Paddy learnt to peak for the bigger games and important phases while maintaining a good level of fitness to get him through what is now a 10-month season. Athletes, like racehorses, are not machines and cannot achieve at optimum level for an entire year. Van der Westhuisen appreciated this and shaped Paddy's training accordingly. They have worked outstandingly together. Paddy found he could be completely honest with Dan, telling him when he was lacking energy at training or going stale without van der Westhuisen ever thinking he was being lazy.

Lewis McGill taught Paddy to believe in himself and Dan van der Westhuisen taught him to be disciplined in his training. Together, they turned a referee's career around in dramatic fashion. By the time of the next World Cup, Paddy, having arrived home from the previous one with his tail firmly between his legs, would be at the peak of his powers.

The call came at 7.30 one morning early in 2000, from Martin Devlin, breakfast host on Radio Sport. 'Paddy,' he said, 'Steve Walsh and Paul Honiss are the only New Zealanders who've received Six Nations appointments. Are you disappointed at being dropped from the international panel?'

Paddy wasn't quite sure what to say, although he was annoyed at Devlin's interpretation of events. He and Colin Hawke hadn't been dropped from any panel. And why wasn't Devlin putting a positive spin on Paul and Steve's achievement in winning such prestigious appointments?

Paddy knew he wouldn't be refereeing Six Nations matches that (New Zealand) summer, because Tim Gresson had told him so. Tim had been brutally honest, reassuring Paddy that the international panel hadn't lost faith in him, but that the ball was now in his court. He needed to regain his confidence and the opportunity was there for him to do that in the Super 12.

Paddy was relieved, in a sense. He didn't feel he was ready to step out on the world stage just yet. There would be too much pressure on him. He kept hearing people saying he was a shit referee. He knew he wasn't, but there was a process he had to go through before he could prove to the world he was competent to handle international appointments again.

In the meantime, he was thrilled for Steve and Paul that they were winning international recognition. He couldn't emphasise that point strongly enough in his interview with Devlin.

Paddy eased back into refereeing with the Chiefs-Crusaders and Blues-Chiefs Super 12 matches in February-March, 2000, games that were mercifully free of 'train smashes'.

But with his next appointment, the Highlanders-Hurricanes contest at Carisbrook, he was thrust back into the limelight when he showed Tana Umaga the red card for a blatantly high tackle on Romi Ropati. Ropati had tried to step Umaga and was heading for the goal-line when Umaga coat-hangered him.

Paddy regarded it as a 'non-negotiable' situation. When he has doubt in his mind, he pulls a yellow card. On this occasion the seriousness of the infringement justified an ordering off. And when Ropati recovered, which was some minutes later, he awarded the Highlanders a penalty try.

Paddy believes that to this day he has never sent a player from the field who didn't deserve to go. 'Because only 20 minutes had been played, Tana going off spoiled the game as a spectacle. He's one of the nicest guys in rugby, but I referee on the facts. I don't think, 'That's Tana, I can't send him off.' At the time I said, '13, you're off!'

The scars hadn't completely re-grown on Paddy's back since Toulouse and he was still sensitive to criticism. It hurt when David White, then chief executive officer of the Hurricanes, turned his back on him at the aftermatch and also when he read in the Sunday papers the following day, as he was heading off to South Africa and his next Super 12 appointment, how outrageous it was that Tana should be treated in such a manner.

The papers made a meal of it. What irked Paddy was that none of them talked of the act, only that it was Tana. Paddy sympathises with critics and fans who argue that reducing a team to 14 damages the contest. He suggests rugby looks at what other codes do. He's adamant the referee should always have the right to send a player from the field for an extremely serious offence. After 10 minutes, during which that player's team must operate with 14 players, a replacement could be permitted, obviously not the individual who's received the red card. The game would continue with 15 against 15.

Paddy was also disappointed that certain commentators, Murray Mexted among them, criticised him for hitting the Hurricanes with a double whammy, an ordering-off and a penalty try. It was claimed the Hurricanes had effectively been penalised twice for the one offence. Paddy doesn't buy that. 'The red card was for the dangerous, high tackle. The penalty try was given because, but for illegal play by the Hurricanes No. 13, a try would probably have been scored.'

When a commentator makes a statement, the public accept it as fact. Trouble is, says Paddy, the commentator isn't always a master of the law book. It was pretty obvious, he felt, that many of the comments from the so-called experts following Umaga's eviction from Carisbrook were driven by their personal association with the Hurricanes team, not from their analysis of what actually happened on the field.

The judicial committee backed the referee, finding Umaga guilty and suspending him for a week. However, Paddy didn't feel he received the same unmitigated support from the NZRU. His boss Keith Lawrence's response to a flood of correspondence expressing concern that Umaga's sending-off had spoilt the game was to e-mail Paddy in South Africa asking him if he had considered using a yellow card rather than the red one.

Paddy harbours no remorse over his actions that day at Carisbrook. In hindsight, he wouldn't have changed a thing. One good aspect out of all the controversy was that it gave the message to New Zealand rugby players that Paddy O'Brien didn't muck around with foul play, especially pertinent given that his action was supported by the judiciary.

It's natural for individuals to interpret events in rugby differently, but what intrigues Paddy is how many people focus on the referee after an ordering-off, rather than the guilty player. 'Occasionally, the referee will get it wrong,' he says, 'but in an overwhelming number of cases, the referee's actions are supported by the judicial committee. Yet you hear countless people jumping to the offending player's defence.'

Paddy fronted Keith Lawrence on his return from South Africa and said he expected him to back his referees.

'What if you make a mistake?' replied Lawrence. 'Should we comment then?'

'Yes,' said Paddy. 'We shouldn't go into hiding. I don't believe in all this political correctness. If we're upfront, we'll earn more respect from the media and, hopefully, the public.'

Paddy believes that by being 'transparent' referees will be more understood, and hopefully appreciated. For example, if while a referee is going through a tough patch he is assigned to an NPC second division match to help get his confidence back, why shouldn't that be made known? Selectors and coaches often drop players because they are low in confidence. That's always made public, but not when referees are stepped down for the identical reason.

Until Colin Cooper sorted out the Hurricanes' discipline in 2003, the Wellington-based team annually topped the yellow card table in Super 12 action. It frustrated Paddy and his colleagues that the referees consistently copped abuse from the Wellington media for what was interpreted as an anti-Hurricanes attitude.

Paddy identifies Dion Waller and Inoke Afeaki as players who repeatedly breached boundaries yet because the team was playing an exciting brand of rugby and possessed a powerful spectator base, there was outrage when yellow cards kept coming. In Paddy's opinion, the Hurricanes fans and their media didn't want facts spoiling a good story!

Murray Mexted is regarded by referees as an enigma. He has boundless enthusiasm but the mistakes he makes with his original interpretations of the laws have a seriously detrimental effect on how the public perceives referees. In a professional world, his errors are unacceptable. Referees are accountable and have to accept their assessors' reports when they make mistakes, but Mexted is seemingly immune. His personal interpretation of the laws often does not equate to what is contained in the law book.

Commentators are privy to the referees' comments and rulings throughout a match. Replays show most decisions at the troublesome tackle ball area are accurate. Not all, but most. Mexted is often oblivious to the referee's rulings. He'll make a comment which often relates to a separate law altogether. And what frustrates the referees is that the multitude sitting at home watching accept his word.

Paddy considers that New Zealand is blessed with quality commentators, individuals like Keith Quinn, John McBeth, Grant Nisbett and Tony Johnson, whose expertise and professionalism he considers to be the best of the Sanzar countries. But unfortunately much of their good work is undone by Mexted who dances to his own tune.

The television match official, or TMO as he is technically known, made its entrance into New Zealand rugby during the 2000 Super 12 competition. A blessing for referees, who now effectively had an extra pair of eyes behind the goal-line to assist them in their judgment, the TMO brought its moments of humour, as in the Hurricanes-Crusaders match in Wellington.

It was a fantastic exhibition of rugby and after one powerful surge by the Crusaders forwards their captain Todd Blackadder, who didn't often feature in the tryscorers' list, contorted his body and grounded the ball back over his head for what his team mates instantly regarded as a try.

Referee O'Brien didn't have a clear view of the grounding so chose to go 'upstairs' to the video referee. No sooner had he indicated his intentions than Norm Hewitt, the Hurricanes captain, came rushing across, declaring, 'No try!'

Blackadder resented this intrusion and it took Paddy 10 seconds to prise the two skippers apart. 'Come on, you guys, control yourselves,' said Paddy.

Blackadder wasn't going to allow a skirmish to detract from his moment of glory. 'Is it a try, if you place the ball on the goal-line?' he asked Paddy.

'Yes.'

'Then it's a f—— try!'

By the time the video referee had confirmed this fact to Paddy, Blackadder had led his team back to halfway, tossing the ball to his goalkicker along the way. The Crusaders, trailing 22–28 with the clock running down and desperate for points, were within sight of the Hurricanes' posts when Paddy blew up an unplayable ruck and gave the put-in to the Hurricanes.

When Blackadder realised this, he lost his cool, something which very rarely happened. One of the game's most even-tempered individuals, Blackadder was a wonderful, calming influence on his teams, always leading by example. But on this occasion, he went ballistic, presumably because he was seeing his team's last opportunity of rescuing the match evaporating on a referee's marginal call. Blackadder was in full flight when he suddenly looked up, saw himself on the giant screen and fell silent.

A moment or two later, after the Hurricanes had scrambled the ball into touch, fulltime was called. Paddy began making his way from the field but as he did so, he became aware of someone hurrying towards him. It was Blackadder.

'Paddy, I want to apologise for going off my nut out there. That was awful. I didn't mean for that to happen.'

No wonder Paddy rates Todd right alongside John Eales as his favourite player. They were, he says, complete gentlemen, both of them. That small blemish at the Cake Tin aside, neither of them ever lost their composure when Paddy was refereeing, not even in the tensest of situations or when events were running cruelly against their sides. Their special strength was their capacity to remain calm and reasoned in the most challenging of circumstances and to inspire their teams to greater effort, more often than not with themselves providing the heroic touch.

If Blackadder had a grizzle about a referee, he detailed it in his captain's report, which, says Paddy, is the right and proper thing to do. He never bagged referees publicly ... 'He accepted that referees, like players, had bad days. Life went on after the final whistle. Personally, I was thrilled when he made the All Blacks. While he would admit he was never one of New Zealand's greatest locks, he was certainly one of the game's characters, and gentlemen.'

Early in April, 2000, Paddy ran touch in Canberra when the Brumbies demolished the Cats 64–nil, an unfortunate result for Laurie Mains' men who had been extremely competitive in their matches in New Zealand.

When Paddy returned to Canberra in mid May to referee the same two combatants in a semi-final, he half expected another one-sided contest. But if proof was needed of Mains' exceptional coaching powers, this was it. Notwithstanding the wearying flights through from Johannesburg, the Cats took the game to the home side, falling away only in the last 10 minutes.

Paddy's return to the international scene was comparatively low key, Scotland against New Zealand Vikings at Whangarei, a game the Vikings, bolstered by such up-and-comers as Steve Devine, Paul Steinmetz, Rico Gear, Chris Jack, Xavier Rush and Justin Collins, won hands down. It was a stepping stone to the test stage. For a player there is surely no greater sense of satisfaction than a recall to the All Blacks. Paddy felt that same surge of achievement when he received notification of his appointment to the Wallabies-Springboks Mandela Cup international at Colonial Stadium in Melbourne.

Two hundred and sixty-five days after his disaster at Toulouse, he was back as a test referee. While it was obviously a momentous occasion in the context of his refereeing career, Paddy didn't consider he had to prove anything except that he belonged in the test arena. To his intense relief, the game was incident free. No train smashes. Not even a slight shunting mishap. Referee O'Brien was very definitely No. 31 on this occasion, exactly where he wanted to be. He came off feeling he was back on the horse.

In the wake of that Melbourne international, Paddy had a vision: that he would go to the 2003 World Cup and come home declaring it a great experience.

In September of 2000, he refereed the Auckland NPC game against Canterbury at Eden Park, won by the southerners 29–26. The next day on talkback radio he heard claims again that Auckland and the Blues couldn't beat the men in red and black while Paddy O'Brien was refereeing. How ironic, thought Paddy, given his one genuine mistake in that game tangibly favoured Auckland. Robin Brooke, in driving for the line, had lost possession of the ball before forcing it. Paddy looked to his touch judge, who gave no indication anything was amiss and so, with no video referee to fall back on, he awarded the try.

It was a classic example of 'what you don't see, you can't rule on'. Breaching that rule had got Paddy into big trouble at Toulouse and although, on this occasion, his sixth sense warned him something was not quite right, he could only adjudicate on what he'd seen.

Notwithstanding that, Aucklanders, stoked up by Mr Deaker, were still somehow accusing him of jinxing their fine side. Paddy laughs off the accusations and can shoot down such ludicrous claims with statistical evidence. Before the balance of power shifted from the City of Sails to the Garden City, Paddy had refereed Auckland on 10 occasions, and in nine of those games the blue and whites were victorious. The solitary loss was to North Harbour in a ripsnorter of a game on Eden Park. He'd also refereed the Blues six times and on each occasion they'd been successful.

Fifteen victories from 16 matches with Paddy on the whistle scarcely suggests that as a Southlander he was waging a personal vendetta against Aucklanders. To those who were trying to lay the blame for Auckland rugby's demise on refereeing, Paddy suggests there were more obvious causes. Such as the retirement or departure overseas of such icons as Sean Fitzpatrick, Zinzan Brooke, Frank Bunce and coach Graham Henry, coinciding with Canterbury and the Crusaders' emergence under such enlightened modern coaches as Robbie Deans, Wayne Smith, Peter Sloane and Steve Hansen.

By the time Paddy journeyed to Hamilton for Canterbury's Ranfurly Shield challenge, he was aware, thanks to a memo from statistician Geoff Miller, that in the nine shield matches he had previously controlled, the trophy had never changed hands. Miller, a Waikato supporter, was obviously wanting the status quo to remain.

Miller had given Paddy's spirits a lift around the time Aucklanders were pointing accusingly at the Southlander, dropping him the following note:

Dear Paddy,

From time to time, one listens with incredulity to Murray Deaker and is reminded of 'the King's new clothes' with such wisdom as 50-50 calls, team culture, winning habit etc. If referees are judged on the number of mistakes they make, why are the public more generous with players? A missed goal kick is a player's mistake, and using this criteria Grant Fox rarely had a good game, for he had about a 70 per cent success rate through his career. If referees were to be punished/dropped for making mistakes, it wouldn't be long before the cupboard was bare. The reaction of the public is determined by their expectation. Usually, it is to see their team win, and therefore they must be disappointed probably 50 per cent of the time. At Rugby Park, the woman behind me has the referee classified within three minutes whereas I go along to see excellence of performance and am rarely disappointed. You remain Miller's number one referee.

On the morning of the Hamilton game, Paddy encountered Canterbury captain Todd Blackadder in a lift. Asked how he was, Paddy mentioned that he was still receiving flak on talkback radio for his handling of the Auckland-Canterbury match.

'You don't listen to that crap,' said Blackadder. 'Why don't you go and buy a CD player?'

When Paddy mentioned this conversation to Canterbury coach Steve Hansen later in the morning, Hansen replied, 'That's rich coming from Toddy. We told him to do exactly the same thing last week!'

After an epic contest, played in the best traditions of Ranfurly Shield rugby, Canterbury lifted the prized 'log', 26 points to 18. Although he had sampled shield fever on those many previous occasions, Paddy only now appreciated what the winning and losing of this precious trophy meant to the unions involved. It was the first occasion the shield had changed hands while he was refereeing.

Because he wanted to be present when his daughter Kylie celebrated her 21st birthday in Christchurch, he had booked himself on the first available flight south that evening. To his surprise, he found himself sharing the plane with the triumphant Canterbury players. And in Christchurch, he had great difficulty clearing the airport, which was packed to the gunwales with euphoric red and black supporters, so he could join his daughter at a mid-city restaurant.

Back on the IRB's test rota, Paddy was assigned one of rugby's most prestigious contests, the Calcutta Cup match between England and Scotland at Twickenham. He decided it would be good if, for the first time, his wife Carolyn accompanied him. They planned a two-week sojourn in the UK following the big match.

A fortnight before the Six Nations encounter, he ran touch at Twickenham at the England-Italy game, refereed by Australia's Stuart Dickinson. During the game, he felt a slight strain in his calf muscle. He didn't consider it cause for great concern and was confident that, with treatment, it would heal quickly. His optimism was not unfounded for, since the commencement of his refereeing career, he had never missed one match through injury or illness.

Unprepared to risk the muscle in such an important encounter, Paddy approached officials of the RFU's referees' committee, requesting an appointment that would allow him to satisfy himself of his readiness for Twickenham. He was assigned to the Bath-Gloucester club fixture at Bath where he was settling nicely into his routine when the calf muscle gave him a sharp reminder that it was far from mended. At the 15 minute mark, he limped to the sideline.

Keith Lawrence at NZRU headquarters back in Wellington was extremely supportive, suggesting Paddy undergo treatment in the UK and, in light of Carolyn's presence, continue with the trip. But Paddy felt uncomfortable about holidaying in the UK when he'd failed to front for his assignment, so the O'Briens packed up and headed home to Invercargill where the troublesome calf muscle was sorted out.

That calf would be the only muscle injured in Paddy's long career. Whether the long flight contributed or whether he'd damaged it in training, Paddy doesn't know. But since then, he's been meticulous in stretching his calf muscles before commencing any training or match.

After three weeks' rehab, he was winging his way off to Durban for the Sharks-Waratahs Super 12 match and was enormously relieved to complete the 80 minutes with no twinges whatsoever in the calf region.

On his way home he controlled the Brumbies-Waratahs match, interesting for the fact that Australian referees had sacrificed the opportunity to control local derbies, preferring to stick with neutral appointees. With only three teams involved, referees found they were subjected to unreasonable media pressure. New Zealand initially reciprocated, using Australians for some local derbies but subsequently changed and now use home talent exclusively for matches among the New Zealand franchises.

Back in Godzone, Paddy was in charge when the Chiefs sensationally disposed of the Hurricanes 51–27 at the Cake Tin, an amazing result given the Chiefs' modest achievements since the advent of Super 12. It was a performance that catapulted the Chiefs' new coach John Mitchell into All Black contention. By season's end he had replaced Wayne Smith.

Bounced in the Capital

Paddy just loves refereeing at the Cake Tin. The place exudes excitement and atmosphere, helped by the Hurricanes' preparedness to play thrill-a-minute rugby which, while not always successful, certainly helps make a night at Wellington's super stadium a memorable occasion. The Chiefs trouncing the Hurricanes was one of these occasions.

Less enchanting, however, was the reception Paddy received when referees Hawke, Honiss and O'Brien headed for a bar on the Wellington waterfront later that evening. Hawke and Honiss were welcome but Paddy suddenly found his progress barred by a massive bouncer.

'Nuh,' said the bouncer.

'Why can't I go in?' asked a startled Paddy.

''Cos I said so.'

'Why's that?' asked Paddy, genuinely confused.

''Cos I don't like you.'

It remains the only occasion in his entire career, embracing his roles as a policeman and a referee, that he has been refused admission. Patently, the bouncer had taken exception to Paddy's refereeing of the Super 12 encounter earlier in the evening, evidently holding him somehow responsible for the Hurricanes' demise.

Paddy's career in the police force had taught him to know when not to be confrontational. And this was such a time. 'He'd have killed me if I'd challenged him, for a start. And I'd seen how players had brought themselves unfavourable publicity by reacting to situations such as this. I could see the headlines in the Sunday papers if I allowed myself to be impetuous. While I wasn't going in, I wasn't going away either. I let Paul and Hawkeye have their drink while I remained outside staring at this great bruiser, letting him know I didn't approve of his attitude.'

When he returned to Invercargill, Paddy telephoned the establishment concerned and complained to the manager who said he would 'follow it up'. Paddy never heard back, leaving it at that. It remains the only occasion he has been personally challenged. Most of his critics hide anonymously behind a pen or talkback radio. While rugby pundits have definite views on referees, until that night Paddy had never been personally abused.

Paddy's next appointment was a prestigious one, the Super 12 final between the Brumbies and the Sharks in Canberra, the occasion being notable for the absence of New Zealand teams (who'd won the title in 1996, 1997, 1998, 1999 and 2000 and would reign supreme again in 2002 and 2003).

On the morning of the game, Paddy had a fax delivered to him at his hotel. It read:

Dear Mr O'Brien,

With respect, sir, regarding the final on Saturday, we request that you please show no bias, or listen to the media. I am sure you are an honourable man with the best of intentions. However, referees have been so influenced by home games and the media of late, particularly when it comes to so-called 'illegal tackles' as opposed to really dangerous tackles. I am also sure that you are aware of the foul language directed at a referee recently by George Gregan, which should have been a red card offence. Due to obvious reasons, it was ignored. Gregan is a great player, but he does, as you are aware, tend to referee matches himself and it would be a great pity to spoil this event by allowing him to undermine your authority. Please don't take this as criticism, no offence is meant. We have respected you over the years as a fair man and one of the best referees and it is our wish that this game reinforces the Paddy O'Brien of the past. May I take this opportunity to wish you the very best for Saturday and the future. Sincerely, Cecil Owen (and on behalf of many South African Super 12 supporters).

Paddy shook his head in disbelief. He couldn't believe someone would send him such a letter. He went out and refereed the game as he saw it. The Brumbies, decisively the best team in the competition, won 36–6, clinching for the Australians at the time just about every major rugby trophy they were eligible for.

When Paddy handled the Pumas match against Counties Manukau at Pukekohe in June 2001, Sky TV commentator Tony Johnson was moved to comment that 'Paddy O'Brien's Spanish has improved.' Which left him more than a little bemused when someone brought the observation to his attention. So he watched a video of the game and was embarrassed to note how when addressing the Argentinians he lapsed into Puma-speak. Scooz me, but when-a you play da ball, you must-a be ona your feet!

The rugby world's focus in the middle of 2001 was firmly set on the Wallabies-Lions series in Australia. With the Wallabies under Rod Macqueen boasting an overflowing trophy cabinet and the best of Britain and Ireland being shaped by the Great Redeemer Graham Henry, it was effectively the battle for world supremacy. And Paddy was honoured to be awarded the third, and, as it turned out, the deciding, international in Sydney. South Africans André Watson and Jonathon Kaplan had charge of the first two tests.

At Brisbane, Watson's test, Paddy ran touch with Kaplan. At Melbourne, when Kaplan had the whistle, Watson and O'Brien were the touch judges. Collectively, they established an excellent rapport, so Paddy was a little disappointed when the IRB broke them up for the decider.

While he was pleased to have his Kiwi colleagues Steve Walsh and Paul Honiss running touch for him at Stadium Australia in Sydney, it mystified him why the IRB appointments panel split up an established threesome that had got the feel of the series.

Paddy was blown away by the extent of the support for the Lions. By the time the tests started, almost 30,000 UK supporters had invaded Australia. He believes if New Zealand's top administrators of the time had crossed the Tasman and noted what that series was doing for the Australian economy, they would never have allowed sub-hosting rights for the World Cup to slip from their grasp.

Outside of the World Cup, there was surely no greater appointment available for a New Zealand referee and Paddy was determined to be at his peak for the contest. Through working with McGill and van der Westhuisen, he felt he was in the best shape of his life. It was also reassuring to know that his boss, Keith Lawrence, and wife, Carolyn, were in town to provide support and encouragement.

On the Friday morning he met with Graham Henry at the Lions' hotel at Manly to discuss law interpretations. As they sat in the lounge drinking coffee, a dove landed on the windowsill, directly in front of them. 'That bloody Rod Macqueen,' quipped Henry. 'He'll stop at nothing to win this series. The dove's obviously wired!'

The test rates as one of the most mentally draining Paddy has ever been involved in. Because the scores were close throughout — indeed, with less than 10 minutes remaining the teams were locked together at 23–all — it was imperative for the referee to retain his concentration to the final whistle. Paddy knew that one bad decision could ruin what had been a classic series. In the event, the Wallabies survived a storming finish from the Lions to claim the match 29–23.

While the Lions were unlucky to have been decimated by injury, Paddy says the Wallabies demonstrated during the series just why they were the world champions ... 'They showed how mentally tough they were, a classic example of which was Justin Harrison winning a crucial lineout against the throw with only two or three minutes remaining.'

At the final whistle, Harrison was so ecstatic he gave the individual closest to him a massive bear hug. That person happened to be Paddy who, while happy for the Aussie, was anxious to disentangle himself, alarmed at how it might appear on British television, the referee embracing a Wallaby on the field!

Silence is golden, we were all taught at school. For a referee controlling a major international rugby fixture silence is indeed golden in the wake of the final whistle. A referee knows when critics, commentators and match officials are talking only about the result, the tries, the heroic individual performances that he has done his job.

'It wasn't a perfect refereeing performance,' he recalls, 'but there's no such thing. However, I knew because everyone was talking about the game and not the referee, it was a satisfactory display.'

In the wash-up, even the unforgiving UK media apportioned no blame for the Lions' defeat to the referee. They were more preoccupied with whether the English 'rebels' Austin Healey and Matt Dawson, who had commented critically on Graham Henry's coaching methods, might have undermined team morale.

Paddy found Henry to be a good loser. 'He had plenty to blame, injuries, the bounce of the ball and rebellious players, but he was magnanimous in defeat, congratulating the Wallabies on their series victory. Deep down, he was obviously hurting like hell.'

Back on the domestic scene, Paddy handled the Otago-Auckland NPC game at Carisbrook, which produced a sensational finish when Brendan Laney, who'd become something of a cult figure in Speight's territory, scored behind the posts in the dying seconds.

It prompted veteran Auckland journalist Don (D.J.) Cameron to ask in his *Rugby News* column, 'How can Auckland ever win with Paddy O'Brien refereeing?' Paddy's response at reading that was a simple, 'Huh!'.

When Auckland then journeyed south to Jade Stadium to challenge for the Ranfurly Shield, in a contest which doubled as an important NPC fixture, there were groans in the north after it was announced that the referee would be P. O'Brien (Southland). Neither Auckland nor the Blues had won against the red and blacks since 1996 with Paddy refereeing, so the editorial tone in the north could be imagined. Paddy himself received a reassuring call from Bob Francis, one of those responsible for the appointment. 'As long as you're refereeing accurately, we have no qualms about putting you in charge of Auckland-Canterbury contests,' said Francis. 'I don't care what the critics are saying.'

Canterbury smashed Auckland 38–10 and if there were Doubting Donalds in the City of Sails who reckoned Mr O'Brien somehow contributed to that one-sided scoreline, their arguments were shot down in flames a couple of weeks later when, in a semi-final rematch on the same turf, Canterbury slaughtered the same Auckland side 53–22. This time the referee was Kelvin Deaker.

Paddy rounded out 2001 with a prestigious appointment, England against Australia at the venue that fascinates him, Twickenham. 'Rugger at Twickers' is as far removed from a game at Rugby Park in Invercargill or Centennial Park in Oamaru, or Memorial Park in Masterton as it is possible to imagine.

The Twickenham occasion starts in the car park where the aristocracy wine and dine out of the boots of their Bentleys and Rolls Royces, many with servants who tend to such menial matters as tidying up and recorking the unfinished wine bottles while the rugby is happening. And for those lucky enough to perform on the hallowed turf, which is always in utterly immaculate condition, there are hot baths to soak in afterwards.

After his match in 2001, Paddy was invited to the president's box for a drink prior to attending the aftermatch function. A committeeman, resplendent in a distinctive jacket and tie, spotted the silver fern on Paddy's breast pocket and came across and shook his hand.

'What has brought you all the way from New Zealand, old chap?'

'I came for the big game today,' replied Paddy.

'My darling,' said the committeeman, beckoning his wife across, 'this gentleman has come all the way from New Zealand. All the way from the Antipodes.'

Turning back to Paddy, he asked why a New Zealander would come all that distance to watch England play Australia.

'I was the referee, that's why.'

'Darling, darling ... he's the bloody referee!'

Paddy loves re-telling that story. To him, it sums up the very best and very worst of English rugby. He can understand why so many New Zealanders detest pompous Poms and yet he concedes there is also something magical about 'rugger at Twickers'.

On his previous visit, when a torn calf muscle had prevented him refereeing the Calcutta Cup match, he attended the game as a spectator, along with his wife Carolyn. Mark Lawrence of South Africa, who was running touch, was also accompanied by his wife, Giselle.

On match day, Nick Bunting, England's referees' boss, inquired where Giselle was.

'She's gone shopping,' said Lawrence.

'You mean she's not going to the game?' replied Bunting, a look of disbelief on his face.

'No,' said Lawrence. 'She'd rather shop.'

Bunting turned to Paddy. 'What do you think of that decision?'

Paddy just shrugged.

'She's turning down an opportunity to attend an international at the home of rugby,' said Bunting.

'No,' quipped Paddy, 'Eden Park is the home of rugby.'

Bunting was about to react when a huge grin broke out on Paddy's face.

When Carolyn accompanied Paddy to the Hong Kong sevens one year, she found herself sitting beside Noel Howcroft, an expat British referee who was working for the police. As the evening unfolded, he inquired of Carolyn's maiden name.

'Wyeth,' replied Carolyn.

'What sort of stock is that?'

Carolyn declined to react but when the same fellow said, 'You must feel privileged being here, you won't have dinners like this in New Zealand,' Carolyn came back with, 'No, but we have really good barbecues!'

On one of Paddy's visits to London, England's president-elect, Robert Horner (who had become president by the time England won the 2003 World Cup), invited the three New Zealand referees, Steve Walsh, Colin Hawke and Paddy, to join him for lunch at his club, Oxford-Cambridge in Pall Mall.

The Kiwis were pretty impressed, membership being reserved exclusively for graduates of the two famous universities. In a time-honoured tradition, the menu disclosed no prices, as the meal is always billed to the member's account. For a boy from Invercargill, it was all a bit overwhelming. But Paddy knew what he wanted from the menu. Mixed grill, please. Which brought untold mirth to the president-to-be who settled for his customary rack of lamb.

As he warmed to the meal in the palatial dining room, Paddy removed his jacket and was about to place it on the back of his chair when president-elect Horner coughed politely.

'Jacket on, if you don't mind.'

'Of course.'

Yellow card, Paddy!

On another day the three New Zealand referees were treated to a round of golf at the Woburn Club. Paddy, a 20-handicap hacker with no ambitions to ever challenge Tiger Woods, approached the first green in borrowed shoes and wearing a colourful shirt.

Noting that after morning rain there was mud about, he decided to tuck his trousers into his socks, creating a sort of poor-man's plus fours. Just as he was on his first backswing, a voice boomed out, 'Get your trousers out of your socks. This is Woburn. We have standards here!'

Second yellow card!

While life in England, particularly among the upper class who abound in rugby circles, is in many respects a million miles removed from the game in New Zealand, Paddy always enjoys his time there. And he has huge respect for Clive Woodward, under whom England in 2003 rose to the No. 1 ranking in the world and then won the World Cup.

Woodward always telephones the referee on the Monday before an international match, inviting him in for a cup of coffee. In the prelude to the match against the Wallabies in 2001, he simply asked Paddy how he was going to referee the tackle area. 'The same as you did for the Blues-Crusaders match? We've got the video of that.'

And that was that. No histrionics. No copious notes like those Bob Dwyer always pulls out of his briefcase.

Paddy admits to being mightily impressed with Woodward because he has his England players so well disciplined. He says they give away far fewer penalties than their opponents, because Woodward is so methodical in his preparation. 'A lot of people are cynical of England's approach, insisting they play boring rugby, relying on Jonny Wilkinson's boot for success. But if you analyse their play, you find they adapt cleverly to opponents and conditions and give away few penalties. A classic example was their game against New Zealand Maori at New Plymouth in 2003, a match I happened to referee. I thought their tactical application that night, in extremely challenging conditions, was masterly. I couldn't believe it when the *Dominion* newspaper the next morning accused them of playing boring rugby. They out-strategised the Maori and won a game everyone was predicting they would lose.'

Obviously, English rugby officials find New Zealanders excessively casual. And Paddy was surprised to discover that they are rather sceptical of the quality of rugby produced in the Super 12. When Australian referee Peter Marshall was addressing a rugby gathering in London, the first question concerned the Super 12.

'It's a rather frivolous competition, don't you feel?' asked one member of the audience. 'I feel there's no structure to it.'

'Do you have a remote for your television?' asked Marshall.

'Yes, why do you ask?'

'We'll, you're not forced to watch it. You can change channels, you know!'

In contrast to many of those connected with rugby in the UK, Paddy finds most of the referees there delightful individuals. He ranks Colin High, the No. 1 assessor, Chris White and Tony Spreadbury among the most down-to-earth people he has ever met.

High, from the north of England, has a refreshing approach to the game and is extremely popular with all international referees. Spreadbury, whose voice is never silent, ensures there is never a dull moment. Paddy was amazed to find he maintained his humour and entertaining line of patter throughout the eight weeks of the 2003 World Cup.

Characters like Spreadbury on the one hand and the pompous brigade on the other definitely make England the most fascinating of all countries to visit for a rugby person, in Paddy's opinion.

The Bodyguard Test

The opening assignment of 2002 for Paddy was the Hurricanes-Blues Super 12 fixture in Wellington. After leaving the referees' changing room at WestpacTrust Stadium for the Friday night fixture, he inadvertently took a wrong turning which he realised only when he heard coach Peter Sloane's voice echoing out of the Blues' changing room.

'You know what O'Brien's f—— like, so don't f— him around!'

Paddy hadn't intended to eavesdrop, but he was secretly delighted with what he'd heard. He concedes that in his formative years as a referee, he'd made the mistake of wanting to be liked. With maturity in the role, he came to realise that that was unrealistic, for on any Saturday afternoon it is truly impossible for one arbiter to satisfy all 15 players on both sides.

What Paddy and other established referees seek is credibility and respect. Sloane's words that night at the Cake Tin, notwithstanding the expletives, were enormously reassuring. They emphasised that the Blues players were going to make every effort to comply with his refereeing.

Given Paddy's recent record with Auckland and Blues teams (it being six years since either had won under him) and the unfavourable publicity emanating from the

Auckland media, the northerners' attitude represented a major breakthrough. By a matter of minutes, Paddy was obviously the first person in Wellington that evening to appreciate that a fresh attitude was sweeping through Auckland rugby. When the final whistle sounded later that evening, every Hurricanes supporter was of the same mind, for Sloane's team, in awesome form, had registered an astonishing 60 points to 7 victory.

Although it would be another 15 months before the Blues would reinstate themselves as the premier combination in the Super 12, a status last achieved way back in 1997 when Graham Henry was at the peak of his powers, it was obvious for all to see in Wellington that evening that they were on the way. It was the first certain indication that the balance of power in New Zealand rugby was beginning to swing north again. Although the Crusaders would come through to reclaim their crown in 2002, within a year both Canterbury and the Crusaders' status had been usurped by the men from the City of Sails.

Starting with that 60-point result in Wellington, Paddy's relationship with the Blues and the Auckland public improved dramatically. This had little to do with his refereeing, he considered, but a lot to do with the strong management of the Blues, and subsequently Auckland, teams.

Paddy found that individuals like Carlos Spencer, who in his youth could be rattled and often take his frustrations out on the referee, and Ali Williams, a real extrovert, were now behaving responsibly. The discipline they had absorbed was obviously a particular strength of the team.

Paddy would accumulate a feast of airpoints in 2002 with Super 12 appointments in Cape Town and Sydney and test assignments in Paris, Nuku'alofa, and Johannesburg. Rugby was, in a clichéd sense, unquestionably the winner in all those destinations, save for the last one when Paddy breezed into South Africa shortly before Irishman Dave McHugh was set upon in Durban by the desperate and inebriated Springbok supporter Pieter van Zyl. For the first time in his sporting career, Paddy would find himself allocated a bodyguard.

Certainly, no bodyguards were necessary in Paris where Paddy refereed, on a serene autumn afternoon, the Six Nations encounter between France and Ireland, the outcome of which secured the championship title for the French. The contest was one-sided but Paddy was captivated by the whole French experience, the colour, the noise, the cacophonous din that celebrated every score by the Tricolores, and there were plenty that afternoon.

The occasion was special for Paddy anyway because a special guest of his at the game was his Invercargill mentor Lewis McGill, who happened to be in Europe on business. Paddy arranged a prime seat for him at the Stade de France for what was his first international.

Paddy recalls with delight that their roles were effectively reversed that weekend. 'Lewis was far more nervous about the game than I was! He had a great seat right near the players' tunnel and was completely blown away by the experience.'

The semi-finals of the 2002 Super 12 pitted the Crusaders against the Highlanders in Christchurch and the Waratahs against the Brumbies in Sydney, one Kiwi derby, one Australian derby. Logically, Paddy should have refereed the Christchurch encounter but because the Sanzar authorities insisted on neutral referees for semi-finals and finals, he was assigned to Sydney, on his Tasman flight passing Stuart Dickinson heading to Christchurch.

Actually, there was a second barrier disqualifying Paddy from controlling the Christchurch game ... he's from Southland, part of the Highlanders franchise. Obviously, certain administrators believe that would render him biased. Paddy considers that thinking to be obscene. 'I can't believe that anyone would believe a referee who has controlled more than 180 first-class appointments would harbour a local bias.'

Before heading for Johannesburg, Paddy refereed the World Cup qualifier between Tonga and Manu Samoa at Teufiva Stadium in Nuku'alofa. Like Paris, it was another total rugby experience to be lapped up. Notwithstanding the hardships experienced by so many of the population, Paddy has found Tongans to be marvellous hosts, totally enraptured in rugby and he has developed a real affinity with them. It was in his favour as a referee that both teams were prepared by New Zealanders, John Boe having charge of the Samoans and Jim Love the home team.

Paddy could have diverted to Durban after landing in South Africa following the long haul through from New Zealand and watched the All Blacks' Tri-Nations encounter with the Springboks from the grandstands. The pair who would be his touch judges at Ellis Park, David McHugh and Chris White, were officiating and the opportunity was there for him to acquaint himself with them.

But knowing he would be jetlagged, he opted for a quieter, if lonelier, weekend on the high veldt, becoming a virtual prisoner in his hotel, venturing no further than the dining room, gymnasium, pool and his own room. Johannesburg, given its alarming crime rate, is not a city you venture out in alone. Smart visitors stay close to their accommodation.

So it was that from his Holiday Inn hotel room 600 miles away, Paddy watched with disbelief as Pieter van Zyl entered the arena at Absa Stadium (previously King's Park) and attacked referee McHugh, in turn being set upon by All Blacks before being forcibly removed by security men.

Perhaps it was the jetlag, but the whole affair seemed somewhat surreal to Paddy and the consequences for himself didn't sink in until he picked up the Sunday newspapers the next morning. As far as the boy from Invercargill was concerned, the Durban incident involved a drunken larrikin who would get what he deserved.

Paddy couldn't believe what he was reading when he opened the Sunday papers. The villainous van Zyl, as Paddy perceived him, was being portrayed in at least two publications as a hero. It was time someone did something about the referees who had been giving South Africa a rough deal for years.

Was this really how the South African public viewed international referees? Paddy was the next cab off the rank. What was in store for him at Ellis Park? Was there a whole pack of Pieter van Zyls ready to invade Ellis Park and sort out the referee if he made a few decisions that didn't find favour with the Springbok supporters?

While Rian Oberholzer, the chief executive officer of the South African Rugby Football Union (SARFU), condemned the attack upon McHugh, it was obvious to Paddy, from statements on television and in the newspapers, that a huge number of South Africans felt the referee had 'got what he deserved'. This was pretty alarming for the individual lined up to referee the next test!

Paddy's phone rang red hot on the Monday, as the media zeroed in on the next potential victim. The media onslaught threatened to become a huge distraction for him. Fortunately, Joe Locke, media co-ordinator with the NZRU, was on the ball and took charge.

One major press conference was set up for the South African media, another for New Zealand, and he gave a live interview to Paul Holmes on his television programme. After that, he was off-limits, left alone to concentrate on his mission of satisfactorily refereeing the Springboks against the Wallabies.

The Bodyguard Test

The headline in one Johannesburg newspaper declared O'BRIEN DOESN'T FEAR FOR HIS SAFETY. Well, he hadn't until then. Suddenly reading such a pronouncement made him feel a trifle uneasy, a situation that intensified when the South African Rugby Union advised him that they were allocating to Paddy and his touch judges, Alain Roland of Ireland and Chris White of England, three bodyguards (or personal protection people, as they were officially known).

Paddy's minder was Pierre Coetzer, a well-performed South African heavyweight boxer who had been close to fighting for the world crown. His brief was to ensure Paddy safely boarded his flight out of Johannesburg International Airport the day following the match.

As a former policeman who knew a thing or two about matters of security and protection of individuals, Paddy was intrigued to now find himself being safeguarded. Whenever the three referees ventured to their favourite restaurant, a half mile from their hotel, the PPPs, who were armed, were never more than five metres away from them. Invariably on these journeys, someone would fire a comment like 'Watch out on Saturday' to Paddy.

The referees' trip from Sandton to Ellis Park on match day was a breathtaking experience. Well, it was for Paddy, who'd burnt his share of rubber in pursuit of crims back in his days in the force, but for Irishman Jim Irvine, Paddy's assessor, the drive at breakneck speed was something he could have done without. A sprightly sixty-something, Jim was in a lather of sweat by the time the group's mini-van pulled up at the stadium. The journey that would normally take half an hour was completed in barely 10 minutes, with the van, light flashing, stopping for no one!

'You better have a good game,' Springbok fans barked at Paddy, as he made his way towards the entrance. In focused mood, he didn't bother to try and identify whether the comments were flippant or deadly serious.

Until that afternoon at Ellis Park, Paddy unhesitatingly labelled the World Cup opener between Wales and Argentina in 1999 and the Lions-Wallabies decider in Sydney in 2001 as the most momentous events of his refereeing career. But unquestionably, the Bodyguard Test was now ranking right up there with them.

Given the sensational prelude to this match created by the belligerent Mr van Zyl, who was unrepentant over his King's Park invasion, some were comparing the atmosphere at Ellis Park as being comparable with the great day of 1995 when, with Nelson Mandela bedecked in Springbok jersey No. 6, the Rainbow Nation's favourite sons had dramatically outlasted the more strongly favoured All Blacks in the World Cup final.

In terms of security, Paddy concluded that that afternoon he was probably the safest referee ever in the history of international rugby. Not only was Ellis Park swarming with security guards, all on the lookout for would-be referee attackers, but a moat between the perimeter fence and the sward of grass made Ellis Park effectively impenetrable, except via the players' tunnel.

The referee factor aside, the match was a critical one in the context of Springbok coach Rudolf Straeuli's career. His team was coming off successive losses at Wellington, Brisbane and Durban and, dubious refereeing or not, was sitting a distant last on the Tri-Nations points table. Very obviously, unless there was a significant turnaround in fortunes this time, coach Straeuli, and probably a good few of his selected players, could be shown the exit door.

It was a cracking game, featuring tries aplenty, with neither side able to establish dominance. The Springboks looked to have a winning break at one stage but the ice-cool Aussies, once again displaying the temperament that had made them world champions, maintained their composure and stayed within striking range.

Although the game was played in good spirit, a sequence of high tackles prompted Paddy to issue a final warning, shortly after which Marius Joubert, the Springbok centre, repeated the offence. De Wet Barry, one centre, had already spent 10 minutes in the sin bin for that very transgression. Enough was enough. Now when his partner in crime, Joubert, felled a Wallaby with another dangerous, head-high tackle, Paddy unhesitatingly produced a red card. The crowd audibly gasped. Their team, clinging to a 26–23 advantage, would have to operate for the final 10 minutes a man short.

It's probable that at this moment some of the more fanatical Springbok supporters in the crowd were beginning to compare referee O'Brien with referee McHugh, who'd got his come-uppance because he hadn't been giving the Springboks a 'fair go'. But Paddy wasn't going there. He was, as always, maintaining his objectivity and refereeing events purely as they unfolded in front of him.

The tension built at Ellis Park. A dropped goal by George Gregan levelled the scores at 26–all. Then with about four minutes remaining, the Wallabies stole a lineout off South Africa's throw and muscled their way through to the goal-line for a try to hooker Brendan Cannon.

Gregan was over the moon and his exaggerated celebrations were plainly winding the crowd up. When Paddy is refereeing, he is normally so focused, to the extent of almost being in a cocoon, that he is totally oblivious to crowd reaction. But on this occasion, as Matt Burke was preparing for his wide-angle conversion, he permitted himself a glance towards the spectators. What he saw startled him. The South African fans, he realised, were utterly desperate for a win. This proud rugby nation, with its great tradition of winning, plainly wasn't in a mood for another defeat. Their desperation was scarily obvious.

When Burke's kick sliced outside the uprights, it meant a converted try could still win the day for South Africa. But less than two minutes of play remained. That, as it turned out, was long enough for Straeuli's men to achieve a dramatic victory, secured by fullback Werner Greeff after the final siren had sounded. Adopting a never-say-die attitude, the South Africans had secured the ball from the restart and created a slender opportunity which Greeff had cashed in on with a scything run to the goal-line.

The try locked the scores at 31–all, conversion to come from a reasonably handy position. Greeff, the kicker, took his time. The IRB had ruled in 2001 that kicks at goal must not exceed one minute, but, given the dramatic circumstances, Paddy wasn't timing this one.

Greeff completed the fairytale ending by slotting the ball directly between the uprights for a 33–31 victory, sending the fans into ecstasy. Paddy immediately blew for full time.

As he began walking towards the players' tunnel, Matt Burke materialised and shook his hand. 'Paddy,' he said, 'that last kick took longer than one minute.'

Forgetting that he still had his microphone on, Paddy replied, 'Matt, I've got balls, but they're not that big!'

Every spectator seemed to be smiling, yet 10 minutes earlier, after Joubert had been ordered off, probably twenty thousand of them had wanted to do a 'van Zyl' on referee O'Brien. Now, no one cared. The referee was a great bloke again. Paddy reflected on how fickle fans could be and how a referee could convert from villain to hero in a remarkably short space of time.

In the excitement of South Africa's thrilling victory, no one mentioned the referee at the aftermatch function, which was just fine by Paddy. A pleasant change from Durban seven days earlier when the referee was almost the exclusive topic of conversation after that game.

Indeed, people were still talking about it. 'Wasn't that terrible, what happened to the referee in Durban?' individuals said. Paddy, his beefy bodyguard close by, could only agree.

After a thoroughly pleasant meal at Tappe Henning's steakhouse restaurant, Paddy was, next morning, safely delivered by Pierre Coetzer to the airport. Having much enjoyed the ex-boxer's company, he presented him with an IRB tracksuit — and has kept in touch since.

As the Qantas jet carried him eastwards back towards his homeland, Paddy reflected on an amazing week, one he never thought he would experience. A rugby referee with a fulltime bodyguard. How about that! Back in Invercargill, he fielded a call from Bob Francis. Was he up to refereeing an NPC first division fixture the following Saturday, or would he prefer something gentler?

Most definitely something gentler, Paddy answered, after his traumatic experiences in Johannesburg and the wearying journey home.

'How about the third division game between Wairarapa-Bush and King Country at Masterton?' asked Bob.

'Done.'

And so, a week after officiating in front of 70,000 fans in the white hot atmosphere of Ellis Park, Paddy found himself running on to Memorial Park in front of barely 250 spectators. He was back in heartland New Zealand, and loving it.

'Hey, Paddy,' said King Country coach Peter Fatialofa, 'you look after us jokers, all right? None of those yellow cards, eh. We play fifteen-a-side in third division!'

Paddy cherished his afternoon. No bodyguards, no video umpires, no yellow cards, no controversies. Plenty of onfield endeavour followed by typical New Zealand aftermatch hospitality, which Paddy had to cut short. A rental car trip through to Wellington Airport got him on the last flight home to Invercargill.

In successive weekends following Masterton, Paddy controlled a spectacular match between Waikato and Canterbury in Hamilton, won 59–41 by the home side, and an equally free-flowing game in New Plymouth in which Taranaki beat Bay of Plenty 73–33. When his next match, Otago against Waikato at Carisbrook, produced a 35–20 final scoreline, statistician Geoff Miller e-mailed him, suggesting he was losing his touch as he'd fallen well short of a hundred points!

Paddy was on a high after the Waikato-Canterbury extravaganza. It was the sort of contest every referee loves to be associated with, producing thrilling, non-stop action, tries galore and a complete absence of controversy. Only a couple of points separated the teams throughout until Waikato spurted clear right at the finish.

Paddy, a pretty slick sprinter in his athletic prime, has always prided himself on his ability to get to the goalposts ahead of any rugby player, except when interceptions wrongfoot everyone, including the referee. Explaining this, Paddy says he is able to fast-track up the middle of the field whereas the speedy threequarter has to negotiate his way around opponents before arcing in towards the goalposts. Given the extra distance the threequarter has to travel, the advantage is always with Paddy.

Until the Northland-Waikato contest in Hamilton in October 2002, only one individual had embarrassed Paddy for speed by beating him to the goalposts hands down, Christian Cullen. When Central Vikings put 90 points on Nelson Bays in an NPC second division match at Palmerston North back in 1997, Cullen scored four tries, three of them tearaway efforts from his own 22. Each time he not only burnt off the opposition but referee O'Brien as well. 'The problem with Cullen,' Paddy recalls, 'is that he ghosts past opponents. A player like Doug Howlett is also blisteringly fast, but it's obvious because of his body movement, whereas Cullen seems to glide. He's gone before you can react.'

At Hamilton, Paddy experienced that Jaguar against a Maserati feeling for the second time in his career. This time the flyer was Rupeni Caucaunibuca, Northland's freakish tryscoring winger. Although Caucaunibuca's team was heavily defeated by Waikato, he collected two tries, each time leaving referee O'Brien in his wake. The frustrating thing for Paddy, purely from a pride viewpoint because the opposition was burnt off just as convincingly, was that he anticipated Caucaunibuca's breaks. But by the time he was into his second stride, Rupeni was gone. Even with the angle in his favour, Paddy found himself arriving at the goalposts almost 10 metres behind the Fijian flyer.

It wasn't as if Paddy needed to be alongside Caucaunibuca to rule on the try, because the opposition were distant figures. Probably the message it did deliver was that Caucaunibuca at 22 was approximately half the age of the referee!

Maybe it was that extra metre of pace that Paddy strived for to keep Caucaunibuca within sight that brought about his undoing at Wellington's WestpacTrust Stadium six days later. Twenty minutes into the Wellington-Auckland match he felt a twinge in his calf muscle. Initially, he thought he would be able to continue if strapping was applied at halftime. But over the next 10 minutes it became apparent he was in trouble. He was reluctant to relinquish his post because, with Wellington's leading referees operating out of town, the two touch judges were inexperienced senior club referees, and this was an important NPC fixture.

Fifteen minutes from the break, Paddy alerted Brent Murray, the more senior of the touch judges, of his predicament and told him he would have to control the second half. It was important, Paddy considered, that Murray had time to mentally prepare himself before taking over the whistle.

Before he exited, Paddy spoke to the rival captains, Tana Umaga and Xavier Rush, and explained the situation. He pleaded with them not to take advantage of the inexperienced referee who would be taking over.

In the event, Brent Murray, a 35-year-old detective, refereed like a veteran, giving a performance that made the assessors take notice. He grasped his opportunity so impressively that, one year on, he was included in the NPC referees squad.

Having to exit a game injured was a major disappointment for Paddy, the first time it had occurred in his refereeing career (he doesn't place Bath in the same category because he was fitness testing himself there). It shouldn't, he reasons, be a cause for embarrassment because it happens to players all the time, but fitness fanatic Paddy felt gutted at the time.

At least the muscle wasn't torn and intensive physiotherapy treatment over the next fortnight had him fully repaired in time to control the NPC final between Waikato and Auckland at the flash new Waikato Stadium in Hamilton.

It was a cracking final. Waikato had been the standout team throughout the competition but Auckland, prepared by Wayne Pivac and Grant Fox, with input from Graham Henry, recently returned from Wales, had timed its run to perfection and, on the evening, proved to be the superior team, winning 40–28.

Paddy saw it as a turning point for Auckland rugby and, as events would show, for New Zealand rugby as well. Importantly, Pivac and Fox had instilled strong discipline into their team which Paddy, better than anyone, was able to identify. One player in particular who had patently mellowed was Carlos Spencer. He was still learning his trade when Zinzan Brooke and Sean Fitzpatrick, strong, inspirational leaders, departed the scene, and for some years he punched beyond his weight with a certain arrogance that didn't endear him to referees. Not now. Carlos' concerns were for the team, not exclusively for Carlos.

One individual who did have a momentary lapse in discipline, and it was the first time Paddy had encountered him, was the towering lock Ali Williams, who got himself involved in a dust-up with his main rival Keith Robinson. Paddy decided the best thing for both of them was 10 minutes of cooling down time in the sin bin.

Shortly after his re-association with his colleagues, Williams shaped up aggressively again at an opponent. Paddy, playing the peacemaker role, reminded him that a second yellow card would represent an ordering off. Quick as a flash, Williams, who possesses great humour and character, came back with, 'Cool down, Paddy, you're already going to the World Cup — it's all right for you!'

As a referee dealing almost exclusively on the field with captains, save for the occasional witty riposte from individuals like Williams, Paddy unhesitatingly brands the Auckland, and Blues leader, Xavier Rush as the most impressive of the New Zealand captains. Why? Because he knows his law book and really puts pressure on the referee if he feels an injustice has been committed. But importantly, says Paddy, he knows when to pull back.

Reuben Thorne, the Canterbury, Crusaders and All Black captain, in contrast, rarely challenges the referee, in Paddy's experience, invariably accepting any explanation offered, while Taine Randell, of Otago, Highlanders and also All Black fame, was often indecisive when he approached the referee. Neither of them confronts the referee in the manner of the Auckland leader. Xavier, Paddy says, really keeps a referee on his toes.

Paddy's final assignment for 2002 was a prestigious one, England against the Springboks at Twickenham. Unfortunately, what could have been a showpiece for the game degenerated into an ugly fiasco with Paddy having to bring out a red card for only the second time in his test refereeing career (Marius Joubert having copped the first one).

Having lost, rather embarrassingly, to Ireland and Scotland, the South Africans were determined to salvage pride from their northern hemisphere tour in this encounter. This was never going to be easy at Fortress Twickenham where Clive Woodward's men were advancing towards a notable hat-trick of victories against the Sanzar Big Three, having edged out the All Blacks and the Wallabies in recent weeks.

The Springboks obviously decided the best way to unsettle the English players was to intimidate them. Paddy had always been an admirer of Corne Krige, the Springbok captain, but felt that on this occasion he let himself, and his country, down by going beyond the pale.

After about 20 minutes, during which there had been several late and high tackles, almost exclusively from the South Africans, Paddy summoned captains Krige and Martin Johnson and warned them that the game was getting out of hand. If they didn't bring their players under control, more drastic action would have to be taken.

Following the very next lineout, which England won, Jonny Wilkinson punted for touch, after which he became the victim of a late shoulder-charge from Jannes Labuschagne.

Paddy says that in different circumstances, the offence might have justified only a yellow card. But in light of his final warning, Labuschagne was shown the red card. Paddy regarded it as a non-negotiable situation, even though he knew that by forcing one team to play the final hour with 14 men he was effectively destroying the game as a spectacle.

'There comes a point,' says Paddy, 'where a referee must say enough is enough. While it's easy to blame the referee, and a lot of people suggested I was excessively tough on Labuschagne, the Springboks let themselves down that afternoon. It was a black day for South African rugby and I'm certain the Springbok coach, Rudolf Straeuli, would have been embarrassed when he later reflected on his team's attitude.'

Paddy's tough line was vindicated twice over. First, the judicial committee acknowledged the seriousness of Labuschagne's offence by suspending him for two matches. Then, after his return to New Zealand, Paddy received a video tape from the Rugby Football Union's referees committee, supplying graphic, irrefutable evidence of the South Africans' illegal tactics.

Unbeknown to Paddy, and very obviously most players, the RFU films all major matches at Twickenham with a camera secured high above the playing surface and providing a spectacular aerial view of the action. The edited film highlighted all the illegal play Paddy had witnessed and acted on, and several other unsavoury incidents as well. To his astonishment, he identified tackles by Corne Krige and his men on England players not just three, four and five seconds late, but sometimes 10 seconds after the ball had been released. And there were other brutal acts, such as the kneeing of players in the back, he'd missed.

It was a most enlightening video tape. He wondered whether a copy had been sent to Rudolf Straeuli!

Given the Springboks' commando mentality that afternoon, he'd expected a trace of remorse, especially given that the final scoreline was a humiliating, and record-smashing, 51 points to 5. But coach Straeuli simply said he felt the referee had been tough while Krige, still in combat mood, had told the English they'd be waiting for them (in the World Cup pool match) at Perth.

Clive Woodward was the only one who backed Paddy, saying he was pleased he'd taken a hard line on foul play. At the function following the game, Clive Woodward's wife told Paddy there was someone she wanted him to meet, leading him towards a pleasant young fellow who offered a handshake.

'Congratulations on your game,' said the young chap. 'I wore sports ears and was amazed at how well you people communicate with each other. I thought you had a great game.'

When he took his leave, Paddy commented to Mrs Woodward on what a delightful child they'd reared.

'Oh, no,' she reacted. 'He's not our boy. That was Prince Harry.'

The dastardly deeds at Twickenham were but a distant memory when Paddy, refreshed after a summer relaxing in the deep south, including a couple of wonderful weeks with his family at the seaside resort of Riverton, swung back into action in the Super 12.

Paddy doesn't know any referee who takes satisfaction from issuing red cards. It's something he'd done only three times since becoming a professional, Umaga, Joubert and Labuschagne being the recipients, and given the infrequency with which such serious offences occur, it was reasonable to presume it would be well into 2003, if at all, that he'd have to go beyond a yellow card. But just two matches into the new year, Paddy found himself exhibiting the red card again, this time in the direction of an All Black, Troy Flavell, for an incident he did not personally witness.

Flavell was 'marched' from the Blues-Chiefs Super 12 match in Hamilton on the report of touch judge Kevin Rowe, who had stood with his flag raised for almost two minutes before play came to a halt.

Rowe didn't embellish his comments to referee O'Brien.

'Five blue trampled on the head of two black,' he reported gravely.

'Are we talking a red card?' asked Paddy.

'Yes.'

And with that, Flavell was dismissed from the field. Such was the seriousness of the offence, Flavell's boot coming down heavily on the head of Chiefs hooker Greg Smith, that he was subsequently suspended for three months, which eliminated him from consideration for John Mitchell's All Black squad, a shattering blow for such a talented footballer in a World Cup year.

Paddy empathises with Flavell, a player of immense talent. Some observers might think that referees pick on him, because he is so consistently in trouble. But that, says Paddy, is a myth. Flavell is fine 98 per cent of the time. It's that other two per cent that causes the problems, a simple matter of knowing where the line is and not going beyond it.

The work of touch judge Rowe drew praise from Paddy. His report was totally endorsed by television replays.

Flavell's dismissal wasn't the only controversy to come out of that Hamilton encounter which the Blues won 30–27, despite having to operate for two-thirds of the game with 14 men. Blues halfback Steve Devine scored a try of dubious origin. Paddy knew it was dubious, and he dearly wanted to refer a questionable ruck to the video referee, but that wasn't possible, because the video referee's powers of adjudication stopped at the goal-line. They didn't extend onto the field of play.

Paddy had tried to get that changed, arguing the case for wider powers for the TMO with the then NZRU chairman Murray McCaw who had dismissed it, believing matches would 'go on forever' as referees sought clarification of onfield events.

He was so wrong, says Paddy. Since the TMO was introduced in 2000, Paddy says there have been only three or four occasions, in all the matches he has controlled involving a video referee, when he would have gone to check on events in the field of play.

In the Hamilton match, Daniel Braid, the Blues flanker, illegally hacked the ball out of a ruck 15 metres from the Chiefs line and Devine scored. Braid should have been penalised; instead, he created a matchwinning try for his team. Although Paddy sensed something was awry, he could only rule on what he saw. Guessing wasn't an option. He dearly wanted to seek guidance from 'above', but that wasn't an option either. So he awarded Devine a five-pointer, a gross injustice, as he would appreciate when he watched the video replay.

Paddy is confident technological assistance for referees will eventually be extended to the field of play. He just hopes it doesn't take a catastrophic mistake in a World Cup final before the game's administrators decide to make that change.

Some administrators are concerned that by extending the TMO's powers, the technology would be used indiscriminately by referees and for such basic matters as whether passes are forward and throws to the lineout accurate. Not so, says Paddy. If such technology was available, senior referees would use it judiciously, in his opinion. Referees who began using it to excess would quickly be hauled into line by their bosses.

The most common question asked of Paddy whenever he promotes this particular discussion is, 'Yes, but how far would you scan back — it could become farcical if you were querying a forward pass 60 metres downfield.'

That's not what it's about, says Paddy. Extending the powers of the TMO would be purely to allow the referee to check on an incident he was confused about, such as the ruck in the Blues-Chiefs game where Braid offended. And it's most certainly not about whether a pass is forward or a lineout throw off-centre. Those matters are ruled on by the referee and the touch judges at the time. Most cameras give a distorted view of passes anyway, because they are not directly in line.

Paddy is confident that, with the professional game's evolution, the use of technology will be extended. Whether that happens before he retires is another issue!

The Super 12 happening that gave Paddy the first inkling that 2003 could be an exciting year for New Zealand rugby was when the Blues demolished the champion Crusaders side 39–5 at North Harbour Stadium. Tryscorers for the Blues included Joe Rokocoko, Doug Howlett and Carlos Spencer, with Steve Devine and Mils Muliaina other backline stars and Ali Williams and Kees Meeuws providing a huge impact up front.

While acknowledging that the Crusaders were a long way away from peaking in March, Paddy identified the qualities and skills that, within a few months, would make John Mitchell's All Blacks the talk of the rugby world. He personally found the rugby the Blues were playing, under the guidance of Peter Sloane and Bruce Robertson (with input from Graham Henry), 'terribly exciting'.

When he addressed a rugby gathering shortly thereafter, he described how the Blues had demonstrated their class in 'a test match atmosphere'. It was an observation he would amend three months later after England edged out the All Blacks in a tough, bruising encounter in Wellington. He conceded then that Super 12 rugby did not equate to test match play at all. It is an entirely different beast. The Super 12, a large percentage of which unfolds in summer temperatures on rock-hard surfaces in what is still the cricket season, is all about entertainment, bonus points and qualifying for the top four.

The high flyers, like the Blues and the Crusaders, prefer to shove the ball into the corners in search of five-pointers rather than settle for penalty goals. You don't get Super 12 contests, except when the weather sometimes packs up, producing 15–12 scorelines. It's more likely to be 62–20, 56–28, 43–37 or 65–37 (actual scores from the 2003 competition).

Clive Woodward's Englishmen would remind the All Blacks in June that test rugby, certainly the way the leading Six Nations teams approach it, is more about dominating the set pieces, making tackles and kicking goals than endeavouring to entertain with razzamatazz. While many astute observers considered the happenings in Wellington to be a timely wake-up call for John Mitchell's men, they would, ultimately, not be heeded. The All Black shortcomings exposed by England would be more embarrassingly exploited by Australia in the World Cup semi-final five months on.

Paddy's next assignment was the Waratahs-Bulls game in Sydney. The Bulls, who'd impressed in New Zealand upsetting the Hurricanes, had the misfortune to lose their experienced and talented halfback Joost van der Westhuizen early with a knee injury, but hung in tenaciously, the outcome remaining in the balance until the finish.

Late in the game, when the Waratahs were defending resolutely, Paddy had cause to issue a yellow card to one Aussie guilty of persistent killing of the ball. As Paddy was exiting the field after the final whistle, the Waratahs a 26–16 winner, the team's coach Bob Dwyer came rushing across, in a patently emotional state.

'What about their killing of the ball?' he barked. 'You sinbin our man, but they were just as guilty.'

Paddy looked at him with amazement. 'F—- off, Bob!' he said, and walked away to the dressing room.

Bob Dwyer had transgressed an unwritten code that coaches don't approach referees in the highly-charged, intensely emotional moments immediately following important contests.

Most inquisitions take place on the Monday following. By then, coaches, referees and players have all had the opportunity to study video replays and to talk dispassionately about what eventuated in the heat of battle. If a coach is still confused or bemused by a referee's rulings, he'll talk it through to hopefully achieve an understanding, important for when they next encounter each other.

On top of that, coaches submit a report on the referee. Dwyer wrote of O'Brien after that Sydney encounter that it was the worst refereeing display he had witnessed in all his years as a coach.

Dwyer, who has retired now, perplexed Paddy by insisting on having a breakfast meeting with him on match days, meetings to which he would bring screeds of notes. Paddy's nonchalant attitude would frustrate hell out of him. 'You know how I referee,' he would say to Dwyer. 'All that stuff you're wanting to quiz me about is bullshit.'

Paddy had the final say about the Waratahs' performance against the Bulls: 'They were obviously jetlagged after their long trip home from South Africa. Their display that night was shabby. They were in disarray, struggling to hold steady in the scrums, which kept collapsing, mishandling a lot and resorting to dubious tactics towards the finish when the Bulls threatened to overhaul their lead. I could understand Bob becoming frustrated with what he was seeing; unfortunately he took that frustration out on me, not his players.'

On the topic of jetlag, Paddy was to suffer an acute attack of it in March and April 2003, hardly surprising given the schedule he undertook. In rapid succession he journeyed from Sydney to Dublin to Paris to New Zealand to Cape Town to Brisbane and back to New Zealand.

He acknowledges now that it was 'utterly crazy' to return to New Zealand after refereeing the France-Wales Six Nations fixture at the Stade de France in Paris, rather than take a direct flight down to Johannesburg. His metabolism was thoroughly jumbled by the time he arrived in South Africa to control the Stormers-Reds game and even more confused by the time he'd lobbed into Brisbane to prepare for the Reds clash with the Cats. He found himself consistently falling asleep late afternoon or early evening but wide awake at 1 a.m. As experienced as he was in international travel, he admits to being 'physically exhausted' by the time he arrived back in Invercargill. It took him fully two weeks to recover.

After Paddy refereed the 1998 Super 12 final between the Blues and the Crusaders at Eden Park, Sanzar bosses ruled that referees for the Super 12 play-offs would be country neutral.

Because New Zealand franchises have continued to dominate the event and have featured in every final, with the exception of 2001 when the Brumbies competed against the Sharks at Canberra, a contest Paddy controlled, Kiwi referees have been disadvantaged regarding these prestigious appointments.

For the 2003 competition, Sanzar ruled that only the top four referees from each country would be appointed to Super 12 contests, the four from New Zealand being Steve Walsh, Paul Honiss, Kelvin Deaker and Paddy.

But they declined to let any country's referee handle a semi-final or final involving two teams from that country. So when the Blues took on the Crusaders at Eden Park in one of the 2003 semi-finals, the game was controlled by an Australian. Paddy found this illogical. They'd let him control the Blues-Crusaders round robin fixture, but for some odd sense of logic, he couldn't take charge of the same two teams in a semi-final. He's asked several administrators to explain to him why that was so. To date, no one has given him a satisfactory explanation.

Plainly, a neutral referee was required for the final involving a New Zealand team, the Blues, and an Australian team, the Brumbies, at Eden Park and that appointment went, predictably, to South Africa's leading exponent André Watson.

Footnote: Interestingly, the final of the Air New Zealand NPC first division championship in 2003, involving Wellington and Auckland, was refereed by Wellington-based referee Lyndon Bray, because both teams requested him. In the absence of the top-line referees at the World Cup, he was clearly the form referee in New Zealand and the NZRU showed it was prepared to break not only with tradition but with its own rules. It raised an interesting issue: in the professional era, should not the best referees be given the major appointments regardless of which province they come from?

The Men Behind the Whistle

There's an apocryphal story about the rematch, in Heaven, of the epic New Zealand-Wales encounter that took place in Cardiff in 1905, a contest that has been shrouded in controversy for almost a century because of the non-award of what the All Blacks involved insisted was a perfectly legitimate try.

When the last survivor of that famous game died in the 1980s and made his way through the Pearly Gates, Dave Gallaher, who had captained New Zealand, declared that finally the two teams could meet again to resolve, once and for all, which was the superior side.

'I'm sorry,' came back St Peter. 'The game cannot take place. All the players are here, for sure, but we don't have any referees!'

Referees are a much maligned lot. While supporters of a winning team will invariably applaud the referees' astute patrolling of off-side play and lineouts, those behind the losing side will condemn the same individual for being inconsistent, incompetent and, if the penalty count seriously favours the other side, patently biased.

If a referee allows a match to flow, some will condemn him for negligence over his policing of the set pieces but the referee who fires out penalties galore for infringements at scrums, rucks and lineouts will stand accused of nitpicking.

Ideally, the referee should be No. 31, not No. 1. Nothing frustrates spectators and, perhaps to a lesser degree, players more than a referee performing a whistling fantasia.

In the 15 years since Paddy made his first-class debut as a referee, at Rugby Park in Invercargill — Bill McLaren, the legendary Scottish commentator once described Invercargill, the southern-most city in the world, as being 'on the main road south to Antarctica', which you can relate to if you've endured a biting midwinter southerly there — he has got to know personally, and in most cases to operate alongside, all the game's leading referees. The shame is that the public, who are fed reams of information on the players, too seldom get to know the personalities who are international rugby's leading arbiters.

Paddy was incredibly fortunate to have Dave Bishop operating in his home province when he was learning the refereeing trade. Bishop's record of 26 test appointments stood as the New Zealand record until Paddy surpassed it just prior to the 2003 World Cup.

Although based in Te Anau, two hour's drive from Invercargill, Bishop belonged to the Southland Rugby Referees Association and regularly regaled members with accounts of his overseas experiences. Nobody soaked his stories up more enthusiastically than Paddy who built up vivid pictures in his mind's eye of the great overseas stadiums and cities where New Zealand's top referee had performed.

Of course, Bishop, whose international career stretched from 1986 to 1995, operated when rugby was completely amateur, with overseas appointments coming along infrequently, based on an antiquated rota system. He retired after the 1995 World Cup, just as rugby was embracing professionalism.

Welshman Derek Bevan, who refereed the World Cup final in 1991 and then in 1995, to his deep embarrassment, was presented with a gold watch by South Africa's notorious rugby boss Louis Luyt, ostensibly as the tournament's best referee, was someone Paddy came to admire immensely. Bevan helped Paddy through the traumatic time that followed his World Cup shocker at Toulouse in 1999. 'Oh, I've had plenty of matches that I couldn't put behind me quickly enough,' he told Paddy. 'It's important not to dwell on them. You can't expect every game you referee to be a good one.'

Paddy came away from the '99 tournament with a resolve to approach his refereeing from that moment in the same manner as Derek Bevan. Bevan always had a couple of beers on a Thursday night and he refused to alter that pattern because he was at the World Cup. 'Paddy, I am who I am,' he told his New Zealand colleague. It was a piece of wisdom Paddy took on board.

Paddy enjoyed Bevan's companionship because of his rich humour and quick repartee. Unbeknown to most rugby followers, he was quite the comedian. And he has a soft touch as well. He would give a colleague the shirt off his back if he needed it.

In contrast, Paddy's relationship with Scotland's Jim Fleming started on a negative note when Fleming criticised him in an interview in an Edinburgh newspaper following his handling of the Calcutta Cup match at Murrayfield in 1998. Paddy doesn't want referees protecting each other, and he acknowledges there were aspects of his refereeing on that occasion that were probably less than ideal, but he felt Fleming could have proffered a 'No comment' to the journalist who began quizzing him about the referee's performance that day.

So it took Paddy some time to warm to Jim Fleming, although he eventually came to appreciate the wisdom he and England's Ed Morrison passed on to the younger group of international referees coming through.

Probably the British referee Paddy has got closest to is Chris White, whom he labels Mr Nice Guy. Paddy says there is no one among the world's top bracket of referees he wouldn't want to have as a touch judge. But there are some he prefers. And at the top end of the list is Chris White.

French rugby players can be volatile, unpredictable and highly entertaining. And the same goes for their referees, particularly Didier Mene. Colin Hawke tells the story of a warm-up match Mene was handling in South Africa, just prior to the start of the 1995 World Cup. Mene took exception to the play of a particular individual and chastised him. The player promptly took exception to Mene.

'F—- you!' he exclaimed.

'What did you say?' responded Mene.

'I said, "F—- you!"'

'Huh,' snorted Mene. 'I'll decide who f—-s me. You're off!'

At the 2001 Australia-England international at Twickenham, Mene and André Watson were running touch for Paddy.

Suddenly, Paddy heard Mene, flag extended, shouting 'Offside, offside, offside.' Which duly led to Paddy awarding a penalty to England.

As Jonny Wilkinson was lining up his kick at goal, George Gregan approached Paddy and asked, 'Who was offside?'

Paddy didn't know, so he questioned Mene whom, with his limited understanding of English, he did not comprehend. Watson picked up on it and, in fractured French, addressed his fellow touch judge.

'Whoo wuz orfside, Didier?'

'All of zem,' barked back the Frenchman. 'All of zem — nine, ten, eleven, twelve ... take your pick!'

Mene had a chequered career and was eventually dropped from the IRB panel. Because he was then confined to touch judge duties, he referred to himself as The Man With The Golden Flag.

He was holidaying at one time when the IRB tracked him down, to advise that he had been appointed to referee a test match in the United States. 'But I've got no whistle,' he declared, 'just a flag!'

It wasn't Mene but one of his compatriots who was running touch when Paddy refereed a match between Pau and Colomiers in France as a warm-up to a Five Nations match in Paris. Paddy was intrigued to have a sophisticated looking armband fitted, one which pulsed when the touch judges activated it. Two buzzes indicated a knock-on, one a forward pass.

During the action Paddy witnessed a high tackle and indicated that he was playing advantage. This escaped the attention of one of the French-speaking touch judges who began buzzing incessantly. Each buzz came through to Paddy like a mini electric shock. Finally, he could stand it no longer. He blew his whistle, left the players to it and strode towards the touchline.

Although the touch judge could understand no English, he unquestionably got the message as an angry Paddy snapped at him, 'If you press that f——— buzzer once more ...!'

As he returned to the action he could see Serge Blanco, the famous fullback who was in the referees' box, killing himself with laughter.

Refereeing humour isn't exclusive to French settings.

At a World Cup match in Christchurch in 1987, Derek Bevan and Roger Quittenton were standing behind the goalposts awaiting a kick when sections of the crowd began chanting 'Pooftah'.

Fotopress

Paddy got sucked into refereeing the IRB way when Ireland played England at Dublin in 1999, dishing out 36 penalties and this yellow card to Lawrence Dallaglio. For all future appointments in the UK, he refereed the Paddy O'Brien way.

Paddy O'Brien collection

Paddy with Scott Young, Jim Fleming and Andrew Cole prior to refereeing the World Cup opener between Wales and Argentina at Cardiff in 1999.

Paddy O'Brien collection

Derek Bevan, as the judge, and Paddy, as the prosecutor, providing entertainment during a referees' mock court session during the 1999 World Cup.

Paddy O'Brien collection

The 1999 World Cup referees. Back row: Derek Bevan (Wales), David McHugh (Ireland), Stuart Dickinson (Australia), Peter Marshall (Australia), Jim Fleming (Scotland), André Watson (South Africa), Joel Dume (France), Wayne Erickson (Australia), Colin Hawke (New Zealand). Front row: Paul Honiss (New Zealand), Andrew Cole (Australia), Brian Campsall (England), Chris White (England), Clayton Thomas (Wales), Paddy O'Brien (New Zealand), Ed Morrison (England).

Fotopress

The day of Paddy's fearful 'train smash' at Toulouse during the 1999 World Cup. Here he awards a penalty to France against Fiji.

Fotopress

Paddy awards Justin Marshall his matchwinning try in Canterbury's NPC clash with Auckland at Eden Park in 2000. It gave the red and blacks a 29–26 victory.

Fotopress

A penalty to Taranaki in the NPC semi-final against Canterbury at Jade Stadium in 2000, a game Canterbury won 31–23.

Paddy O'Brien collection

Paddy and his team of helpers for the Australia-British Lions third test in Sydney in 2001. From left, John McCarthy, Paul Honiss, Steve Walsh and Wayne Erickson.

Fotopress

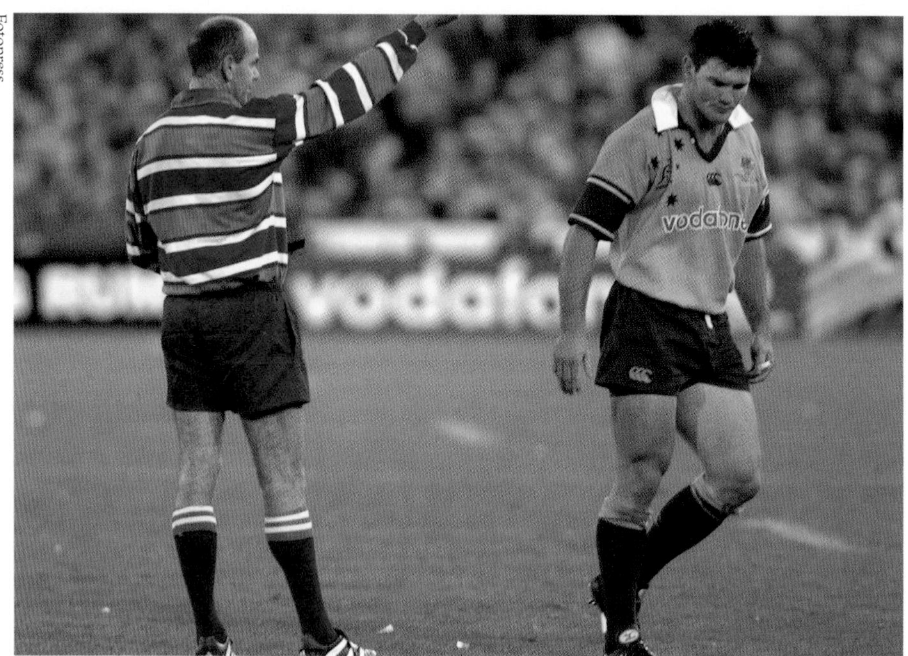

Wallaby centre Daniel Herbert is despatched to the sin bin for a high tackle during the deciding third test against the British Lions in Sydney in 2001. Herbert returned to help his team claim a thrilling series victory.

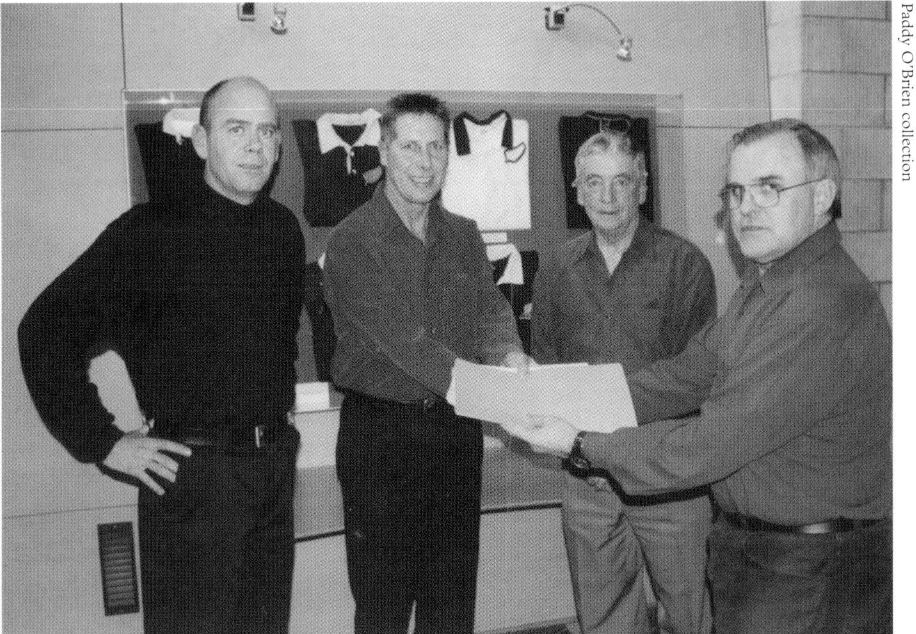

Paddy O'Brien collection

Paddy, Colin Hawke, Bob Francis (second from right) and Keith Lawrence along to celebrate Colin Hawke's 'This is Your Life' evening following his retirement in 2002.

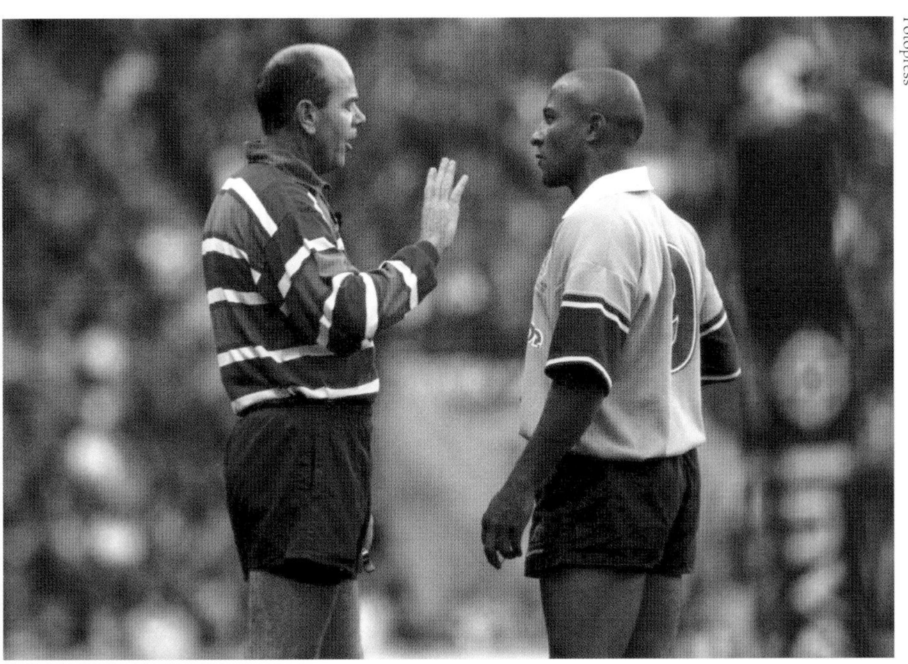

Fotopress

Paddy is animated with Australian captain George Gregan during the Cook Cup match against England at Twickenham in 2001.

Fotopress

New Zealand referee of the year for 2002, Paddy at the microphone after receiving his trophy at the Steinlager awards function in Auckland. He would win the trophy again in 2003.

Fotopress

Blues flanker Troy Flavell receives the red card from Paddy after his reckless trampling of Chiefs hooker Greg Smith in the Super 12 match in Hamilton in 2003. He would receive a 12-week suspension.

'Ignore them, Derek,' said Quittenton, the ultimate showman with his collar up and sporting brief, tight shorts. He was the senior touch judge that day.

'But they're not talking to me, Roger!' came back Bevan, quick as a flash.

The first time Paddy ran touch at an overseas international was for a Wallabies-Ireland game at Brisbane, sharing the role with fellow Southlander Dave Bishop. As they stood behind the goalposts while Michael Lynagh was lining up a kick at goal from right out in front, the crowd fell silent whereupon a wag shouted, 'Hey, touch judge, put up your flag if you're homosexual.'

Lynagh slotted the goal and Paddy raised his flag, although he was laughing so much it was quite an effort to do so.

Because of the interaction among the Sanzar nations on an annual basis, Paddy has developed a close relationship with several of the Australian and South African referees, particularly Scott Young, André Watson and Tappe Henning. Paddy and Young talk to each other by phone regularly, discussing trends and aspects of refereeing. Their friendship grew out of the 1995 World Cup preliminaries in Kuala Lumpur where they operated in tandem. Paddy labels Young 'one of nature's good guys' and describes him as 'a very loyal friend'.

Andrew Cole is regarded as a down-to-earth good bloke and Peter Marshall, the most senior of the current crop of top-ranking Australian referees, as seriously laidback. What you see with Marshall is apparently what you get.

Paddy and André Watson have forged a close relationship. They met in Hong Kong at the sevens in the early 1990s and their careers have largely paralleled each other's. Appropriately, they finished up ranked the top two referees at the 2003 World Cup.

In Paddy's opinion, Watson was without peer from 1999 to 2003. He considered Watson's poor games were still the equal of most other referees' good games. He is still the referee who sets the standards for others to follow. That's why Paddy was disappointed that André awarded the last minute scrum penalty to Australia in the World Cup final. It was just not the André he knows.

Paddy was terribly saddened when Tappe Henning missed selection for the 2003 World Cup, largely because he had not treated an act of foul play involving AJ Venter seriously enough in an early-season Super 12 match. Venter crudely headbutted an opponent, for which Tappe sent him to the sin bin. Tappe's view of the incident had not allowed him to appreciate its full seriousness, TV replays later revealing it was definitely a red card offence.

Venter was subsequently suspended for four weeks and Tappe also suffered. Having also been involved in a couple of domestic situations, he did not receive backing from the South African referees administration and was dropped off the IRB panel.

Paddy regards Henning as a magnificently loyal team member and says his input during the World Cup in Australia could have been immense. While he gives the impression of being a tough guy, underneath the surface he is a big-hearted, very human individual who would offer you his last dollar if you'd demonstrated to him you were just as loyal.

Events in South Africa have made the leading New Zealand referees appreciate the support they receive from bosses such as Keith Lawrence, Tom Doocey and Bob Francis who have remained loyal at all times. Paddy recognises that there have been times when they could easily have dropped certain individuals to save flak. Henning has maintained his dignity and Paddy, for one, won't be surprised to see him rebound and even be involved come the 2007 Rugby World Cup.

Rugby relationships between South Africa and New Zealand deteriorated after Keith Lawrence, the NZRU referees boss, sent an e-mail to his Australian equivalent Russell Trotter a few years back, a copy of which was inadvertently forwarded to Frik Burger in Cape Town. Lawrence's text concluded with the words, 'We've got to teach these Jaapies a lesson'.

While it might have been an innocent comment, it provoked outrage in South Africa at the time, and Paddy finds it still festers there. He believes South Africans haven't trusted New Zealanders or Australians since that time. They consider Kiwis and Ockers have got it in for them, and therefore the relationship at administrative level is not healthy, although among the referees themselves, it has never been an issue.

From a hospitality viewpoint, South Africa is the ultimate place for a referee to visit, with Henning, who is a part owner of a restaurant, and Watson really laying it on for their overseas visitors. Paddy and co. find themselves being treated like royalty in South Africa.

Colin Hawke and Paddy combined like brothers from 1997 when they were installed as New Zealand's first two professional referees. The best of mates beforehand, they decided they couldn't make it on their own. So from the time of their 'investiture' as professionals they shared everything, interpretations of the law book, information culled on overseas trips, even their salaries. They would not hear of individual contracts. Whatever was budgeted by the NZRU for them was to be shared.

It was a relationship that functioned without a hitch and which was only strengthened when the IRB decided that for major international appointments referees should be accompanied by touch judges from their own country. As a consequence, Messrs O'Brien and Hawke made as many as 10 overseas trips together, to South Africa, to the UK and France and to Australia.

Hawke retired after the 2001 season (having controlled no fewer than 175 first-class fixtures, including 24 tests) but remains loyal to and a faithful fan of Paddy's. Never a major appointment goes by without Paddy receiving a message of goodwill from his old buddy.

Steve Walsh junior and Paddy took a lot longer to become buddies, for the simple reason their egos intruded. They laugh about it now, but for a couple of seasons, as a pair of extremely ambitious referees, they regarded each other suspiciously.

But now they are extremely close; indeed, in the thick of the rugby season they telephone each other most days. Paddy always used to refer to Steve Walsh as Junior, stemming from the fact that back in the 1990s there were two top-ranking referees of that name on the New Zealand scene. The other one, of Welsh ancestry, who also achieved test status, operated out of Wellington.

Walsh, who is from North Harbour, broke into the first-class refereeing scene when he was still in his mid-twenties, a remarkable achievement. In 2003 while still only 32 he claimed a spot among the world's 16 leading referees at the World Cup. Notwithstanding a verbal dust-up with England's trainer when Clive Woodward's side was slipping a 16th player onto the field, which brought Walsh a three-day suspension, he was highly enough regarded to win a quarter-final appointment.

Possessed of exciting raw talent, Walsh took a while to appreciate that the referee's road is not always straight. He encountered a few sharpish bends, most notably when controlling Wellington's Ranfurly Shield challenge against Canterbury at Jade Stadium in 2001. Wellington appeared headed for a famous victory but, assisted in no small manner by an outrageously lopsided penalty count (26–4 to Canterbury), the red and blacks got up to win 31–29 in the final seconds.

The Wellington players and supporters were outraged that Walsh could find fault with only one team, in such an important, closely-contested encounter and he was caned by many in the media. For a long time he was *persona non grata* in the capital.

Paddy, who'd been through it all two years previously, at the World Cup, empathised with him. It was a turning point in his career. He's now more receptive to criticism and appreciates that it's a lonely world out there if, as a referee, you don't take someone along for the ride with you.

Paddy considers that as Steve's refereeing continues to mature, he has the potential to become the number one referee in the world. One issue confronting Steve is that all his professional life he has been single and should he eventually marry and have a family then it could alter his outlook on refereeing. Both Colin Hawke, Paul Honiss and Paddy already had established families when they turned pro and it takes a special woman to understand the role of a full-time referee and to operate as a solo parent whilst their husband travels the world.

Paul Honiss almost merits a chapter on his own. He is certainly the most misunderstood of New Zealand's top referees. Of all the referees Paddy has worked with, Honiss has the most professional training habits. And he's arguably the sharpest referee in world rugby. Although stockily built, he can outsprint Paddy, and that's saying something.

Unfortunately for Honiss, controversy has followed him throughout his career, much of which, it must be said, he has brought on himself — as when he awarded three penalty tries in one NPC encounter between Otago and North Harbour at Carisbrook — and as when he penalised the Highlanders' lineout at the death in Christchurch in 2002, allowing the Crusaders to snatch an unlikely victory.

Paddy is of the view that Honiss needs to relax more, which would help make him more streetwise in his refereeing, and he needs to build relationships with members of the media who have tended to ostracise him. He tends to be more a letter-of-the-law referee than Steve Walsh and Paddy and as a result, perhaps, has not achieved the same affinity with players and coaches.

It frustrates Paddy that on the occasions he and Colin Hawke tried to help Honiss, using Keith Lawrence as a medium, they were chopped back. It's certainly Paddy's belief that the best individuals to lend help in such circumstances are your peers.

Paddy says that he would always choose Honiss to run touch for him because for any appointment, in whatever capacity, he is always fired up. 'I think Steve and I tend to lose focus a bit when we're touch judges, but Paul is always totally focused. You know that if he's running touch for you, he's not going to miss anything.'

Kelvin Deaker, who makes up the current New Zealand test panel, has impressed Paddy with his willingness to learn. A genuinely affable bloke, he took some scarring when a test match between Australia and Argentina in 2002 didn't go quite the way he would have liked. But he listened to the advice, bit the bullet and, through his positive attitude, picked up a World Cup appointment when Scott Young dropped out with a hamstring injury. Deaker is in the early stages of his career and has the right attitude to ensure he remains a test referee for many years to come.

In 2003 the NZRU employed three more full-timers, Lyndon Bray, Gary Wise and Bryce Lawrence, who were kept extremely busy during the NPC competition with the top guns away at the World Cup. Bray made such an impact that both coaches requested him to referee the NPC final, a remarkable achievement given that Bray's home team Wellington was involved. Paddy feels it is too soon to say whether any of this trio will achieve test status, but the opportunity is there for all of them.

Glenn Wahlstrom, the only Aucklander to achieve test status in recent times, probably didn't progress as far as he might have because he kept challenging the administration. If he found fault with refereeing appointments, he would let the NZRU know. And he wasn't prepared to compromise.

Glenn and Paddy didn't start off as the best of buddies, having a couple of early fallouts. But as they matured they became supportive of each other, and Paddy was delighted when, late in 2003, Glenn was appointed to the board of the Auckland Rugby Union as a director. Paddy considers he has a huge future in New Zealand rugby administration.

Steve Griffiths is the IRB referees manager and has held the position for seven years. Prior to that he held a similar position with the RFU at Twickenham. Colin Hawke and Paddy took a little while to warm to him, at first finding him a little too 'British' for their liking, as when he prevented them wearing their New Zealand blazers to a test dinner in London, ordering them into dinner suits instead. They survived that experience to become extremely fond of their big boss.

Paddy has developed a special relationship with Griffiths and was amazed to find some of his World Cup colleagues in awe of him because he was their boss. Some seemed scared to get to know him.

Griffiths is a champion organiser whose attention to detail is second to none. He was far more relaxed at the 2003 World Cup than four years previously, Paddy putting that down to the fact he didn't have Clive Norling functioning as his liaison officer this time. Norling's attitude served to undermine Griffiths when Wales was hosting the event.

Paddy had regarded Norling as a legend prior to 1999 but felt he let himself down badly. He has since resigned as Wales' referee manager, his position being taken over by Bob Yeman, a former test referee, who Paddy regards as one of the nicest guys he has ever encountered in rugby.

Yeman has a similar affable approach to life as his countryman Derek Bevan and, like Bevan, he's at his best when spinning a yarn or pulling someone's leg.

After the treatment Colin Hawke and Paddy received in Wales in 1999 it's fair to say they'd gone off Welsh people big time, but since then charming individuals like Bob Yeman, Derek Bevan, Clayton Thomas and Nigel Whitehouse, all extroverts, have more than balanced the scales.

At Australia's World Cup, Griffiths was totally in control, yet he allowed his appointees to dictate onfield policy, preferring to operate almost exclusively as a facilitator. When Steve Walsh got into strife over England fielding a 16th man against Samoa, Griffiths, as referees manager, handled the inquiry. Walsh received a three-day suspension, which cost him a touch judge appointment, but Paddy believes that had it not been for Griffiths' astute handling of the affair, Walsh may have come out of it far worse off.

Some of those referees who missed out on quarter-final appointments were heard to mutter that André Watson and Paddy were too close to Steve Griffiths, which was a load of nonsense. The play-off appointments were based on individual assessments compiled independently of Griffiths. Besides which, he was not one of the tournament selectors.

Paddy's reaction is that he'll befriend who he goddamn likes and if someone doesn't appreciate his relationship with Griffiths, then that is their problem. Paddy suggests a look in the mirror might reveal why some individuals haven't won prestige appointments, more than who's befriending whom. Griffiths cops a lot of criticism at times from national referee associations but, in Paddy's view, he does an outstanding job in what are, at times, extremely trying circumstances.

THE MEN BEHIND THE WHISTLE

While referees through the nature of their role are conspicuous individuals, their assessors are largely anonymous, even though many of them can boast distinguished careers as men behind the whistle.

In New Zealand, for every match from NPC up, the referee is appraised by a qualified assessor. To the layman, it is a complicated business, but in essence the referee is awarded marks for his handling of all aspects of the game, from set pieces (lineouts and scrums) to contact areas (tackles, rucks and mauls) his communication and overall management of the game.

Generally speaking, a mark of 85 to 89 out of 100 is acceptable, 90–92 means the referee has made an excellent fist of controlling his match while anything from 93 up is outstanding. At the 2003 World Cup, Paddy scored 94 twice and 93 twice from four different assessors; hence his appointment to a semi-final. Over the past four years, he has refereed approximately 80 matches from NPC up and only twice has been scored at less than 90.

Paddy's IRB assessment form from the 2003 World Cup pool match between Australia and Ireland.

IRB REFEREE ASSESSMENT

NAME OF REFEREE: PADDY O'BRIEN **UNION:** NEW ZEALAND

FIXTURE: AUSTRALIA (17 PTS)
IRELAND (16 PTS)

TOUCH JUDGE 1: JONATHAN KAPLAN (SOUTH AFRICA) **TOUCH JUDGE 2:** IAIN RAMAGE (SCOTLAND)

TMO: NIGEL WHITEHOUSE (WALES) **4TH MATCH OFFICIAL:** PABLO DELUCA (ARGENTINA)

DATE: 1 NOVEMBER 2003 **Degree of Difficulty** 7

WEATHER AND GROUND CONDITIONS: TELSTRA DOME STADIUM, ROOF CLOSED, FLOODLIT, EXCELLENT SURFACE.

TYPE OF FIXTURE: RUGBY WORLD CUP INTERNATIONAL MATCH.

DESCRIPTION OF THE GAME:

Australia scored a thrilling one point victory over a gallant Ireland in the Rugby World Cup to the delight of a 54 204 crowd in Melbourne, cementing its position at the head of Pool A and ensuring a quarter-final against Scotland in Brisbane next weekend.

Tensions ran high during the first half, with both teams playing with verve and sometimes excessive venom. It boiled over just before halftime when both sides lost a player to the sin bin. At halftime the Wallabies led by 11-6.

Australia had to withstand a fierce second-half storm, after Brian O'Driscoll brought the Irish back into the game with a try and drop goal.

No one could predict the winner until the final whistle. Australia looked in control for so long, but yet again, the fighting spirit of the Irish turned the final few minutes into the ultimate of International competition.

Australia's only try of the match had come from George Smith in the first half and it was enough to help them to a 17-16 victory.

The referee had one Irish parent and the other an Australian, by birth a New Zealander. He addressed the players as "gentlemen", even when he sent two off. On the day his contribution was outstanding. In a quiet, firm manner, he took complete control, yet never imposed himself on the game. Well done Paddy.

- [x] VIDEO WITH VOICE
- [ ] TELEVISION BROADCAST
- [ ] NO VIDEO

CRITICAL INCIDENTS DESCRIPTION:
None.

NUMBER OF CRITICAL INCIDENTS: 0

TOTAL SCORE: 93.45

ASSESSOR: F. MULLER **SIGNATURE:** ....

ASSESSOR RDO: STEVE GRIFFITHS **SIGNATURE:** ....

UNION: SARFU **DATE:** 3 NOVEMBER 2003

The system used in New Zealand is the same as used by the IRB. It is the best system devised in that all areas of the game are covered and it is supported by statistics and input from the assessor.

Of course, the validity of any assessment comes down to the ability of the individual completing the form. New Zealand referees have been fortunate to have had Bob Francis and Tom Doocey heading the assessment team. Both are former test referees who have a real understanding of what it is like to be out in the middle. They can empathise with referees who are having a tough day at the office.

Dick Haigh of Dunedin, although not a test referee, is another with a genuine feel for the game while Trevor McLachlan of Auckland and Alan Bateman of Canterbury, both distinguished provincial referees, have served as assessors with distinction over a 10-year period.

Stu Beissel from Taranaki is the latest New Zealander to assess at IRB level — he was in action at the 2003 World Cup — but unlike Francis and Doocey, he has not refereed to test level. He is methodical and accurate but, in Paddy's opinion, will be a better assessor because of his experience at the World Cup. He has tended to write his reports based on the letter, rather than the spirit, of the law, which is contrary to Paddy's philosophy of refereeing.

If all the assessor is doing is playing 'Gotcha' then it would be impossible to receive a good score unless you refereed the same way. Anyone can referee the 'Gotcha' way because there is no skill in that, but it takes an understanding and an acquired skill to know which offences have a material impact on a game. Paddy will always believe the best referees are the ones who know when not to blow their whistles.

The IRB has appointed almost 30 assessors throughout the world, which the leading referees consider an excessive number.

Whenever the referees' test schedule is released, the first thing they do, after identifying where their next appointment is, is look to see who will be assessing them. Fortunately, cream always rises to the top and Paddy considers that at the two World Cup tournaments he has attended the assessors involved have sung from the same hymn sheet as the referees.

Steve Hilditch (Ireland), Bob Yeman (Wales), Doug Kerr (Scotland), Colin High (England), Michel Lamoulie (France), Ian Scotney (Australia), Frans Muller (South

Africa) and Beissel formed a tight relationship amongst themselves at the 2003 World Cup to ensure a consistency in assessment was achieved. What Paddy found refreshing was that they not only offered assessment, they also tendered coaching advice when they felt it was appropriate.

Frans Muller from South Africa has assessed Paddy on about six occasions and is someone Paddy says he would like to 'bottle up' and take with him because he always seems to nail games that Muller is observing.

While Paddy is reluctant to single out individuals among the assessors, his favourite is a gentleman from Belfast, Jim Irvine, who had the unfortunate task of giving Paddy the worst assessment he ever received, following the France-Fiji debacle at the 1999 World Cup. Paddy says he's not sure who felt worse about what happened at Toulouse. Irvine was possessed of such a gentle nature and had such a wonderful way with words, that he still managed to deliver his report on that forgettable game with dignity. Paddy and Jim Irvine each derived immense satisfaction when, three years on, Paddy controlled the South Africa-Australia Tri-Nations fixture at Johannesburg, the game for which he was allocated a bodyguard, and came through with flying colours. Irvine didn't need to take a deep breath before he delivered his assessment on that occasion.

Like many rugby personalities from northern Ireland, Irvine is a larger-than-life character who entertains his colleagues with story-telling. And many's the time he's assisted referees with well thought-out words of advice.

Paddy has always enjoyed working with the Australian assessors, Ian Scotney, Sandy Macneill and Brian Kinsey, during the Super 12. South Africa is a different story because their head assessor, Steve Strydom, has fallen out with the New Zealand and Australian referees, which makes for an uncomfortable environment when you are refereeing there, says Paddy.

Because Strydom wields such power there is a sense that some of the South African assessors are actually scared of him and some won't file a report unless he has approved it first. Frans Muller is the exception. He has been prepared to stand up to Strydom, refusing to toe the party line. He sends his reports direct to the country involved or to the IRB.

The NZRU's referees manager since Graeme Harrison's untimely death in 1996 has been Keith Lawrence. A former test referee, he is little short of being a workaholic.

It was never going to be easy for him to replace Harrison but he has succeeded by being himself.

One of the biggest problems Lawrence had to face was that he was managing professional referees, for which there had been no blueprint. Both Lawrence and his men have been the pioneers in this field.

Everything Lawrence does is with the referees' best interests at heart. Like the practitioners who have had to learn from their mistakes as the professional era unfolds, he has had to keep re-evaluating trends.

When Keith Lawrence and Paddy tend to frustrate each other is in their philosophies of the game. Lawrence, a former schoolteacher, is meticulous in his work but tends to dramatise the small problems that occur in refereeing while Paddy is more *laissez-faire*. Paddy considers that striving for perfection in refereeing is unrealistic.

Lawrence was a far more technical referee than the Walshs and O'Briens of today. In fact, he probably compares more with Paul Honiss.

As far as Paddy is concerned, neither way is necessarily right or wrong. He considers all referees should be encouraged to develop their own warts-and-all styles, as long as they are not detracting from the games they are refereeing.

Lawrence being an ex-schoolteacher and Paddy being an ex-copper probably sums up their differences. Paddy tends to make 10 decisions quickly and get eight of them right — and learn from the other two — while Lawrence will spend many hours making one decision, ensuring he achieves the right solution, before advancing to the next problem.

The good thing about rugby is that there is room for all kinds in the game, as long as all parties respect each others' differences. Paddy believes he and Lawrence have each other's respect.

Lawrence's equivalent in Australia, through until virtually the eve of the 2003 World Cup, was Russell Trotter, who has been succeeded by Peter Marshall. While Trotter was not everyone's cup of tea, Paddy found he really challenged him in aspects of his refereeing and was invaluable as someone to bounce ideas off.

He lived close to the hotel in Sydney where the referees were based at World Cup time and Paddy joined him on a couple of occasions at his local club where they had a couple of quiet pints away from the hustle and bustle of the tournament.

'Trots' always approached games from a different perspective which Paddy, for one, found stimulating. Certainly, he never went away from a session with Trotter without something to muse over. While Paddy was sad to see him vacate the referees manager's chair, he is delighted that his replacement is veteran test referee Marshall whom he knows will be excellent value for Australia.

Lawrence and Trotter were, in Paddy's opinion, streets ahead in their thinking compared with some of their counterparts in other countries.

While Paddy has had the opportunity to work in tandem with and to socialise with referees and assessors from almost every corner of the globe, several NPC referees, who will probably never reach those dizzy heights, are among his closest colleagues.

When he is controlling a test match overseas, Paddy is aware he is operating on behalf of all the referees in New Zealand because of the support he receives from people like Matt Peters, Vinny Munro, Jonathon White, Kevin Rowe, Bryce Lawrence and Chris Morgan who never overlook his international appointments.

One individual who Paddy is indebted to is capable club referee Chris Jansen of Wanganui who took it on himself to compile scrapbooks and statistics on Paddy's behalf. The complete summary of Paddy's first-class appointments, which feature on the final pages of this book, have been painstakingly compiled by Jansen who is affectionately known to everyone as 'Sarge' through his New Zealand Army connections. A rugby junky, he pops up all over the world and hardly ever misses a rugby test in his home country. His efforts have been mightily appreciated by Paddy.

In 1997, on the recommendation of Colin Hawke, Paddy made contact with Danny Brown, a stalwart of the Counties Manukau union. Paddy didn't have a coach at the time and Brown was able to offer invaluable assistance regarding positional play and onfield demeanour, which was important following his run-in with Zinzan Brooke.

Although Paddy later linked up with Lewis McGill, his relationship with Brown has continued, to the extent that he regards Brown virtually as a mentor. They talk on the phone regularly, and not always purely on refereeing matters. Brown, like Paddy, is a racing enthusiast and the two of them have finished up as fellow members of the Dukes of Hazard syndicate which in 2002/03 had two fillies prepared by leading South Island trainer Ken Barron.

Steve Walsh senior, who was affectionately know as Skylab, a nickname given to him by Graeme Harrison because of his solid build, came on to the New Zealand referees Top 10 panel at the same time as Paddy. Because they were the two new kids on the block, they quickly developed a rapport which continues today.

Steve was a capable referee who now and again seemed to get flustered under pressure which probably cost him several of the important appointments that went instead to Paddy, Colin Hawke and Paul Honiss. Although he must have been disappointed at missing the big ones, he never allowed it to show and was always totally supportive of the man in the middle.

With such a big frame, it would have been understandable if his fitness had dropped away, but he compensated by training harder than anyone and fitness became his special strength. Steve retired at the still young age of 41, on the realisation he was not going to advance further as a referee and after his marriage to Julie in 2001 caused a rearrangement of the priorities in his life.

Paddy found him a great tourist and says the overseas trips involving Steve, Colin Hawke and himself were the most enjoyable of his career.

The final word in this chapter comes as a suggestion from Paddy: why not do away with referees' social rooms at grounds because they create a them-and-us situation? Why shouldn't players, administrators and referees all socialise together after matches? Surely, says Paddy, it would build relationships. He sometimes hears referees described as being 'incestuous', a claim he finds hard to defend while they are tucked away in their own social setting.

Paddy does acknowledge that the relationship among players, referees and coaches has taken a quantum leap from when he first picked up the whistle, for in his earliest days as a referee there was no communication at all. At least now the referee and the coaches have a compulsory chat on the Monday following a big game. That's progress, and Paddy believes the next logical step forward would be to integrate players and referees. Watch this space!

World Cup Agony

You have to give the Aussies their due. They stage-managed the 2003 Rugby World Cup magnificently. Notwithstanding the stringent demands placed on them by the IRB's organising committee, the tournament ran almost without a hitch. Stadiums in such remote rugby outposts as Launceston, Wollongong, Townsville and Gosford North were chocker even for clashes between teams of minnow status such as Namibia and Romania.

What percentage of the spectators at many of these encounters actually understood the rudiments of the game is irrelevant. The Australian Rugby Union (ARU), through brilliant marketing ploys, at least got the people to turn up.

The rugby generally was high calibre with the top-seeded teams all progressing to the quarter-finals. Both the Australian economy and the ARU coffers benefited by countless millions of dollars and the game received a huge boost in a country where rugby has through the decades played second, or sometimes third, fiddle to league and Australian rules.

Most New Zealanders who crossed the Tasman to help celebrate the occasion came away with mixed emotions. They relished the pageantry and the onfield action (if not the All Blacks' shock loss to the Wallabies) but were left with a lingering sense of regret that New Zealand wasn't sharing in the hosting of this gala rugby occasion.

Paddy's wife Carolyn and their children were among those who soaked up the wonderful atmosphere that surrounded the semi-finals, the play-off and the final. Seeing the delight on his children's faces caused him to reflect on what New Zealand rugby had lost out on.

Much has been written about the NZRU's bungled attempt to co-host the 2003 tournament and Paddy says he is no more aware of what happened at the table of the Rugby World Cup board than any other New Zealander.

However, he is in a unique position to talk about several of the main players at the IRB. As an international referee he regularly mixes with the world's leading administrators and he has functioned on a number of IRB working parties which involve select groups of coaches, players, referees and administrators. These sessions have brought him into contact with such distinguished individuals as Syd Millar and the late Vernon Pugh.

Paddy has on more than one occasion received a dismissive, 'What would you know about it, you're only a referee.' Well, he might only be a referee, but as one of international stature whose appointments annually embrace the world's foremost events in Europe, South Africa and Australasia he has as much exposure to the game's leading administrators and media as anyone in the game.

He considered the saddest part of all the bickering relating to the co-hosting issue was that the New Zealand media led their nation down a path of hatred towards individuals who had given a lifetime to rugby and who, previously, had nothing but the best interests of New Zealand rugby at heart.

Paddy first met Vernon Pugh QC prior to the 1999 World Cup in the UK. His first impression was that Pugh retained a deep understanding of the game, having coached at club level in Wales, but, more pertinently, he possessed a huge passion for rugby. He was determined that while he was at the helm rugby would be a game enjoyed by all those who wanted to partake.

Paddy was pleasantly surprised to find how knowledgeable Pugh was on the mechanics of the game and he engaged him several times in earnest discussion on such technical issues as straight put-ins at the scrum. Pugh's reply was always that if the law was not appropriate for the modern game, then it was up to the member unions to go through the proper channels to effect change. Until that happened, the law should be properly adhered to. Paddy found it hard to argue against such logical reasoning.

John O'Neill was the other individual pilloried in New Zealand when the co-hosting rights were taken away. In Paddy's view, he had only one fault when the hosting issue was being hotly debated — he lived on the wrong side of the Tasman. He is a straight shooter whose intention was, purely and simply, to get the best possible deal for Australian rugby. And when New Zealand's negotiators, Murray McCaw and David Rutherford, began prevaricating that's precisely what he did. He told them to stuff off. His Australian union would go it alone.

While many New Zealanders plainly hold him in contempt, Paddy has always found him to be extremely professional and a thorough gentleman. He never ignored referees or touch judges at aftermatch functions where many others of his status found an excuse to be otherwise occupied. O'Neill always made a point of coming over and thanking the match officials for their efforts, whether the Wallabies won or lost. He always inquired whether they were being well hosted in his country.

Following the Wales-Australia quarter-final at the 1999 World Cup, when Colin Hawke was left out to dry at the aftermatch event, it was O'Neill, along with Tim Gresson and his wife Jo, who ensured Colin received the respect and support he merited after such an intense game. Those occasions are not easily forgotten by referees.

Syd Millar, who has taken over as IRB chairman, is one of the game's true gentlemen. A typically amiable Irishman, he has a pair of 'Colin Meads' hands and threatens to dislodge your arm from its socket so heartily does he greet you. Like O'Neill, he makes a point of seeking out the referee at functions and, whilst not shy in proffering his view on happenings that afternoon, Paddy has always found him to be fair in his judgment.

It grated on Paddy that some sections of the media wrote or spoke about Pugh and O'Neill, particularly, as if they were ogres out to destroy New Zealand rugby. When such powerful claims are made, in some instances by journalists who had never come face to face with either individual, it becomes the perceived truth.

Other prominent administrators like Bernard Lappaset from France, Rian Oberholzer (who resigned in the wake of the Springboks' disappointing World Cup campaign in 2003), Noel Murphy from Ireland and Robert Horner from England have come across as down-to-earth rugby people whom one could warm to easily.

Paddy was embarrassed and upset in 2002 when NZRU chairman Murray McCaw and CEO David Rutherford began making demeaning comments about Pugh, Millar and co. during the hosting negotiations.

New Zealand rugby had down the years gained the utmost respect from other rugby nations, making Paddy proud to wear his New Zealand blazer wherever his rugby travels took him. Such mighty onfield achievers as George Nepia, Fred Allen, Bob Scott, Charlie Saxton, Colin Meads, Wilson Whineray, Brian Lochore, Sean Fitzpatrick and Jonah Lomu were spoken of in awe. Wherever Paddy went, once identified as a New Zealander, he found he was treated like royalty.

All that changed with McCaw in charge.

Paddy attended a dinner in Paris after refereeing the France-Ireland Six Nations match and was embarrassed at the way some of the world's leading administrators were interpreting the arrogant stance being adopted by the NZRU.

Trevor Mallard's entirely inappropriate beer bottle comment only added fuel to the conflagration. For McCaw to call Pugh and Millar 'yesterday's men' was a massive insult to two of the world's foremost sports administrators.

Paddy is convinced Pugh desperately wanted New Zealand to co-host the World Cup as he, personally, believed it was inappropriate for one nation to host such a major tournament, but when McCaw launched into such a personal attack through the media his sentiments obviously changed.

In Paddy's view, all the talk about New Zealand losing millions by giving in to the IRB's requests, was a smokescreen to the real issue. That was that McCaw and Rutherford did not understand that New Zealand is but a contributing part to the world rugby scene and not the dominating part, as they misguidedly preferred to believe.

Paddy says he would like to think that New Zealanders now appreciate that losing the co-hosting rights was of our own doing and that the challenge facing New Zealand rugby is to repair the damage that has been done.

Paddy had no problems dealing with Rutherford. He was always pleasant enough at their infrequent meetings. But it was a different story whenever he encountered McCaw who promoted himself as an authority on most matters, including refereeing. His often-derogatory comments about referees were not appreciated by Paddy and his colleagues who considered that McCaw's knowledge of the laws was less than complete. He often ribbed Paddy and co. for wearing NZRU branded gear, obviously believing that only the All Blacks had the right to step out in it.

Jonathan Kaplan's first major test appointment was the Bledisloe Cup game at Wellington's Cake Tin in 2000, the occasion when Ice Cool Eales slotted a penalty goal after the final siren for a famous Australian victory. Kaplan gave an accomplished performance, encouraged by his very experienced touch judges Ed Morrison and Reg Dickson. Paddy was the TMO and so was privy to all their communications.

At the aftermatch function, McCaw, who had also been listening to the dialogue between the referee and his touch judge, approached Paddy and said Morrison was out of line with comments such as 'Great call, Jono' and 'Keep it going, Jono.'

Paddy reacted strongly to McCaw's comments, reminding him that it was a bloody hard and lonely job out there in the middle and that Ed Morrison's comments were excellent and appropriate. He put it to McCaw that it was no different to Todd Blackadder patting Jonah Lomu on the backside after he'd executed a great tackle.

McCaw declined to acknowledge Paddy's response, leaving Paddy with the impression he didn't know where he was coming from.

Paddy believes New Zealand rugby went through a phase under McCaw's directorship where several administrators encroached well beyond their level of expertise. Suddenly, they were experts on refereeing when clearly they had no true appreciation of what constituted a good or bad refereeing performance.

A couple of members of the board weren't content to confine themselves to financial and marketing matters. They seemed to think that because of their status they could also pass judgment on all rugby issues, including refereeing.

Paddy grew up believing that Kiwis were generally a humble people. He hopes that the rugby experiences of the past couple of seasons have reminded those who were being deluded into believing New Zealanders are God's gift to sport might now appreciate that they are one component of this great game of rugby. If New Zealand works alongside all the other IRB countries, not independent of them, the game will prosper.

Paddy often hears the Air New Zealand NPC referred to as the world's premier provincial competition. Sounds good, he says, but has anyone thought to tell that to the Western Province supporters at Newlands in Cape Town or to the Leicester fans in England or to the boisterous followers of Toulouse in France?

Some of them wouldn't even know of the NPC's existence and neither would they care. New Zealanders need to enjoy what they possess and keep improving on it but always to remember that they are just a small fish in a big pond, notwithstanding their proud history and the amazing exploits through the decades of the All Blacks.

Paddy has mentioned earlier in the book his great respect for Tim Gresson. He makes no apologies for the fact that twice in the past handful of years he has campaigned vigorously through his contacts in the game to try and keep him on the NZRU board.

On the first occasion, he was successful but, following the World Cup fiasco, the entire NZRU board was thrown out. Gresson stood again but lost out to Mike Eagles and Mark Peters.

It's Paddy's belief that the baby inadvertently got thrown out with the bath water in the desperation to create a fresh image after McCaw and his cronies had stuffed up so badly.

Paddy's reason for going in to bat for Gresson was simply because he identified him as an individual with a vast knowledge of the game who was held in the highest regard by the Pughs, Millars and O'Neills of the world.

Gresson might have been better advised to have taken a stand against McCaw and Rutherford, in Paddy's opinion, although he concedes he was in a difficult situation. It didn't stop Paddy continuing with his crusade.

After he'd met with the Southland union, he received a phone call from Steve Tew, who was the acting CEO at the time, warning him that as an employee of the NZRU he should not be getting himself involved in political issues.

Paddy heard Tew out but didn't agree with him and told him so. He says he will always fight for a cause if he believes it is a worthy one. As he didn't know Mike Eagles or Mark Peters personally, he says he could not be accused of discrediting them. He was simply promoting the individual he believed would bring integrity and knowledge to the NZRU and on to the IRB.

Paddy's campaigning didn't save Gresson. Democracy took its course and the entire board, save for Maori representative Paul Quinn, was replaced. Paddy has no regrets about his stand.

Notwithstanding their disagreement over the Gresson issue, Paddy has always enjoyed his dealings with Steve Tew whom he labels a man's man. Paddy finds him someone he can have a verbal dust-up with, as over Gresson, but knows where he stands when the matter is finished. Paddy considers that if everyone else involved in rugby operated in that manner, it would be a perfect world!

Tew is supportive of referees and will fight their causes when he believes it is justified. He's also not scared to voice his concerns when things aren't going appropriately, but only after he's accumulated all the facts. Since he has been on the NZRU, referees believe they are getting a fair crack from the board.

With Chris Moller and Jock Hobbs now at the head of the NZRU, Paddy is hopeful that relationships with other countries and the IRB will quickly be restored because under McCaw and Rutherford, New Zealand was losing ground at breakneck speed.

One administrator who has exited the top level is Richie Guy. Paddy always enjoyed his input. They worked together on the NZRU laws committee. Paddy and co. would be putting the finishing touches to the latest bright idea they had to make the game better when Richie would pipe up.

'How is this going to impact on the under-12s in Northland and Southland?' he would ask.

He never forgot the grass roots and his input into that area of the game was invaluable.

World Cup Diary

October

Wednesday 1: Departed Invercargill at midday for Sydney via Christchurch, flying business class, which wasn't normal. Usually, international referees only get upgraded for flights of longer than five hours. Arrived at Brighton Beach, where the World Cup referees were quartered, and caught up with all the officials before hitting the sack.

Thursday 2: All match officials and assessors met for the official welcome from Rugby World Cup organisers. Protocols were set in place for the No.s 4 and 5 match officials. Outfitting for all referees was followed by personal physical assessments by the World Cup physio. The purpose of this was to collect data for future assistance for referees.

The doctor established whether any of us had weaknesses in particular areas so they could prescribe rehab work to prevent future injuries. I was told I needed to strengthen my abdomen to prevent back problems.

Friday 3: A full-on day discussing the various aspects of the game and how the tournament matches would be refereed. Really pleased that no changes were to be made to the 'aide memoir' put in place at the referees meeting in Singapore in 2001. Areas covered included the tackle, lineout, ruck and maul and foul play plus a full session on the importance of touch judging.

Saturday 4: Up at 6 a.m. for a day of team building. There was a 90-minute drive and ferry trip to Paloga Beach where we split into six teams. Three teams attempted to solve challenges during a beach walk while the other three went kayaking for two hours and then solved problems from cryptic clues. After lunch the teams swapped roles. A fantastic day where the spirit which existed within the group came to the fore.

Even in those early days, I could confidently say there was a better feel within the 'twenty-first team' than at the 1999 tournament. Steve Griffiths, the IRB referees manager, had gone out of his way to ensure the hiccups of 1999 wouldn't recur. It appears all egos had been left behind. For the record, Team 3 (Wye Woks), of which I happened to be the leader, tied for first place in the team-building exercises with Six Blind Mice, led by Stu Dickinson, and the Support Team, led by Steve Griffiths. The day was not about coming first but about assisting others when they were taken out of their comfort zones. Overall, the '21st team' was gelling well.

Sunday 5: D Day for all as fitness tests were undertaken. Disappointing results for some, but an excellent day for the Kiwis. Steve Walsh, Kelvin Deaker and Paul Honiss were among the five individuals who registered the top mark of 12.5 in the dreaded beep test. Yours truly was among the next group to finish on 11.8. In the sprints, it was again the New Zealanders who were to the fore, with Paddy on top followed by Paul Honiss. The top six also featured Kelvin Deaker, Steve Walsh and South African Mark Lawrence. Four of the participants were clearly not up to standard in the aerobic test and three struggled in the sprints where there is a very liberal pass target. There were concerns over a couple of the referees who injured themselves whilst undertaking the sprints.

Monday 6: Realisation that the World Cup kicked off within a week, so it was time to start getting urgent. A day off from official activities for the referees whilst the assessors had a full-on training day. Decision taken to re-test in a 12-minute track run those referees who came up short in the beep and sprint tests.

Tuesday 7: A full day at Stadium Australia for everyone for a briefing on TMO protocol and to familiarise everyone with match communication equipment. Team photo shoot, then back to the hotel to prepare for the final fitness assessment. Kelvin, Steve and Paul were asked to assist those struggling at the back of the field during the 12-minute run whilst the rest of us went flat out. Really pleased with my performance as I led the fast pack home from André Watson and Dave McHugh.

Wednesday 8: Final meeting regarding outfitting. Some more work on scrums followed by an official welcome (drinks included) at the Sydney Opera House. Got home in time to pack and get ready for my flight to Perth the following day.

Thursday 9: Trained with Kelvin Deaker and Steve Walsh, concentrating on sprinting, before heading for the airport. Arrived in Perth after a pleasant five-hour flight. Must say, it was great to break into smaller groups and start concentrating on the real reason we were there, to referee. Only 48 hours out from my opening game and I started to prepare mentally for South Africa versus Uruguay.

Friday 10: Quiet day catching up on sleep and correspondence. Kelvin Deaker and Bob Yeman went to the WACA and saw Matthew Hayden smash Brian Lara's world test record, scoring 380 against Zimbabwe.

Saturday 11: Match day. Great to finally involve myself in what I'd spent four years preparing for. Subiaco Oval attracted a large crowd who enjoyed the Springbok romp. The Boks gave a disciplined display. Uruguay tried hard but they were in a different league.

Sunday 12: Recovery day: a bit sore in the back, which is the norm for me after 80 minutes these days. Did a pool recovery session, then spent an hour going over the previous night's game with Bob Yeman, my assessor. Bob is a delight to work with. He's a man's man who reads the game well. Couple of points that needed polishing but overall he was pleased with my performance. That evening I was the No. 4 official for the England-Georgia game which Pablo Deluca from Argentina was refereeing.

Monday 13: A day for relaxation. Trained at Perry Lakes Stadium, on the athletic track, doing 4 x 1200 metre intervals. Detest them, but felt really good when they were completed. Barbecue at the liaison officer's house. First opportunity to let our hair down since our arrival. Lots of laughter and the chance to completely relax out of the public eye. Spoke to John Mitchell by cell phone and updated him on refereeing trends thus far.

Tuesday 14: Free day, an opportunity to take in the sights of Perth and Fremantle, and to catch up on laundry, e-mails and phone calls. Fitted in a 40-minute run along the river bank. Lots of South Africans and Poms were arriving in town for Saturday's big match.

Wednesday 15: Another quiet day. Had another good training run around the riverbank and then spent some time at the TAB with Jonathan Kaplan trying to pick winners at the races. Operated as the No. 4 official at the Samoa-Uruguay game which David McHugh of Ireland refereed.

Thursday 16: Up early for another run along the river bank, then went off to the airport to catch a flight through to Canberra. The temperatures were starting to climb in Perth, so it was probably a good time to depart. We'd been a good team in Perth, so it was sad to be pulling out, but I was looking forward to my next game, Italy versus Canada the following Tuesday.

Friday 17: In Canberra on my own for 24 hours before the other team members arrived. Quite nice to have time out. Went on a 70-minute run around the lakefront and felt really strong. Had my first decent sleep since arriving in Australia. Even though there's only a three-hour time difference between Perth and Canberra, it takes time for the body to adjust. Had an evening meal at our liaison officer's house. Was nice to sample home cooked food again, and Alan Casey and his wife were excellent company. Watched the All Blacks beat Canada before retiring for the night.

Saturday 18: After an early morning run, I spent a little time studying the Caulfield Cup field and decided to invest on the New Zealand hope, Distinctly Secret, who ran bravely and finished third. Probably got a better return than if I'd backed him in New

Zealand. Paul Honiss, George Ayoub and Steve Hilditch arrived for Sunday's game, so we dined together and prepared for the late-evening kick-off in the tournament's first heavyweight battle between England and South Africa across in Perth. Peter Marshall showed all his experience in ensuring what was potentially a fiery encounter was kept under firm control. Whilst Peter has obviously lost his pace, his top two inches are as good as any referee around, which was obvious during this game.

Sunday 19: Lazy morning catching up on the Sunday papers, then a training run. Took in some of the sights of Canberra during the afternoon, then went off to Canberra Stadium to be No. 4 for the Tonga-Wales game. Was good to catch up with Steve Hansen again. He's a breath of fresh air amongst the coaches. Always time for a chat regardless of the circumstances, and is obviously building Wales into a formidable team. A phone call from son Hamish advised that Paddy O'Brien, the horse, had won at the Gore trots.

Monday 20: No training. Visited the physiotherapist for my twice-weekly back manipulation and then played golf at Royal Canberra Golf Club, a magnificent course. Mick Keogh, the Australian referees coach, and I lost on the 18th to Paul Honiss and Steve Hilditch. What's $30 amongst friends! A nice, relaxing day and perfect build-up to the Italy-Canada game. Felt in great nick but needed to nail this game to be mentally right for Ireland versus Australia, one of the key contests of the tournament.

Tuesday 21: Refereed Italy against Canada. An intense game with plenty of desire but not a lot of finesse. Not the sort of game I altogether appreciate as a referee, with so many stoppages, but I held my concentration for the 80 minutes. Italy got home 19–14 to keep its play-off hopes alive. The winner of the Canada-Wales will advance to the quarter-finals.

Wednesday 22: Packed up again and flew to Adelaide via Melbourne. Went over the previous night's performance with my assessor, Steve Hilditch from Ireland. He's a delightful person, with a real understanding of the game from a referee's perspective. I was feeling physically good but mentally tired from my game. Caught up on e-mails and laundry.

Thursday 23: Had an enjoyable training run along the beachfront. Uplifted from our hotel by Steve Kinsman, the head of the homicide squad with the Adelaide police. After a pleasant lunch, we took in the sights of the city before adjourning to his favourite watering hole. Over a few beers we swapped CIB experiences. After a pleasant meal he dropped me back at the hotel around 10 p.m. Was nice to relax and have a blow out.

Friday 24: Training was an effort as I'd developed some flu-like symptoms. Put antibiotics into my body as I didn't want to be crook for the following weekend's big game. Health improved enough for me to play golf with André Watson and Mark Lawrence. Another loss to 'Wattie' but it filled in the day nicely. In the evening, we watched the All Blacks demolish Tonga and the Springboks score a patchy win over Georgia.

Saturday 25: Took a morning walk along the beach before breakfast. My first touch judge appointment, for Joel Jutge who was refereeing Australia against Namibia. God, what a bore: Australia 142, Namibia nil! Felt sorry for Joel as the game was a joke. Got the impression the Namibians didn't want to be on the paddock.

Sunday 26: Another touch judge appointment, this time at the Argentina-Ireland game which André Watson refereed. We knew this would be a real contest, not like the previous day's farce. The Irish, who looked to have dug themselves into a hole, sneaked out with a one-point victory. André needed all his experience to control this tight, tense game, and turned in an excellent performance. Retired to a pub to watch the Samoa-England game which was an absolute stunner. Looked for a long while as if Samoa could pull off the upset of all time. The Samoans were awesome and were cheered all the way by the Irish supporters who packed the pub.

Monday 27: Flew from Adelaide to Sydney. My first day back at base after three weeks on the road. Really enjoyed going 'walkabout' because I find there are too many distractions when I'm amongst a large assembly of fellow referees.

Tuesday 28: Spent most of the day with Steve Walsh who had come under fire from the England team management for his part in an incident where England wrongfully allowed a 16th player onto the field against Samoa. At the conclusion of the game Dave Reddin, England's fitness trainer responsible for their bench, had an altercation with Brett Bowden, subs controller for England. Steve went to Bowden's assistance and he and Reddin exchanged unpleasantries. Strong words were uttered, but nothing worse than happens from time to time at Super 12 or test matches. Unfortunately for Steve, because England was in trouble for fielding the 16th man, he became implicated. Whilst England's actions were dealt with by the IRB judiciary, Steve's situation was handled by Steve Griffiths, the referees manager. Because Steve had interfered in a problem which was not his, he was suspended for three days. In reality, all that happened was that he was taken off touch judge duties for the upcoming Friday night pool game. All other referees knew that 'there but for the grace of God go I'. The lesson learnt was that in today's professional environment every move we make is heavily scrutinised.

Wednesday 29: Played golf in the morning with Russell Trotter, Mick Keogh and André Watson. Lost again. What's new! Went training in the afternoon and then was entertained by Russell Trotter at his local workingmen's club. Again, nice to relax away from the crowd.

Thursday 30: Was starting to build into game mode for Ireland-Australia. Looked at a couple of things on DVD concerning both sides, mostly scrums and tackle entry. Advised that a meeting with Wallaby coach Eddie Jones had been arranged for the following day in Melbourne. Journeyed into the Sydney CBD for the first time and purchased some boots and jeans from the store of R M Williams who were our clothes sponsor at the tournament. Trained in the afternoon and packed my bags in readiness for my morning flight to Melbourne. It's a pain having to continually re-pack, especially when you're only away for 48 hours, but them's the rules.

Friday 31: Flew to Melbourne where the weather was wet and cold. Luckily, the game was to be staged at Telstra Stadium where we would be enclosed. Immediately noticed that the city was full of Irish supporters, in town for the rugby and the races.

November

Saturday 1: A quiet day preparing for the game which didn't kick off until 8.30 p.m. It made it a long day. No point in winding myself up too early. Ate breakfast out with friends of Jonathan Kaplan's. Had a couple of bets on the Melbourne races, then spent the afternoon reading a book and snoozing. In my test career, which stretches back a decade, I doubt I had ever heard a louder, more enthusiastic crowd. The Irish fans were out in force and, obviously, there were plenty of Australian supporters on hand as well, although Melbourne isn't a rugby stronghold. Even though my touch judges and TMO were connected through the best gear available, I struggled to hear them, such was the hubbub. A fantastic match which was in doubt till the final whistle. The Irish did everything to win, which would have represented a massive boil-over, but the Wallabies, like the champions they are, weathered the storm and got home by a point. By the time I returned to my hotel it was 2 a.m. and I was exhausted.

Sunday 2: Still really tired from my game, but satisfied that my three pool games had gone off well. Felt so much more satisfied than in 1999. Flew back into Sydney mid-afternoon and re-established myself at HQ. Caught up with my laundry and e-mails before settling down to watch the All Blacks-Wales game. Had an allocation of tickets for the match which I'd given to daughter Kylie and her fiancé.

Monday 3: All the referees are now back in Sydney and we spent the day reviewing the tournament to date. The assessors and selectors then staged their own meeting, at which they made the appointments for the quarter-finals. Told we would be advised of those the next day. While I was pleased with my performances, I wasn't getting too excited about future appointments, because that was now out of my hands. Either they would select me or they wouldn't. Control the controllables, Paddy, and let other matters take their course. Went out to a local restaurant with the entire referees team, including the eight guys who were along as touch judges only. As they were all departing the next day, we concluded proceedings with a hilarious court session. Ian Scotney played the judge and I was the prosecutor. One of the best nights I can remember and reinforced how well the Rugby World Cup refereeing team had gelled together.

Tuesday 4: I was suffering the effects of the huge night out. It had taken me this long to realise I can't drink like a young fella anymore, although it was still good fun trying! All Australia seemed to be focused on the Melbourne Cup. Delighted to show my loyalty by backing the only Kiwi horse involved, Distinctly Secret, but he was among the also-rans. Each of us was individually summoned to Steve Griffiths' room where we were informed of our status for the remainder of the tournament. A nervous time for all of us. I was advised that if the Springboks beat the All Blacks, I would referee the final. However, if the Springboks lost, I would be appointed to a semi-final (obviously not the one involving the All Blacks). Naturally, I was over the moon and quite emotional. The four years of hard work since the disasters of '99 had reaped their reward. Steve Walsh was excited, too, because he had been appointed to a quarter-final, an indication he was now fulfilling the potential he had shown since he first came into refereeing. Paul Honiss was advised he would not get a semi-final or the final but that if the All Blacks kept winning, he would control the play-off for third. Altogether, a sensational day for New Zealand referees, with three being ranked in the top eight. It doesn't come much better than that.

Wednesday 5: I trained with Steve Walsh. It was bloody hot and energy sapping, but good to get focused on the job ahead. Steve showed he was up for his game and determined to nail it. Notwithstanding the skirmish with the English camp in Adelaide, he showed he was in good nick and in a positive frame of mind. Spent the afternoon at Coogee Beach. We don't get many days in high summer like this in Invercargill. The temperature was in the high twenties, the water just gorgeous. In the evening we all attended the New South Wales referees' dinner.

Thursday 6: Quiet day. Caught up on a few housekeeping matters. Trained well in preparation for a big weekend ahead.

Friday 7: My 16th wedding anniversary, so I arranged for flowers to be delivered to Carolyn. Only four days till the family arrives in Sydney. Another good training session followed by a midday flight to Brisbane to prepare for the quarter-finals. The other half of the referees headed for Melbourne. Dined out with André Watson and some of his South African friends.

Saturday 8: Played golf at the exclusive Gold Coast course. Our hosts were fantastic and spared no expense to make us welcome. I teamed up with Greg Cornelsen, famous for his four tries against the All Blacks at Eden Park in 1978. A top bloke. André and I were allowed to choose any shirt we liked from the Golf Shop. Returned to our hotel at 2 p.m. for a briefing, with Steve Walsh, for the Australia-Scotland game. Watched the first half of the All Blacks-Springboks game and whilst a Springboks win would have allowed me to referee the final, I must admit I was cheering for New Zealand. After this performance, I genuinely felt the All Blacks were the best team at the tournament. Sad to see empty seats at Brisbane for the Scotland-Australia quarter-final. Steve Walsh refereed well and must be in a great position to go to the top over the next four years. To referee a World Cup quarter-final at the age of 31 was unprecedented. With a few more scars on his back, I'm sure he will be at the top for a long time.

Sunday 9: Played golf with André Watson, Paul Honiss and Greg Hinton before returning to the hotel for a briefing with Alain Roland, who was refereeing the England-Wales game that night. Alain, like Steve Walsh, has the refereeing world at his feet. A former Irish halfback, he has a lovely nature and a cool head for a guy who is relatively new to the international game. Spoke to Carolyn and the kids who said they were all organised for their flight across the Tasman the following day.

Monday 10: Flew down to Sydney, arriving at 3 p.m. Just enough time to drop off my luggage and get back to the airport to uplift Carolyn, Danielle and Hamish. So good to embrace the family again after being parted for six weeks. All looking well with the kids pretty excited about going to the semis and the final. I'm told to report to Steve Griffiths' room at 6 p.m. where he explains the selectors' thinking for the last four games. I have been appointed to the France-England semi-final with Chris White given the New Zealand-Australia game. André, Chris and myself are all in consideration for the final, dependent, obviously, on the outcome of the semis (although not a concern for André because the Springboks are already back in South Africa). Paul Honiss and Alain Roland are under consideration for the Thursday play-off, again dependent on the outcome of the semis. I am thrilled with my appointment and now really want to referee well in what will be the biggest game of my career. I also want the All Blacks to win, which would be the icing on the cake of a wonderful tournament.

Paddy O'Brien collection

The wedding of Jeremy, the youngest of the nine O'Brien children, in New Plymouth in 2003 to Courtney O'Sullivan, daughter of former All Black, the late Terry O'Sullivan. The other O'Briens are Tim and Kevin (standing, behind) and Casey, Margot, Anne, parents Valerie and Ray, Paddy and Gabrielle.

Paddy O'Brien collection

The O'Brien children suitably decked out for the All Blacks' big semi-final clash with the Wallabies at the 2003 World Cup. Eldest daughter Kylie, who lives in Australia, is flanked by Danielle, left, and Hamish.

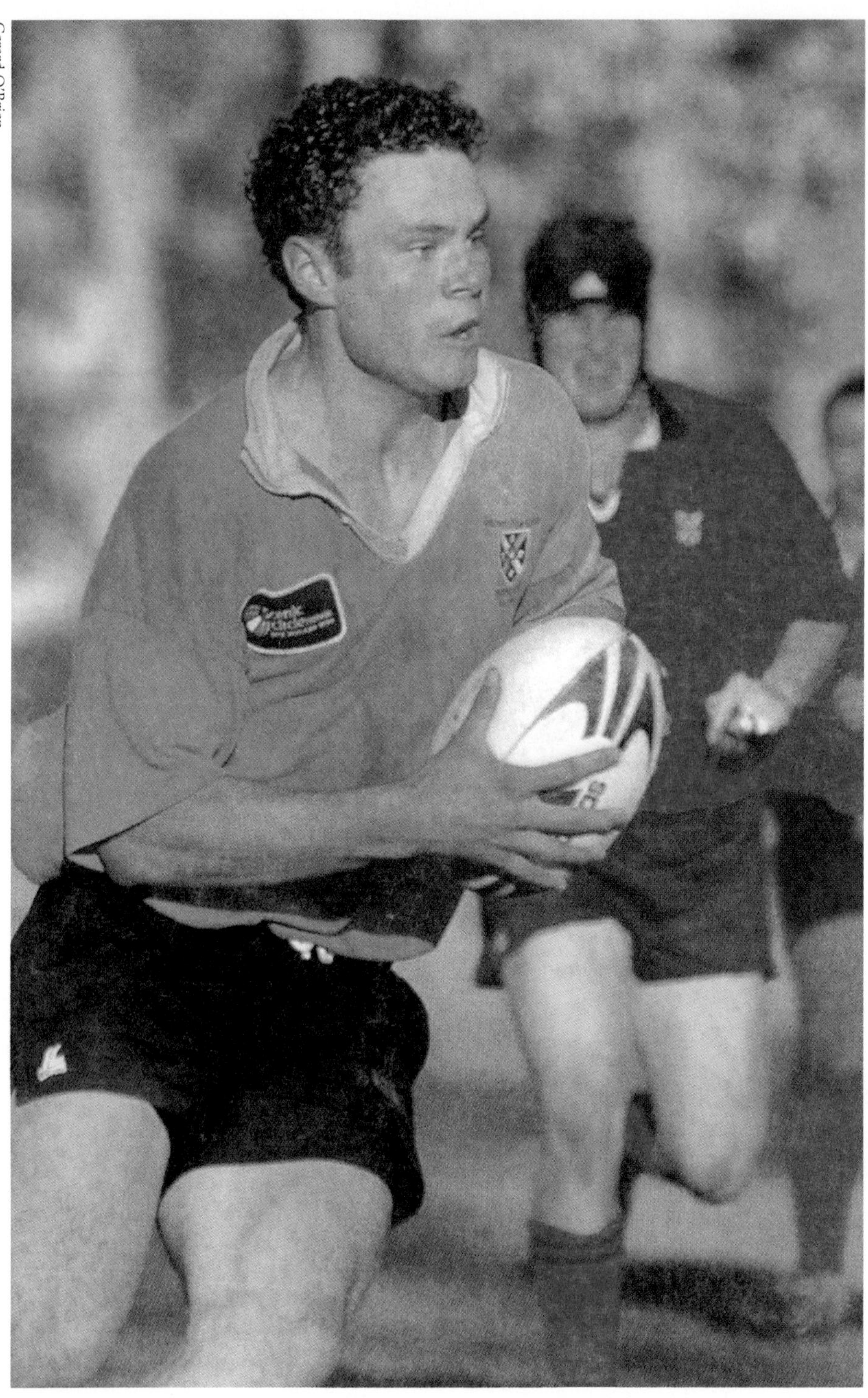

Gerard O'Brien

Paddy's eldest son Matthew in action for University A in the Dunedin senior club competition in 2003.

Paddy O'Brien collection

Readying for World Cup action in Perth in 2003. From left, Mattie Goddard, Peter Marshall, referee Pablo Deluca, Kelvin Deaker and Paddy. Their game was England against Romania.

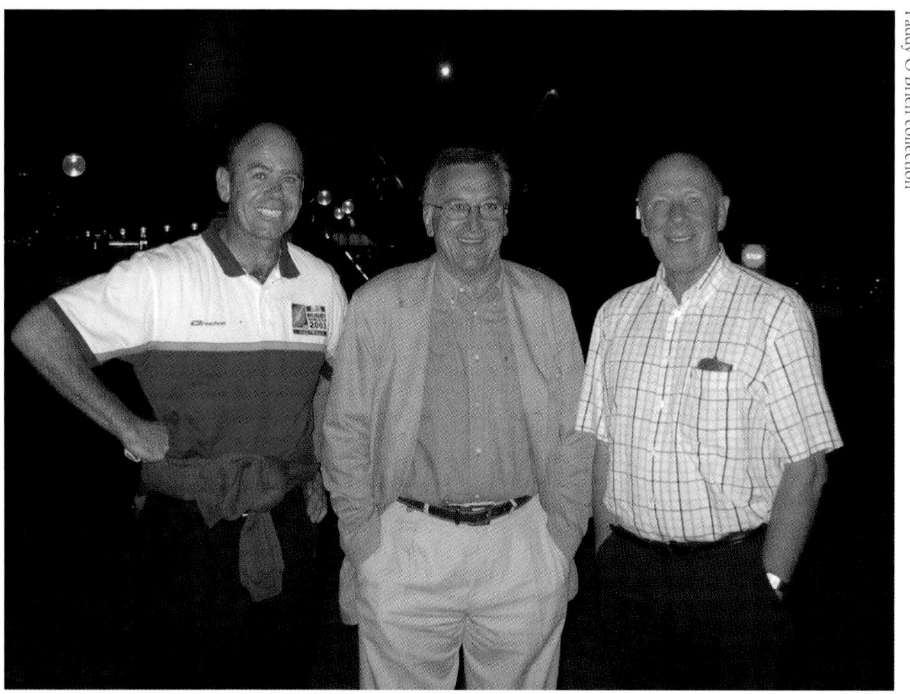

Paddy O'Brien collection

Paddy with World Cup assessors Michel Lamoulie (France) and Steve Hilditch (Ireland).

Paddy O'Brien collection

The sponsor's fine product helps Paddy and Steve Walsh celebrate worthily at a Steinlager awards function in Auckland.

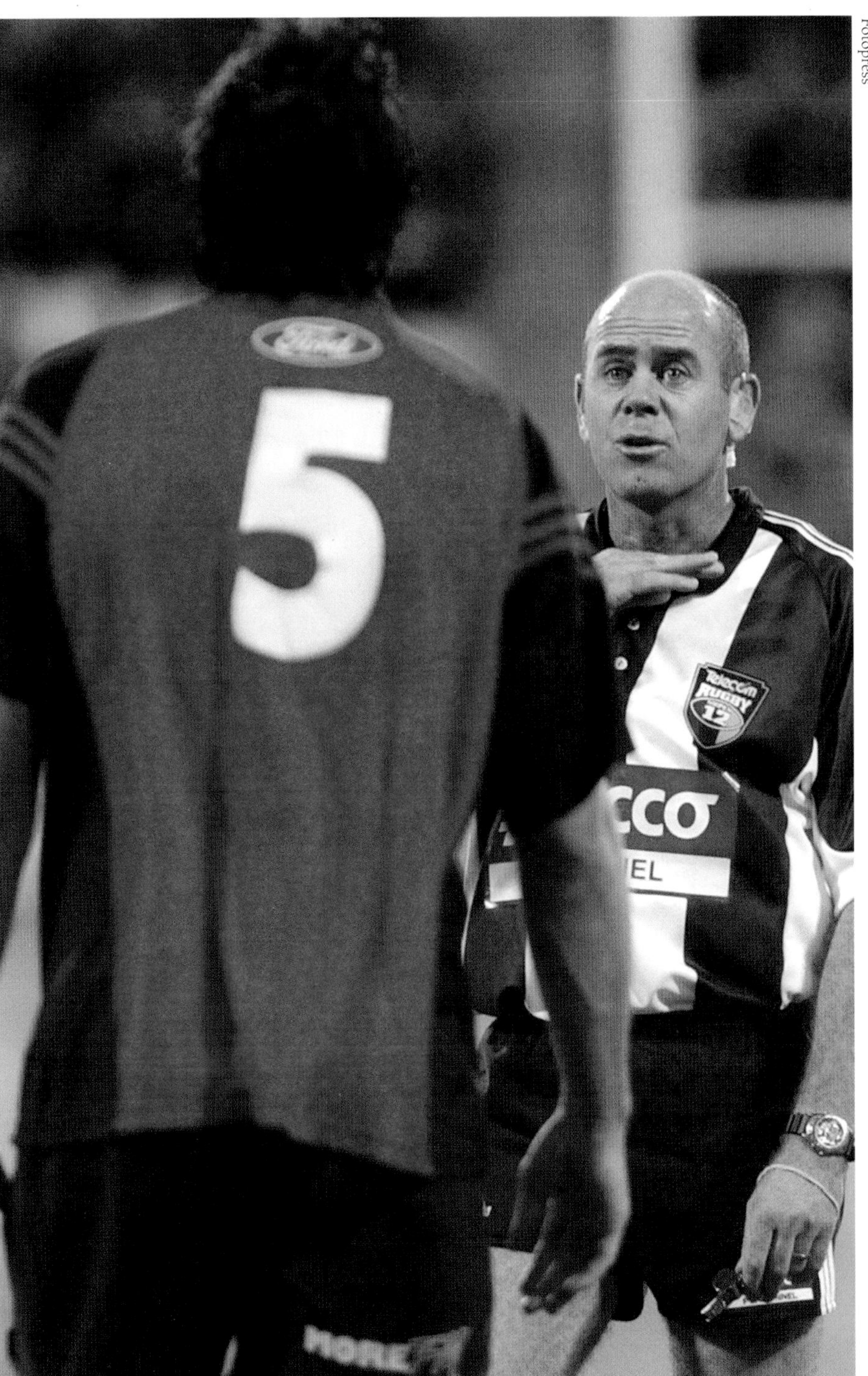

Fotopress

'Keep it down, Norm,' Paddy tells Norm Maxwell during a Crusaders-Hurricanes Super 12 match in Wellington.

Paddy O'Brien collection

Judge Ian Scotney of Australia and prosecutor Paddy O'Brien of New Zealand at the referees' mock court session in Sydney during the 2003 World Cup.

Paddy O'Brien collection

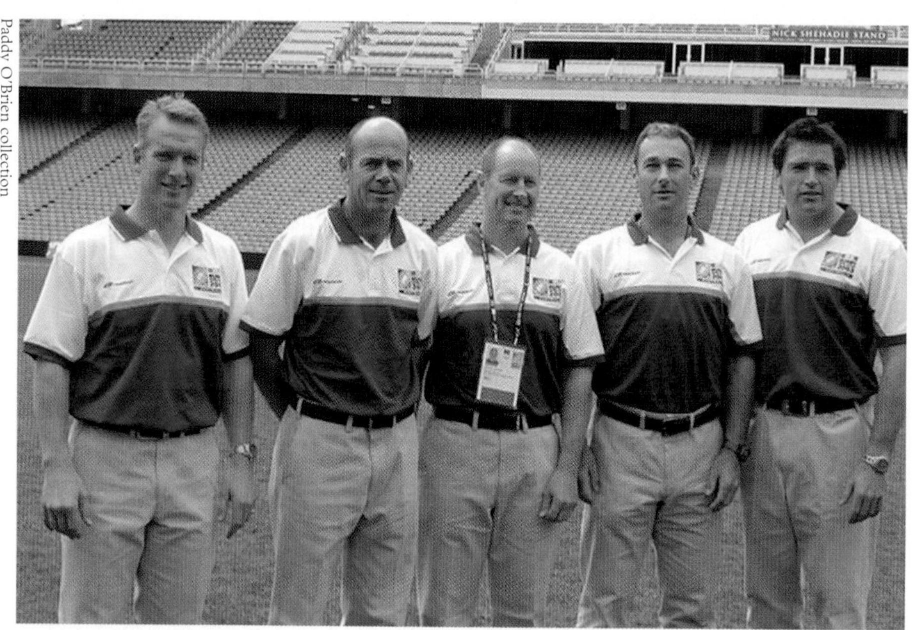

The New Zealand refereeing contingent at the 2003 World Cup. From left: Paul Honiss, Paddy O'Brien, assessor Stu Beissel, Kelvin Deaker, Steve Walsh.

Fotopress

Paddy monitors a scrum during the World Cup semi-final between France and England at Telstra Stadium in Sydney. He became the first New Zealander to referee a World Cup semi-final in five tournaments.

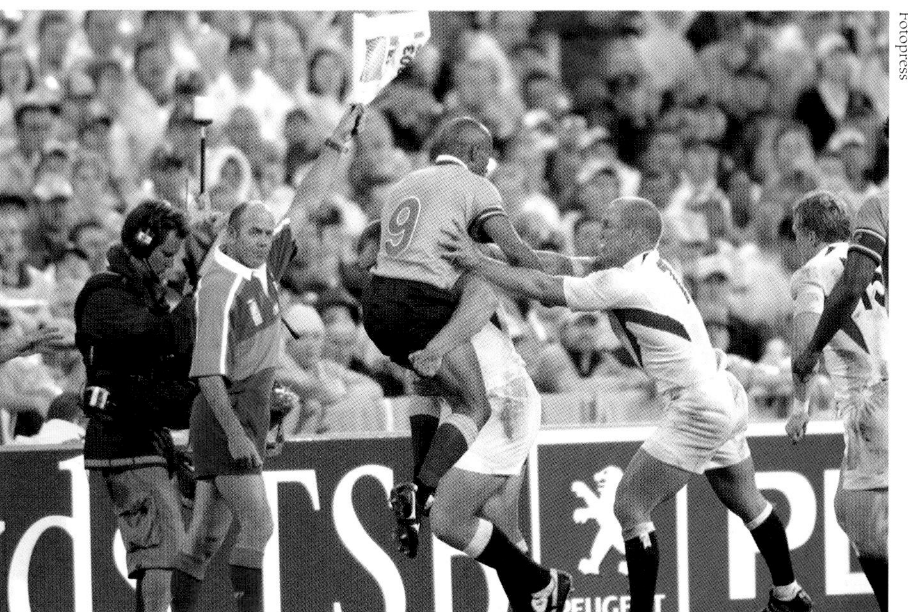

Fotopress

Paddy signals play has gone into touch as George Gregan heads for a dumping in the World Cup final between England and Australia in Sydney.

Fotopress

New Zealand's four World Cup referees in 2003 with their boss Keith Lawrence. From left, Paul Honiss, Paddy, Steve Walsh and Kelvin Deaker.

Fotopress

Paddy with author Bob Howitt at the 2003 Steinlager rugby awards. Bob was a judge while Paddy took away the referees' trophy.

Tuesday 11: Trained in the morning with Steve Walsh and Andy Cole. We did ten 150-metre sprints which were hard work. But it's easier when you have competitive mates like Andy and Steve operating alongside you. In the afternoon, I journeyed with Carolyn and the children to Coogee where we had an apartment booked for the remainder of the tournament. Great to get away from hotel life for a brief while. It was a beautiful day and the kids loved the beach.

Wednesday 12: Had a quiet run in Coogee in the morning before returning to HQ to link with the 'team' for a barbecue at the home of Brian Kinsey, an ex-Australian test referee. Home late with Hamish very tired. Stayed the night at the hotel.

Thursday 13: Returned to Coogee in time to train with Steve Walsh. This time we did 60-metre sprints. I was feeling a little off-colour, hoping it wasn't the flu. Spent the afternoon in the city showing the children the sights.

Friday 14: Still didn't feel 100 per cent, but better than on Thursday. While Carolyn and the children went shopping at East Gardens, I attended the semi-final luncheon in the city. Peter Marshall, Nigel Williams and I represented the referees at a function where Eric Rush was the guest speaker. The second time I've heard him and he was hugely impressive and funny again. We three referees were introduced to the guests and interviewed on stage for 10 minutes.

Saturday 15: D Day for the All Blacks and the Wallabies. Danielle and Hamish were both excited and Hamish used his pocket money to buy an All Black jersey. Fortunately, I was back to full health, having ditched the 24-hour bug. It was an unbelievably hot day, which attracted the family to the beach. But with my big game coming up, I remained in the cool of the apartment. With the conditions ideal, I was confident the All Blacks would run the Wallabies around Telstra Stadium, as they had in July. But it didn't work out that way. The Wallabies upped their performance 200 per cent and never let the All Blacks into the game. We were massively disappointed and felt sorry for the players and John Mitchell. I knew how hard they had worked and to have it collapse like this must have devastated them. I also knew what the reaction would be back home. The O'Briens arrived back at Coogee at midnight and had a great sleep.

Sunday 16: Headed back to HQ to rejoin the referees and spend a quiet day preparing for the game. Arrived at Telstra Stadium around 6 p.m. for the 8 p.m. kick-off, disappointed that the weather had caved in. Heavy, almost torrential, rain was falling. The body language of the French players as they went through the warm-ups told me they were frustrated that the weather was not hot and fine like the previous evening. It was a very special occasion refereeing a World Cup semi-final and I became a tad emotional during the anthems as I thought of all that had gone into the four years since 1999. I thought how proud my Mum and Dad and my other loved ones would be. I know that when I'm in that nostalgic mood, I am ready for a big one. England basically strangled the French to death and ran out a deserved 22–7 winner. I was pleased with my performance in what was a tense, tight, error-ridden game. Had a big night of celebrations.

Monday 17: Summoned to Steve Griffiths' room at 11.45 a.m. to be told I was the reserve referee for the final and that André Watson had won the major appointment. Steve advised that what should have been a five minute selection meeting took two hours and it was a 'very, very tight' decision. Five per cent of me was disappointed as I am a competitive athlete but 95 per cent of me was not. At this tournament I controlled the controllables by refereeing well. Appointments were something I couldn't control. Went to André's room and congratulated him, then went to the team room where all the appointments were announced. Really impressed that Steve Griffiths had spoken personally to André and me before the appointments were made public.

Tuesday 18: Kylie, my eldest daughter, had kindly taken a day off work to introduce Danielle and Hamish to the Wonderland theme park. It allowed Carolyn and me to go into Sydney for a free afternoon. Shared a coffee and a chat with Tim Gresson which was really appreciated.

Wednesday 19: Returned to Coogee for a day in the sun and in the evening attended the final referees court session. Put together my obligatory race call in which I took the mickey out of everyone. Caused plenty of mirth. Overall, an excellent night's entertainment, put together by Ian Scotney, Andrew Cole and Tony Spreadbury. The '21st team' really did have its share of entertainers.

Thursday 20: André Watson, Tony Spreadbury and I attended the finals luncheon in Sydney (with Carolyn and Antionette also invited). In the evening it was back to Telstra Stadium where this time the All Blacks constructed the tries that had eluded them against Australia, securing third place. Difficult for both sets of players to get up after the disappointment of their semi-final losses. The atmosphere at the ground was awful. The IRB really needs to have a serious look at the merits of such a contest taking place. Mind you, third is better than fourth, although I saw enough in the All Blacks' performance against France to convince me they would not have been good enough to have won the Cup. I was convinced England would win the final because of the potency of its tight five.

Friday 21: Spent all day reviewing the tournament and catching up on a swag of e-mails and other correspondence. In the evening the O'Briens attended the *Lion King* show which was wonderful. Danielle and Hamish thoroughly enjoyed it.

Saturday 22: Finals day. Spent a quiet day relaxing before moving out to Telstra Stadium, Paul Honiss and I having had a briefing with André Watson at midday. It was an overcast, drizzly night which was welcomed by England. The atmosphere was fantastic and the final was a classic, the drama enhanced when the game went into extra time. André had an excellent game, although I questioned the last minute scrum penalty that allowed Australia to equalise and take the match into extra time. From my touch judge position, I felt England clearly had the dominant scrum and to pluck a technical penalty out at such a crucial moment was, in my view, wrong. Andy Robinson, the assistant coach of England, was livid, as was Clive Woodward, and I had to verbally ensure Robinson stayed away from André as the teams regrouped for extra time. Jonny Wilkinson nailed the dropped goal in the 99th minute and England was a deserving winner of the 2003 World Cup. I was greatly impressed by the humility with which the England squad handled their new status as world champions and equally impressed at the sportsmanship shown by Eddie Jones, George Gregan and the Australian players after such a gut-wrenching loss. After the medal presentations we returned to the referees' hotel and celebrated what had been a wonderful eight weeks of rugby.

Sunday 23: A quiet day after such a momentous evening. Sunday night attended the IRB awards dinner. An excellent function at which I was lucky enough to sit next to Derek Bevan who was awarded the Distinguished Services to Refereeing award. Derek is all class and will always remain, in my view, the best referee encountered in my career.

Monday 24: Time for everyone to disperse. The Great Adventure that was World Cup 2003 was over. This time I could return home with my head held high.

Have You Heard The One About . . . ?

When your name is Paddy O'Brien it's inevitable you will be mistaken for an Irishman. On more than one occasion when Paddy has been assigned to a match in Dublin, the Irish Rugby Union has fielded calls from people wanting to know why the upcoming international wasn't being controlled by a neutral referee.

Not surprisingly, Paddy's after-dinner speaking routine bears a strong Irish theme. While some of his stories are ever so slightly exaggerated, many are from actual experiences in Ireland where he relates to the delightfully whimsical approach to life.

On his first trip to Dublin, Paddy fell into conversation with an Irish farmer.

'How big's your farm, then?' inquired Paddy.

'More than five hundred acres.'

'You'll be one of the biggest farmers around then?'

'No, I'm only fourteen stone!'

Pat Murray was an Irishman who worked in Invercargill for a couple of years and played fullback for the Marist club. Paddy caught up with him in Dublin following his return home and was shown around his clubrooms.

'Very nice,' said Paddy. 'Do you play all your games here?'

'No, not the away ones!'

Commentator Jim Neilly dines out on the story of the Leinster-Munster match played before a massive audience at Lansdowne Road. The final score was 2–nil to Leinster.

'How on earth could the game be won by that score?' he was asked.

'Well, there was no TMO operating that day and Leinster's solitary try was a highly controversial affair; in fact, Munster appealed to the Irish Rugby Union that it should never have been awarded.

'The Irish committee studied a video of the try and ruled that the player had indeed put his foot into touch before grounding the ball.

'But they also ruled there was nothing wrong with the conversion!'

When a group of New Zealand supporters were in Limerick following the All Blacks many years ago, they decided they would walk from their downtown hotel to Thomond Park. After a short while they stopped to ask a local storekeeper for directions.

'Well,' he said, scratching his head. 'You head straight down here for two blocks, then turn left, then right, then left again, go straight ahead for four blocks, then right, go over the bridge and veer right.

'But if I was you,' he said, 'I wouldn't be starting from here!'

While Paddy, who has been described as a third generation Irishman living in New Zealand, has a close affinity with Ireland, his heart is very much in Southland where he's lived for all of his 44 years.

You can take the boy out of Southland but you can never take Southland out of the boy. It's a line Paddy uses regularly.

He's enormously proud of the city where he lives and although Invercargill is the butt of many jokes about its climate, Paddy retaliates by assuring sceptics that the city has sporting facilities second to none in New Zealand. Thanks to the financial support of the Invercargill Licensing Trust, Invercargill hosts Davis Cup tennis matches, netball and badminton tests and Super 12 rugby encounters.

A bold initiative to offer free education to students attending the Southland Institute of Technology has helped turn around the economy of the city quite dramatically. A decade ago, Invercargill looked to be doomed but now it is prosperous again, real estate prices are soaring and there's a feel-good atmosphere in evidence.

Paddy flourishes in the deep south where he's surrounded by his kind of down-to-earth, honest people. Anyone who comes to Southland with thoughts of grandeur, he says, is in for a shock. The place is too small for that.

While he might live in a comparatively remote part of New Zealand, thanks to the media and a rugby-mad population Paddy maintains a high profile. While he's learnt to live with that, sometimes he's envious of Australian test referee Scott Young who lives in Brisbane and goes about his business totally unrecognised. He's told Paddy that he could sprint naked down the main street and no one would have the foggiest who he was.

How different in New Zealand where every NPC match, every Super 12 encounter, every international is beamed live into hundreds of thousands of New Zealand homes. Paddy O'Brien is as well known as Justin Marshall or Andrew Mehrtens or Christian Cullen.

Because of Paddy's placid nature, he learnt at an early age not to concern himself with what was written or said about him, believing it was important people expressed their views. Some of the more acerbic critics of referees are coaches. Colin Hawke and Paddy used to joke that the last resort of coaches, before they disappeared over the cliff, was to have a crack at a referee.

While Paddy does have some sympathy with coaches, acknowledging that in an extremely tight game one crucial decision could possibly swing the outcome, he suggests that losing coaches would be better advised to focus on their team's shortcomings. Paddy proudly declares that as a referee he has never missed a tackle, knocked on, dropped a pass or sliced a kick outside the uprights. So to apportion blame to a referee when a team loses is unfair. The referee's decisions might be a factor, he concedes, but they are never the sole reason why a team hasn't emerged triumphant.

When it comes to the media, Paddy believes a more open stance should be taken by those involved in the game. He thinks they spend too much time defending the indefensible. If Paddy O'Brien misses an important knock-on and it's obvious, then admit it. Like players and coaches, referees make mistakes too. They are only human.

Some of the player interviews he hears make him cringe, they are so politically correct. If the players and the coaches told it the way it was, they would gain far more credibility. He finds Andrew Mehrtens and Anton Oliver, who express themselves honestly, humorously and from the heart, so refreshing.

He gets annoyed at times when his bosses try to censor what he can and cannot say to the media. Paddy is always available and is always prepared to discuss matters openly. It's a two-way thing and he's developed strong relationships with people like Murray Deaker, Wynne Gray of the *New Zealand Herald* and John Matheson, formerly of *NZ Rugby World*, through being up front.

Paddy does get annoyed with reporters who, with scant knowledge of the laws, launch attacks on referees, sensationalising events unnecessarily. However, he does consider that New Zealand is generally well served by its leading television commentators and its most experienced journalists.

He was always a fan of Keith Quinn and John McBeth but since Sky's takeover of the rugby screening rights (the 2003 World Cup excepted) they have been pushed into the background. The front-runners now are Grant Nisbett and Tony Johnson, two of the nicest guys around. Paddy rates their standard of commentary the best by far among the Tri-Nations countries.

A danger, in Paddy's view, is TV decision makers concluding that because an individual has been a good player he will automatically become an expert comments person. John Drake, Grant Fox and Ian Smith (who excelled in cricket, not rugby but has been a revelation as a sideline rugby person) have successfully made the transition but there have been several who haven't.

The referees' arch critic is Murray Mexted. He's someone Paddy could never get angry with because he enjoys his company so much and he is such an enthusiastic student of the game, but Mexted has an infuriating tendency on camera to criticise referees who are accurately ruling according to the law book. Mexted renders a unique interpretation of some of the game's laws, to support his own image of events.

Paddy is not a fan of tabloid type sensationalism. It saddened him that during 2003 a prominent New Zealand sportsman featured big in a Sunday newspaper because his uncle was in court. 'If my uncle ended up in court, I'd be horrified if I rated a mention,' he argues. He regards such journalism as dishonest.

As for talkback, Paddy listens to it intermittently but without ever taking it too seriously. He regards it as a medium for the public to vent their frustrations. It's important to remember, he says, that what you're hearing is only one person's opinion. If you listen too long you'll get hung up. He enjoys the theatre of it all.

He's convinced Brendan Telfer deliberately takes stances to provoke callers and enjoys Martin Devlin's entertaining opinions on the breakfast show. The only Radio Sport presenter who's upset him is Bryan Waddle, the voice of cricket. Paddy enjoys his commentaries when he's dealing with his favourite sport of cricket but finds that if his favourite Hurricanes team gets beaten he invariably lays the blame on the referee.

Paddy believes the referees should use Radio Sport to get their message across. Why not give the referees' point of view? he asks. Instead of leaving listeners guessing about happenings in the previous day's big match, get the referee on to explain it all. He doesn't want referees to take centre stage, but he does emphasise that they do have personalities and should be free to express their views.

Whenever he features as a guest speaker, he finds members of the audience come up afterwards and make comments like, 'I never realised referees had a sense of humour' or 'I've changed my mind about you — you are human.'

Paddy's award for the funniest rugby commentator he knows goes to Southland's Lee Piper, who, as part of the Scream Team, provided a live but thoroughly irreverent commentary on the Gore-based Hokonui Gold radio station. Piper is now station manager at Newstalk ZB. He provided an outrageously biased commentary, so entertaining that if Paddy happened to be at home he'd turn the television sound down to listen. Such was Piper's wit that Paddy often finished up with tears rolling down his cheeks.

The overseas correspondent who regularly stirs New Zealanders up is Stephen Jones who writes for the London *Sunday Times* and occasionally as a special correspondent for the *New Zealand Herald*. Having met him, Paddy realises that he writes to deliberately wind the New Zealand public up, which he does most effectively. How dare anyone criticise our glorious Super 12 competition?

Readers should always remember it is only one person's opinion. That's Paddy's sage advice now. As he says, try telling him that four years ago — Colin Hawke commented in the wake of the Toulouse Train Smash that there was no room on Paddy's back for any more scars! These days Paddy takes notice only if the criticism is from someone he respects.

Paddy gets upset when he sees a former All Black, in particular, writing columns and criticising the sport that has given them so much. He says rugby owes him nothing and his challenge over the next four years is to be able to slide gracefully into retirement, saying he in turn owes rugby nothing.

Paddy believes that many New Zealanders are still struggling to come to grips with the fact that rugby is professional. Callers to radio say how come the All Blacks, now that they're professional and rich, still lose to Australia? Well, one obvious answer is that the Wallabies are professional also. As for the 'rich' bit, well, try drawing a comparison with Michael Campbell. If he finishes fourth in a major tournament, he'll take home for one week's effort more than an All Black will earn in a year.

Paddy is pleased he made it to the top in the amateur days. Now he referees for fun and the fact he's paid, he regards as a huge bonus.

He receives many offers from members of the public to 'carry your bags' on his next overseas trip. What the public don't realise is how exhausting world travel can be and that the life of a professional referee is not always as appealing as it might appear to be. On average, he spends 180 days a year on referee duties. Most of these days are spent on aircraft or in foreign hotels.

If it sounds glamorous, he says there is no greater feeling than kicking back in his own home, with his feet on the furniture and spaghetti on toast for lunch and a mattress his body understands to sleep on. Not that Paddy wants his book to portray the fact he's complaining about his job. He appreciates that there are more than 4000 other referees in New Zealand who would gladly swap their positions with him. He considers himself extremely lucky to have received the opportunities that have come his way and sometimes wonders just how it all came about.

What makes a good referee? Aside from the obvious attributes of being physically fit, energetic, enthusiastic and knowing the rule book, Paddy says there is no substitute for experience. At the top level it's about more than the ability to simply blow a game. It's about credibility, about earning the respect of the players and, like everything else in life, if commonsense is applied one will never go far wrong. Paddy says there are a lot theories about refereeing but nothing he's ever read mentions the word 'commonsense'.

A referee like Steve Walsh has an enormous advantage over many others because he took up refereeing in his mid-twenties. Another aspiring referee is Jonathon White who at 21 had the maturity of a 30-year-old. Like Walsh, he's an exciting talent and Paddy believes he should be encouraged and given important appointments. He'll receive knockbacks but because he is mentally tough he'll survive and by the time he's 26 he'll be a seasoned campaigner.

In Paddy's world, it's people who have always mattered most — like his Mum and Dad. His Dad worked the extra hours to ensure there was always food on the table for the ever-increasing family. His Mum was the rock of the house, someone who never passed judgment and never took sides.

Now and again in life, most people encounter someone who carries a special aura with them. Paddy regards his Mum as such a person. She has a great presence about her and an inner happiness. She radiates peace. Saint Val seems an entirely appropriate title.

Paddy's wife Carolyn has been totally supportive. Whenever he is copping verbals on television or the radio, she either turns it off or offers words of encouragement. Life has not always been easy for them, with Paddy overseas on refereeing assignments for weeks at a time but, like her mother, Carolyn has always just got on with life and made things happen. Her parents Norma and Lloyd Wyeth have also been a tower of support, especially after rugby turned professional. Carolyn and Paddy's two children Danielle, 12, and Hamish, 9, are proud of their Dad and hugely understanding of the time he's had to spend away from home. Both children are heavily involved in sport themselves and receive strong encouragement from their parents.

It is said you only need a handful of really close friends. Besides Carolyn, Paddy has three people he terms great mates with whom he would share anything.

Two of them are former police colleagues, Dave Evans and Brian Hewett. Brian, or Brains as he is popularly known, is a sports nutter who has similar interests to Paddy. A rugby, racing and beer man, he loves nothing better than a good argument on a Friday night at the Police Club and he certainly lets Paddy know if he thinks he's had a poor game or made a rough call. Conversely, if someone else starts giving Paddy a hard time, they will cop it from Brains. An extremely loyal individual, he headed the police investigation into the Maureen McKinnel homicide at Arrowtown that produced an arrest after 14 years.

Dave Evans was best man at Paddy and Carolyn's wedding. Married to Sue, another police officer, he rates as the best policeman Paddy ever worked alongside. Highly intelligent with an eye for detail and a sharp brain, he broke down many an offender in the interview room.

Dave enjoys questioning authority, particularly when it involves politically correct nonsense. Paddy still laughs when he recalls the time Dave was recruited as a hostage negotiator for the Armed Offenders Squad and claimed he should be paid a full call-out allowance. The department compromised and said they would pay half the allowance. Dave's response was to supply them with half his phone number.

Don and Isobel Radka are the O'Briens' neighbours, sharing a driveway with them. To reach the O'Briens a car must pass their lounge window and Don is out, quick as a flash, if it's not one he recognises. The lawns are always mowed and the garden up to date whenever Paddy returns home from his latest trip while Isobel is like a second mother to Hamish and Danielle who wander in and out of the Radka house as they do their own.

After two World Cups, 32 tests (the most by a New Zealand referee) and 196 first-class games (also a record for a New Zealander), when is Paddy going to retire? It's a question he gets asked often.

The best answer he can give at the moment is that he is contracted to the NZRU through till December 2005 and hopes to referee at the 2007 Rugby World Cup. After that, he plans to retire.

He is also realistic and has enormous confidence in individuals like Tom Doocey and Bob Francis who, he knows, will whisper in his ear if they believe he is trying to stretch out too far.

While he possesses speed (he is still the quickest referee on the international panel), he will need to work on his aerobic fitness if the body is to stand up for another four years. He believes he will know the day his body and mind realise enough is enough. The passion is still there and he knows he is a far better referee than he was four years ago. He is also a great believer that you should only step aside when there is someone better waiting to take your place.

He sees Lyndon Bray, Gary Wise, Bryce Lawrence and a couple of up-and-comers Chris Pollock and Jonathan White as the referees most likely to break into the test ranks over the next four years. If they do, they are mistaken if they think that, starting now at 44, Paddy is going to step aside and let them win by default. He's ready for the challenge.

Dream Teams

It is conventional for players and coaches who have biographies published to incorporate a chapter highlighting the finest players they have encountered in their careers. The two don't always overlap, for players often perceive talented team-mates and opponents differently from coaches.

It's rare for referees to identify their standout players but Paddy considers that being the man in the middle at more than 200 first-class fixtures over 15 seasons, and touch judge on another 100 occasions, has presented him with a unique opportunity to assess both the talents and attitudes of most of the game's leading performers.

Paddy perceives players from a different perspective and felt it would be a worthwhile exercise to choose two teams, one selected purely on playing ability, the other chosen from individuals he most enjoyed refereeing.

So he's come up with a DREAM TEAM of obvious achievers and a REFEREE'S team of what he describes as 'good buggers', which doesn't mean to say those in the Dream Team aren't 'good buggers'. But the 'good buggers' Paddy enjoyed working with weren't necessarily the greatest players in their respective positions.

So here, in Paddy's own words, are the teams:

THE DREAM TEAM

FULLBACK

When Christian Cullen was at his best, around 1998 and 1999, there was no better fullback in world rugby. He had everything and was one of a small group of players with the ability to glide when he ran, allowing him to leave opponents — and referees! — in his wake whilst giving the impression he wasn't going flat out. His record of 46 tries from 58 internationals speaks for itself.

WINGERS

It never ceases to amaze me how swift people were to criticise Jonah Lomu when he was sometimes bumbling around on defence or occasionally having trouble with his hands. Jonah was the face of rugby at two World Cups and scored tries no other player in the entire history of the game was capable of. Whilst I never got close to him personally, I will never forget watching him signing autographs some three hours after New Zealand had won the Sevens World Cup at Mar del Plata in Argentina. All the officials and his team-mates were showered and enjoying celebratory drinks and here was Jonah still in the middle surrounded by hundreds of kids willingly signing away. He was a phenomenon, nothing less.

On the other wing I would install a fit Rupeni Caucaunibuca, another freak. Some of the tries he scored in NPC and Super 12 matches in 2002 and 2003 bordered on the unbelievable. Like Cullen, he is deceptively swift, with amazing acceleration and the ability to step defenders at speed. I just hope he continues to stay focused and we see a lot more of his talents.

CENTRE

The standout player wearing the No. 13 jersey on the world scene in recent seasons has been Brian O'Driscoll of Ireland. I thought he was simply superb for the British Lions against Australia in 2001 and, along with Keith Wood, helped transform Ireland from a mediocre team into an extremely competitive one.

SECOND FIVE

Several players of exceptional talent have featured in this position during my refereeing career, not the least of whom would be the Frenchman Philippe Sella who made 100 test appearances, an amazing achievement. But my selection would be Wallaby Jason Little. Besides being enormously talented, and never more lethal than when operating in tandem with his great mate Tim Horan, he was a fantastic bloke who always found time to thank the referee after the match. A genuine, down-to-earth individual.

FIRST FIVE

Now while I'm a huge fan of Carlos Spencer and Andrew Mehrtens, I have to select Jonny Wilkinson, even before he popped over the winning dropped goal in the 2003 World Cup final. He is the complete footballer. He kicks with precision, both in general play and for goal, is a fearless tackler and a dangerous runner with the ball. He's also a hell of a nice guy. At times I feel for individuals like Wilkinson and other English stars whose image is unfortunately driven by their own pompous media and the wannabes that drink in the members bars at Twickenham.

HALFBACK

After refereeing nearly 200 first-class fixtures, I can declare there are few poor halfbacks. The very nature of the position calls for brave, talented and courageous individuals and the game abounds in players with these qualities, guys like Joost van der Westhuizen, Graeme Bachop, Matt Dawson, Rob Howley, Byron Kelleher and Justin Marshall. However, the player I rate No. 1 is Australian captain George Gregan. He is a deceptive runner with a quick pair of hands, a huge ticker and a fast-moving mouth. George has always been super competitive but I like that in a player. He is my vice-captain.

NUMBER EIGHT

I always rated Gary Teichmann from South Africa and Wallaby Toutai Kefu as two of the real hard men of rugby, but no one, in my view, comes close to Zinzan Brooke in the position. One of the most skilful footballers I have ever seen, Zinny's only concern was winning. There has surely never been a more competitive rugby player. He hated losing. Whilst much has been written about Zinny and me crossing swords in the 1998 NPC semi-final, I had the utmost respect for him as a player and a person, and I think we both now see the funny side of that particular game.

FLANKERS

Openside: This is the hardest position for which to select one individual because, in my time, there was an absolute truckload of talent available from all over the world. Michael Jones was obviously the standout in the late 1980s and early 1990s but when I refereed him, he was mostly operating as a No. 6. Quality specialist opensiders during my time included George Smith and Phil Waugh (Australia), Rassie Erasmus and Joe van Niekerk (South Africa), Olivier Magne (France), Neil Back (England) and Richard McCaw and Marty Holah (New Zealand). But the player I would want in my dream team is Josh Kronfeld. He was interesting to referee because he was his own biggest critic. If he thought you as a referee had got it wrong, his body language was worth the price of admission. He was relentless as a footballer and a master at securing turnover ball for his team. No one gave more for 80 minutes than Josh.

Blindside: Although I rate highly South Africa's World Cup winning captain Francois Pienaar and a fit Owen Finegan, the one who stands out above all others is England's Lawrence Dallaglio. Perhaps a fraction past his best at the 2003 World Cup but still hugely competitive and a key member of the successful England team. I would always want him playing for my team rather than against it.

LOCKS

The easiest selections of the lot — Martin Johnson and John Eales. Johnson has become the Colin Meads of the modern game, completely dominating opponents (and trying to do the same with referees!). He is, like Zinny, another with a must-win attitude. Conversely, Eales, a rugby rarity who combined leadership with lineout prowess, ball skills, deadly tackling and goalkicking ability, would actually qualify for selection in both my teams. He rivals Todd Blackadder as my all-time favourite player to referee. Eales was a freak. His only fault was that he was not born a Kiwi!

PROPS

All Black Olo Brown and Springbok Os du Randt were the two strongest props I refereed. Actually, a more accurate description may be that they were the two props with the best technique. Given that the scrum is the most challenging area of rugby for referees, I want them both in my team. Next in line would be the Frenchman Jean-Jacques Crenca.

HOOKER

Another position offering a rich selection of talent, players like Keith Wood (Ireland), Phil Kearns (Australia), Anton Oliver (New Zealand), Raphael Ibanez (France) and James Dalton (South Africa), but none of them came close to matching Sean Fitzpatrick. He was an incredible guy to referee. There is a popular perception that Sean refereed the referees, but I can assure you that was not the case. He was an intelligent player who established where the line in the sand was, and then went and stood on it for the rest of the game. He was never in front of it, never behind, always on it. Definitely the captain of my team.

RESERVES

Backs: Jeff Wilson (New Zealand), unlucky not to be in the starting line-up, would cover wing and fullback, Brian Lima (Samoa), the most potent tackler at the 2003 World Cup whose career dates back to the 1991 World Cup, could fill in anywhere from second-five to wing, and Joost van der Westhuizen (South Africa) would be the ideal back-up to Gregan at halfback. Of the forwards on the bench, three would be All Blacks, flanker Richie McCaw, lock Chris Jack and hooker Anton Oliver with Frenchman Jean-Jacques Crenca the standby prop.

COACH

The Dream Team would be prepared jointly by Graham Henry and Laurie Mains, the two most astute coaches I encountered. What's more, after the final whistle I would get an honest feedback on my performance. Graham, with that wry grin, would observe that, 'We all have good days and bad days', without telling me which one he considered I'd just had, while Laurie would telephone me the next morning and shoot straight from the hip. Other coaches would tell everyone else what they thought, but never me. Graham and Laurie would share a beer with you after the match, which is important. On standby, in case either suddenly took up an overseas appointment, would be Ian McIntosh. He's a unique character who is passionate about winning and losing. I would need to keep out of his firing line for an hour after the game. But then he would undergo a personality change and be thoroughly pleasant to deal with. Graham Henry and Ian McIntosh would be great at media conferences, because they played the media better than any other coaches I've known.

MANAGER

Des Smith of the Highlanders was the most competent manager, by a country mile, of all those I dealt with in my career. His team could be fuming over a referee's decision which they probably believed cost them a victory, yet Des would always make a point of coming into the referees' room to thank the man who'd controlled the game. A thorough gentleman, he was greatly respected among all those involved in rugby. He would, in my opinion, be an excellent manager of any team he was given control of.

THE REFEREE'S TEAM

This team is chosen from players I really enjoyed refereeing, guys who were personalities who, at the appropriate moment, would have a yarn. And, when the whistle blew for full time, they left what had happened on the pitch right out there where it belonged.

FULLBACK

Chris Latham of the Queensland Reds and Australia gets the vote. A real free spirit who usually operated with his socks down, he was a super talent. Either never got a fair crack at test level or struggled to make the step up, but at Super 12 level and below he was sensational, and a real good bloke with it.

WINGERS

Jeff 'Goldie' Wilson was always good for a chat during the game, but as I have named him as a reserve in the Dream Team, I have gone for Inga Tuigamala (New Zealand and Samoa) and Brendan Laney (Scotland). Inga spent every minute of every game I refereed with him involved with a grin on his face. A real solid, humble guy. Rugby would be less of a challenge for referees if there were a lot more Ingas about. Brendan Laney likewise. Not the swiftest of backs but full of bubble and fun. Another who never uttered a bad word about referees or opponents. A hugely entertaining fellow to share a beer with after the game, and he always brought extra cigarettes along!

CENTRE

Tana Umaga has always been the ultimate competitor but neither his ego nor his status have prevented him acknowledging referees. Considering I once showed him the red card, that's really saying something. I can think of a lot of players who have harboured resentments towards referees, but not Tana. He's a really humble bloke who may not have always agreed with referees' decisions but has always accepted them. A class player. I would love to invite him home for a barbecue.

SECOND FIVE

Matt Cooper, a prolific point scorer for Waikato who made just eight test appearances, was one of those players who always had something nice to say both during and after matches. The ultimate gentleman, whether he thought he was hard done by with a refereeing decision or not. The sort of player who inspired you to continue refereeing even after a bad day at the office.

FIRST FIVE

Along with halfbacks, first fives usually have a lot to say and most of them are true characters. Carlos Spencer has matured as a player and a person in the past few seasons. Early on, he was bloody hard going for referees, but now he is full of bubble and energy. Andrew Mehrtens, who is possessed of a wicked sense of humour, always keeps referees honest. Not only does he challenge you frequently, but he's nearly always right! Seems more familiar with the law book than most referees. Of them all, however, I'll plump for Ian Foster, who made a record number of appearances for Waikato. He could be passionate, serious, funny and competitive all in one afternoon. He has carried those traits through into coaching and is refreshingly honest to deal with.

HALFBACK

Matt Dawson, one of the stars of England's 2003 World Cup triumph, has always been fun to work with on the field and so has Jason Spice of Wellington and the Hurricanes who always found humour in the game. While both are extremely competitive, they knew where the line in the sand was and never crossed it. On the short list, and I'm allowed a little Southland bias, is Jimmy Cowan, the New Zealand Colt. He's ultra competitive, possesses a really dry sense of humour and manages to retain a deadpan face after uttering witty or sarcastic comments. An All Black waiting to happen, he will bring plenty to whichever team he is selected for. Dawson gets my vote.

NUMBER EIGHT

One of the easier ones to select. Stunningly successful in 2003 as captain of the Blues and Auckland, Xavier Rush is one of the unsung heroes of New Zealand rugby. He's as good a provincial captain as I have encountered in my career. He always showed respect for me as a referee and was a catalyst in helping me lose the 'I hate Auckland' tag.

FLANKERS

Players wearing No. 6 and No. 7 on their back are always in the firing line of referees through the very nature or their positions. They are probably the victims of more refereeing injustices than those in any other positions. All Black Richie McCaw is a hell of a nice guy to referee and much the same can be said for former All Black captain Taine Randell, Highlanders leader Kelvin Middleton, Wallaby George Smith and former Springbok Rassie Erasmus. But the two I'd select are Springbok Corne Krige and All Black Marty Holah. Krige because he is tough and uncompromising but had the balls to apologise for his team's wrongdoings in the bitter encounter against England at Twickenham in 2002. Holah accepts the referee's decisions as he goes about his business. He's refreshing because he simply concentrates on playing his game. In contrast, I can think of some players who seem to think it's their personal duty to needle the referee.

LOCKS

John Eales would be one of the first selected, but he's already in my Dream Team. The first choice is easy: Todd Blackadder. He is simply the nicest man to have played the game in my era. What you see with Toddy is what you get. I never once heard him blame the referee for a loss and yet I am sure there were occasions when such a comment would have been justified. He would simply say, 'If we'd been good enough, we would have won'. He's obviously the captain of my team, but I won't allow him to do the media interviews. To partner him would be another red and black trooper Norm Maxwell. He's ultra-competitive and gives away some stupid penalties but always accepts your rulings. He has a droll sense of humour. Once, when Auckland prop Paul Thomson, who twitches his head alot, was down being treated for a neck injury, Maxwell inquired of his well-being. I assured Norm he'd be okay. 'Thank goodness,' he said. 'I thought his head was going to fall off!' Norm would always come and join you for a beer at the aftermatch, regardless of the outcome.

PROPS

It's difficult to find props who appreciate referees as they have their own club, and referees are most definitely not part of it. However, Jason Leonard, who has racked up an amazing 118 test appearances, was always a pleasure to deal with. You always felt Leonard was trying to make your job easier. If you were having a hard day at the office, a whisper in his ear and he would work with you in trying to remedy the problem. All Blacks Carl Hoeft and Kees Meeuws were another pair who never caused referees problems, and the same could be said for the 2003 World Cup pair, Greg Somerville and Dave Hewett. Others in the 'good bloke' category are Aussies Glenn Panoho, Bill Young and Ben Darwin. But I'd go for former Wallaby Richard Harry who was always happy to work with the referee, much as Leonard did.

HOOKER

Anton Oliver was fantastic to work with and I was disappointed when he and coach Laurie Mains had their much publicised fall-out, as I admired them both. Anton always had something worthwhile to say when he met you. As a player, he was extremely physical but never dirty. Mark Hammett was another extremely competitive 'gentleman', the same as James Dalton of South Africa. However, the hooker for my 'good buggers' team is Frenchman Raphael Ibanez. This English speaker was an important man to have on your side if you were having problems controlling his team. He was a wonderfully handy player in his own right.

RESERVES

Glen Osborne has to be there, because he's the butt of so many jokes, and no team would be complete without Andrew Mehrtens, who's a delight when he's not quoting the rule book at you. The spare halfback would be Jimmy Cowan. Forwards on the bench would be Wallabies George Smith and Justin Harrison — who caused me great embarrassment when he engaged me in a full body embrace at the final whistle of the Lions series in 2001 — along with All Black front rowers Carl Hoeft and Mark Hammett.

COACHES

This team would be prepared by Steve Hansen and John Boe, who would work with the referees. Steve taught me more about forward play, particularly scrummaging, than any other coach. Importantly, he was always honest in his conversations and was prepared to listen to a referee's perspective. John Boe has built an outstanding record as a coach. I have never worked out who he upset at the NZRU because he has never achieved the recognition he deserves. He is a mild-mannered man with a real passion for the game, a passion he has successfully passed on to the Samoan team he coached at the 2003 World Cup.

MANAGER

Who better than Eric Rush? There's no better after-dinner speaker on the circuit and the 'good buggers' will be demanding entertainment from their boss. And anything the team needs, you can be sure Rushy will know where to find it.

REFEREES

André Watson would normally be in charge but for this cherished encounter I would have the whistle — hey, this is my moment in the spotlight — and I would ask Colin Hawke of New Zealand and Chris White of England to run touch, as I could rely on them totally. Steve Walsh would be my No. 4, which would ensure we had a great night out afterwards, and Derek Bevan could monitor the substitutions for one of the teams, so humour would always be present. Jonathon White could monitor the subs bench for the good guys. Glenn Wahlstrom would be my TMO, ensuring that if any tight calls had to be made I would receive accurate and professional feedback. André Watson would be our bus driver because we can't have a Dream Team game without the man who's refereed the two best games of rugby I have seen, the 39-35 thriller between New Zealand and Australia in 2000 and the World Cup final in 2003. André and I often joke we are the world's two worst touch judges, so I wouldn't risk him in that role.

ASSESSORS

Bob Francis, the mayor of Masterton these days and my early mentor, would assess the game, taking in the big picture when making his judgment. His assistants would be Bob Yeman (Wales), Steve Hilditch (Ireland) and Frans Muller (South Africa). The stats would be compiled by Tom Doocey. You know that when he and Bob Francis are operating together, you will get the perfect balance between letter of the law and spirit of the game. Both Tom and Bob have been the backbone of New Zealand refereeing throughout my career and I couldn't have asked for better. They encouraged and cajoled me at appropriate times but didn't hesitate to offer constructive criticism when it was deserved. Through it all, they remained damned good mates. They're going to be hellishly hard to replace when they finally decide to quit. If this fictional match were to be staged overseas, then I would want Steve Hilditch, Jim Irvine, Bob Yeman, Frans Muller, Colin High, Doug Kerr and Michelle Lamolie to be involved, but if I had to narrow it to one assessor I'd choose Jim Irvine of Scotland, a magnificently humble man.

EXTRAS

Again, if the match was played overseas, I'd get Chris White and André Watson involved, Chris because he's Mr Reliable and André because we've had such a great journey together. And the TMO would be Australia's Andrew Cole, who is Mr Reliable of world rugby.

The Last Word

I met Paddy for the first time at the Hong Kong sevens in 1996. He was at the beginning of his international career, having controlled his first test just prior.

Also, he had refereed the Super 10 final in Johannesburg, so he already had a reputation as a top-class referee. I, on the other hand, was on my first ever overseas duty as a referee.

We were both hungry and keen to make our mark in international rugby. We 'clicked' from the word go and saw things in a similar way. As Paddy was not shy to speak his mind, nor I, we were soon identified as two 'stirrers'. That was never our intention, but the label stuck, so much so that we were eventually referred to as 'The Terrible Twins'.

It was during the Hong Kong tournament in '96 that we made a deal. We decided that we were going to go for the top. As young and eager referees, we weren't scared to aim for the stars, so we stated our goals for the medium term. These were that both of us should be at the 1999 World Cup and that we should both at least referee one of the finals. We also said that we did not want to be followers but pacesetters and that we would do so at Super 12 and international level.

We both got to the World Cup in 1999 and were both on the park during the final and Paddy, by that time, was the pacesetter in the Super 12, without any doubt.

We then set new goals for 2003 and again both of us were involved in the final play-offs. Paddy was simply brilliant throughout the 2003 World Cup.

Paddy's career is well covered in this book, but people out there need to know what Paddy the person is like. We have become tremendously close over the past eight years, simply because we shared the highs and lows with each other. We were brutally honest with each other and this, to me, is the single most important reason that we have survived at this level for such a considerable time.

Paddy is a very sensitive person. He hides it well, but he 'bleeds' easily. Only his wife Carolyn and his close friends will know this. But despite his sensitivity he does not want to be bullshitted, as he is honest to the core, and he expects people to be honest with him.

In this, perhaps, lies one weakness, as people have not always been honest to Paddy. They chose to be nice rather than honest and therein lies the reason that Paddy has been led astray on one or two occasions in his career. We have spent hours consoling each other, but man, out of this and our idea-swapping rose two referees that were noticed all over the world.

Paddy is like a rubber ball. He has bounced back from disappointments in his career on more than one occasion, but none so telling as at the World Cup in 1999. He had an unfortunate game, whereby certain mistakes were made by the team of three. Not all the mistakes were of his own doing, yet he had to carry the can and did exactly that.

Paddy has confidence in abundance, so much so that I had to suck some off him at times. He does not doubt his own ability, although perhaps he doubts the system, but that is another subject.

Paddy is an extrovert so mixes easily. He has friends all over the world, of which his biggest international fan without any doubt is me. I would simply not have achieved all that I did without the sincere support, advice and kicks in the butt that Paddy gave in abundance. For this, I am in debt to one Paddy O'Brien and look forward to repaying him for the rest of my life.

As we traditionally say in South Africa, Paddy is a 'huuuuuge' man, not only as a referee, for there he is a legend, but as a person.

God bless, Paddilack.

André Watson, South Africa

Paddy's Appointments

1988

1 Southland v Otago, Rugby Park, Invercargill, 27 June

2 Southland v Counties, Rugby Park, Invercargill, 27 September

1989

3 West Coast v Wanganui, Rugby Park, Greymouth, 26 August Div 2

4 Southland v North Harbour, Rugby Park, Invercargill, 13 September

5 South Canterbury v Nelson Bays, Fraser Park, Timaru, 16 September Div 2

1990

6 North Otago v Southland, Centennial Park, Oamaru, 26 May

7 Hanan Shield XV v Otago, Centennial Park, Oamaru, 15 July

8 Nelson Bays v West Coast, Trafalgar Park, Nelson, 14 August Div 3

9 South Canterbury v Horowhenua, Fraser Park, Timaru, 15 September Div 3

10 South Canterbury v Mid Canterbury, Fraser Park, Timaru, 29 September

1991

11 South Canterbury v Mid Canterbury, Fraser Park, Timaru, 1 June

12 Southland v Thames Valley, Rugby Park, Invercargill, 27 July Div 2

13 Nelson Bays v Horowhenua, Trafalgar Park, Nelson, 14 September Div 3

14 Canterbury v Hawke's Bay, Lancaster Park, Christchurch, 21 September Div 1

1992

15 South Canterbury v Mid Canterbury, Fraser Park, Timaru, 31 May
16 NZ Universities v England B, Athletic Park, Wellington, 17 June
17 South Canterbury v Wairarapa Bush, Fraser Park, Timaru, 12 August Div 2
18 Mid Canterbury v Wanganui, Showgrounds, Ashburton, 15 August Div 3
19 Waikato v King Country, Rugby Park, Hamilton, 5 September Div 1
20 Nelson Bays v Mid Canterbury, Trafalgar Park, Nelson, 26 September Div 3

1993

21 Horowhenua v Auckland, The Domain, Levin, 3 April RS
22 Hawke's Bay v British Lions, McLean Park, Napier, 22 June
23 Marlborough v Western Samoa, Lansdowne Park, Blenheim, 7 July
24 Canterbury v Auckland, Lancaster Park, Christchurch, 4 September Div 1
25 Otago v Canterbury, Carisbrook, Dunedin, 11 September Div 1
26 North Harbour v Taranaki, Onewa Domain, Takapuna, 25 September Div 1
27 Wanganui v Horowhenua, Spriggens Park, Wanganui, 9 October Div 3 final

1994

28 Southland v New South Wales, Rugby Park, Invercargill, 23 March
29 Otago v Eastern Province, Carisbrook, Dunedin, 30 April
30 North Harbour v Otago, Onewa Domain, Takapuna, 21 May Div 1
31 New Zealand XV v France, Cooks Gardens, Wanganui, 18 June
32 Wellington v South Africa, Athletic Park, Wellington, 28 June
33 Otago v Waikato, Carisbrook, Dunedin, 20 August Div 1
34 Auckland v North Harbour, Eden Park, Auckland, 4 September Div 1
35 Wellington v Canterbury, Athletic Park, Wellington, 24 September Div 1
36 Otago v Auckland, Carisbrook, Dunedin, 9 October Div 1
37 Korea v Hong Kong, Petaling Jaya Stadium, Kuala Lumpur, 22 October
38 Japan v Korea, Petaling Jaya Stadium, Kuala Lumpur, 29 October

1995

39 Canterbury v Tonga, Lancaster Park, Christchurch, 25 March S10
40 Transvaal v Queensland, Ellis Park, Johannesburg, 8 April S10 final
41 Western Samoa v Fiji, Apia Park, Apia, 1 July
42 Auckland v Wellington, Eden Park, Auckland, 5 August Div 1
43 Canterbury v Waikato, Lancaster Park, Christchurch, 19 August Div 1/RS
44 King Country v Canterbury, Rugby Park, Te Kuiti, 2 September Div 1
45 Wellington v King Country, Athletic Park, Wellington, 17 September Div 1
46 Waikato v Wellington, Rugby Park, Hamilton, 23 September Div 1
47 Otago v North Harbour, Carisbrook, Dunedin, 30 September Div 1
48 Auckland v North Harbour, Eden Park, Auckland, 7 October Div 1
49 Wales v Fiji, Arms Park, Cardiff, 11 November
50 Ireland v Fiji, Lansdowne Road, Dublin, 18 November

1996

51 Hurricanes v Blues, Showgrounds, Palmerston North, 1 March S12
52 Crusaders v Blues, Lancaster Park, Christchurch, 10 March S12
53 Crusaders v Western Province, Lancaster Park, Christchurch, 22 March S12
54 Hurricanes v Crusaders, Rugby Park, New Plymouth, 14 April S12
55 Blues v New South Wales, Eden Park, Auckland, 1 May S12
56 Queensland Reds v Natal, Ballymore, Brisbane, 18 May S12
57 All Black trial, McLean Park, Napier, 1 June
58 Bay of Plenty v Scotland, International Stadium, Rotorua, 18 June
59 Otago v NZ Divisional XV, Carisbrook, Dunedin, 10 July
60 Fiji v Western Samoa, National Stadium, Suva, 20 July
61 King Country v Wellington, Owen Delany Stadium, Taupo, 24 August Div 1
62 Southland v Otago, Homestead Stadium, Invercargill, 31 August
63 Otago v Counties Manukau, Carisbrook, Dunedin, 8 September Div 1
64 Waikato v North Harbour, Rugby Park, Hamilton, 13 September Div 1/RS
65 Taranaki v Otago, Rugby Park, New Plymouth, 6 October Div 1
66 Auckland v North Harbour, Eden Park, Auckland, 12 October Div 1/RS
67 Auckland v Counties Manukau, Eden Park, Auckland, 27 October Div 1 final

1997

68 England v Scotland, Twickenham, London, 1 February
69 Crusaders v Hurricanes, Lancaster Park, Christchurch, 7 March S12
70 Chiefs v Blues, North Harbour Stadium, Albany, 15 March S12
71 Blues v Reds, Eden Park, Auckland, 31 March S12
72 Chiefs v Sharks, North Harbour Stadium, Albany, 11 April S12
73 Crusaders v Sharks, Lancaster Park, Christchurch, 19 April S12
74 Blues v Sharks, Eden Park, Auckland, 27 April S12
75 Crusaders v Reds, Lancaster Park, Christchurch, 17 May S12
76 NZ Barbarians v New Zealand A, International Stadium, Rotorua, 8 June
77 Nelson Bays/Marlborough v Argentina, Trafalgar Park, Nelson, 17 June
78 Australia v England, Sydney Football Stadium, Sydney, 12 July
79 South Africa v Australia, Loftus Versfeld, Pretoria, 23 August Tri-N
80 Otago v North Harbour, Carisbrook, Dunedin, 6 September Div 1
81 Cent Vikings v Nelson Bays, Showgrounds, Palmerston Nth, 13 September Div 2
82 Poverty Bay v Mid Canterbury, Rugby Park, Gisborne, 20 September Div 3
83 Otago v Auckland, Carisbrook, Dunedin, 29 September Div 1
84 North Harbour v Taranaki, North Harbour Stadium, Albany, 3 October Div 1
85 Auckland v Wellington, Eden Park, Auckland, 11 October Div 1
86 Canterbury v Auckland, Lancaster Park, Christchurch, 18 October Div 1
87 France v South Africa, Parc des Princes, Paris, 22 November

1998

88 Scotland v France, Murrayfield, Edinburgh, 21 February 5 Nations
89 Northern Bulls v Waratahs, Riebeeck Stadium, Witbank, 21 March S12
90 Waratahs v Coastal Sharks, Sydney Football Stadium, Sydney, 5 April S12
91 Reds v Northern Bulls, Ballymore, Brisbane, 25 April S12
92 Coastal Sharks v Reds, Kings Park, Durban, 10 May S12
93 Blues v Crusaders, Eden Park, Auckland, 30 May S12 final
94 New Zealand A v England, Rugby Park, Hamilton, 13 June
95 South Africa v Wales, Loftus Versfeld, Pretoria, 27 July
96 Waikato v Auckland, Rugby Park, Hamilton, 15 August Div 1/RS
97 North Harbour v Wellington, North Harbour Stadium, Albany, 22 August Div 1
98 Otago v Waikato, Carisbrook, Dunedin, 22 August Div 1
99 Auckland v Canterbury, Eden Park, Auckland, 5 September Div 1
100 Otago v Northland, Carisbrook, Dunedin, 20 September Div 1
101 Waikato v Canterbury, Rugby Park, Hamilton, 3 October Div 1
102 North Harbour v Otago, North Harbour Stadium, Albany, 11 October Div 1
103 Otago v Waikato, Carisbrook, Dunedin, 25 October Div 1 final
104 England v South Africa, Twickenham, London, 5 December

1999

105 Golden Cats v Brumbies, Ellis Park, Johannesburg, 26 February S12
106 Ireland v England, Lansdowne Road, Dublin, 6 March 5 Nations
107 Chiefs v Blues, Rugby Park, Hamilton, 27 March S12
108 Highlanders v Crusaders, Carisbrook, Dunedin, 9 April S12
109 Hurricanes v Chiefs, Rugby Park, New Plymouth, 16 April S12
110 Hurricanes v Highlanders, Athletic Park, Wellington, 15 May S12
111 Australia v South Africa, Suncorp Stadium, Brisbane, 17 July Tri-N
112 North Harbour v Waikato, North Harbour Stadium, Albany, 14 August Div 1/RS
113 Waikato v Counties Manukau, Rugby Park, Hamilton, 21 August Div 1
114 Taranaki v Northland, Rugby Park, New Plymouth, 29 August Div 1
115 Counties Manukau v Canterbury, Stadium, Pukekohe, 4 September Div 1
116 North Harbour v Northland, North Harbour Stadium, Albany, 11 Sept Div 1
117 Otago v Auckland, Carisbrook, Dunedin, 18 September Div 1
118 Wales v Argentina, Millennium Stadium, Cardiff, 1 October RWC
119 France v Fiji, Stade Municipal, Toulouse, 16 October RWC

2000

120 Chiefs v Crusaders, Rugby Park, Hamilton, 27 February S12
121 Blues v Chiefs, North Harbour Stadium, Albany, 5 March S12
122 Highlanders v Hurricanes, Carisbrook, Dunedin, 12 March S12
123 Stormers v Brumbies, Newlands, Cape Town, 18 March S12
124 Hurricanes v Crusaders, WestpacTrust Stadium, Wellington, 7 April S12
125 Highlanders v Chiefs, Carisbrook, Dunedin, 20 April S12
126 Brumbies v Cats, Bruce Stadium, Canberra, 20 May S12

127 Scotland v Vikings XV, Okara Park, Whangarei, 9 June
128 Australia v South Africa, Colonial Stadium, Melbourne, 8 July Mandela Cup
129 Otago v Waikato, Carisbrook, Dunedin, 13 August Div 1
130 Counties Manukau v Auckland, Stadium, Pukekohe, 20 August Div 1
131 Mid Canterbury v King Country, Showgrounds, Ashburton, 26 August Div 2
132 Auckland v Canterbury, Eden Park, Auckland, 1 September Div 1
133 North Harbour v Wellington, North Harbour Stadium, Albany, 16 Sept Div 1
134 Waikato v Canterbury, Rugby Park, Hamilton, 23 September Div 1/RS
135 Thames Valley v Hawke's Bay, Domain, Paeroa, 30 September Div 2
136 Wellington v Waikato, WestpacTrust Stadium, Wellington, 7 October Div 1
137 Canterbury v Taranaki, Jade Stadium, Christchurch, 14 October Div 1

2001

138 Sharks v Waratahs, ABSA Stadium, Durban, 24 March S12
139 Brumbies v Waratahs, Bruce Stadium, Canberra, 13 April S12
140 Hurricanes v Chiefs, WestpacTrust Stadium, Wellington, 4 May S12
141 Brumbies v Sharks, Bruce Stadium, Canberra, 26 May S12 final
142 Counties Manukau v Argentina, Stadium, Pukekohe, 17 June
143 Samoa v Fiji, Apia Park, Apia, 23 June
144 Australia v British Lions, Homebush Stadium, Sydney, 14 July
145 Wellington v Bay of Plenty, WestpacTrust Stadium, Wellington, 12 August Div 1
146 North Harbour v Waikato, North Harbour Stadium, Albany, 18 August Div 1
147 Taranaki v Auckland, Rugby Park, New Plymouth, 24 August Div 1
148 Canterbury v Bay of Plenty, Jade Stadium, Christchurch, 31 August Div 1/RS
149 Hawke's Bay v Thames Valley, McLean Park, Napier, 8 September Div 2
150 Otago v Auckland, Carisbrook, Dunedin, 22 September Div 1
151 Taranaki v Counties Manukau, Rugby Park, New Plymouth, 29 Sept Div 1
152 North Harbour v Northland, North Harbour Stadium, Albany, 6 October Div 1
153 Canterbury v Auckland, Jade Stadium, Christchurch, 13 October Div 1/RS
154 Wellington v Otago, WestpacTrust Stadium, Wellington, 20 October Div 1
155 North Harbour v Otago, North Harbour Stadium, Albany, 27 October Div 1
156 England v Australia, Twickenham, London, 10 November

2002

157 Hurricanes v Blues, WestpacTrust Stadium, Wellington, 22 February S12
158 Stormers v Waratahs, Newlands, Cape Town, 2 March S12
159 Waratahs v Cats, Sydney Football Stadium, Sydney, 16 March S12
160 France v Ireland, Stade de France, Paris, 4 April 6 Nations
161 Hurricanes v Crusaders, WestpacTrust Stadium, Wellington, 4 May S12
162 Waratahs v Brumbies, Stadium Australia, Sydney, 16 May S12
163 Tonga v Samoa, Teufiva Stadium, Nuku'alofa, 15 June RWCQ
164 Samoa v Tonga, Apia Park, Apia, 26 June RWCQ
165 Mid Canterbury v Canterbury, Showgrounds, Ashburton, 24 July RS
166 South Africa v Australia, Ellis Park, Johannesburg, 17 August Tri-N

167 Wairarapa Bush v King Country, Memorial Park, Masterton, 24 August Div 3
168 Auckland v North Harbour, Eden Park, Auckland, 31 August Div 1
169 Waikato v Canterbury, Waikato Stadium, Hamilton, 7 September Div 1
170 Taranaki v Bay of Plenty, Rugby Park, New Plymouth, 15 September Div 1
171 Otago v Waikato, Carisbrook, Dunedin, 21 September Div 1
172 Northland v Bay of Plenty, Northland Stadium, Whangarei, 28 September Div 1
173 Waikato v Northland, Waikato Stadium, Northland, 5 October Div 1
174 Wellington v Auckland, WestpacTrust Stadium, Wellington, 11 October Div 1*
175 Waikato v Auckland, Waikato Stadium, Hamilton, 26 October Div 1 final
176 England v South Africa, Twickenham, London, 23 November

2003

177 Crusaders v Hurricanes, Jade Stadium, Christchurch, 22 February S12
178 Chiefs v Blues, Waikato Stadium, Hamilton, 28 February S12
179 Blues v Crusaders, North Harbour Stadium, Albany, 8 March S12
180 Waratahs v Bulls, Stadium Australia, Sydney, 15 March S12
181 France v Wales, Stade de France, Paris, 29 March 6 Nations
182 Stormers v Reds, Newlands, Cape Town, 12 April S12
183 Reds v Cats, Ballymore, Brisbane, 26 April S12
184 New Zealand Maori v England, Rugby Park, New Plymouth, 9 June
185 Canterbury v Hawke's Bay, Jade Stadium, Christchurch, 9 July RS
186 Australia v South Africa, Suncorp Stadium, Brisbane, 2 August Tri-N
187 Bay of Plenty v North Harbour, Bay Stadium, Mt Maunganui, 17 August Div 1
188 Wellington v Waikato, Waikato Stadium, Hamilton, 11 August Div 1
189 Canterbury v Taranaki, Jade Stadium, Christchurch, 30 August Div 1/RS
190 Auckland v Waikato, Eden Park, Auckland, 6 September Div 1
191 East Coast v Manawatu, Whararua Park, Ruatoria, 13 September Div 2
192 Otago v North Harbour, Carisbrook, Dunedin, 20 September Div 1
193 South Africa v Uruguay, Subiaco Oval, Perth, 11 October RWC
194 Italy v Canada, Bruce Stadium, Canberra, 21 October RWC
195 Australia v Ireland, Millennium Stadium, Melbourne, 1 November RWC
196 England v France, Stadium Australia, Sydney, 16 November RWC semi

*	Left field injured
RWC	Rugby World Cup
RWCQ	Rugby World Cup qualifier
RS	Ranfurly Shield
S10	Super 10
S12	Super 12
Div 1	NPC First Division
Div 2	NPC Second Division
Div 3	NPC Third Division